Old Las Vegas

Collected and translated by

Nasario García

Recuerdos hispanos de la an

Old Las Vegas

*Hispanic Memories from the
New Mexico Meadowlands*

Spanish/**English**

na Las Vegas, Nuevo México

Texas Tech University Press

This book is typeset in Stone Serif. The paper used in this book meets the minimum requirements of ANSI/NISO Z39.48–1992 (R1997). ∞

Printed in the United States of America

Library of Congress Cataloging-in-Publication Data
García, Nasario.
   Old Las Vegas : Hispanic memories from the New Mexico meadowlands / collected and translated by Nasario García.
       p.   cm.
   Text in English and Spanish.
   ISBN 0-89672-539-1 (cloth : acid-free paper)
   ISBN 0-89672-595-2 (pbk : alk paper)
   1. Hispanic Americans—New Mexico—Las Vegas Region—Biography. 2. Older people—New Mexico—Las Vegas Region—Biography. 3. Country life—New Mexico—Las Vegas Region—Anecdotes. 4. Country life—New Mexico—Anecdotes. 5. Folklore—New Mexico—Las Vegas Region. 6. Folklore—New Mexico. 7. Oral history. 8. Las Vegas Region (N.M.)—Social life and customs—Anecdotes. 9. New Mexico—Social life and customs—Anecdotes. 10. Las Vegas Region (N.M.)—Biography. I. Title.
   F804.L3G37 2005
   305.868'073'0978955—dc22

                                                                          2004014193
   ISBN-13 978-0-89672-539-3 (cloth)
   ISBN-13 978-089672-595-9 (paper)

06   07   08   09   10   11   12   13 14 / 9   8   7   6   5   4   3   2   1
E B

Texas Tech University Press
Box 41037
Lubbock, Texas 79409–1037 USA
800.832.4042
www.ttup.ttu.edu

Al tiempo le pido tiempo, y el tiempo, tiempo me da.
Y el mismo tiempo me dice, que él me desengañará.

I ask time for more time, and time, time it grants me.
And it is time itself that will enlighten me.
ALFREDO TRUJILLO

Contents

Preface

Oral history projects are not an overnight proposition. Interviewing old-timers (*viejitos*) whose native language is Spanish is a wonderful and rewarding experience but a time-consuming endeavor. Setting up appointments, which many times are cancelled without notice, conducting interviews and transcribing, translating, and editing them demand time, self-discipline, and infinite patience.

Above and beyond all else, however, it is the old folks (*ancianos*) who take center stage and make a difference in the scheme of things. It is they who determine success or failure in an enterprise in which one seeks information critical to the goals and objectives of a particular project. Only rarely have they failed to provide me with at least a modicum of workable and valuable information. Seeing the fruits of one's labor in published form attests to the consummate joy of interaction with old-timers whose daily experience at times can be as unpredictable as life itself.

Old Las Vegas: Hispanic Memories from the New Mexico Meadowlands encapsulates the pleasure as well as the frustration inherent in producing a work of this kind. When it became evident to me that there was no published oral history about Las Vegas and its environs that addressed politics, education, religion, and folk healing, the idea of a book about a town with a fascinating history was born.

Once the overall intent of a work is decided and it is understood that preconceptions are liable to change as the project unfolds, then and only then can the project be launched. Of utmost importance for the investigator is targeting a geographic location (i.e., a valley, a city, or a village), preferably one known for its history, and a preliminary list of informants who are most likely to provide reliable information central to the focus and intricacies of the project.

A number of students in my folklore classes at New Mexico Highlands University suggested their grandparents as potential sources of *dichos* (folk sayings), *adivinanzas* (riddles), and other cultural attributes central to my undertaking. Thereafter the "snowball effect" came into play whereby an interviewee recommended a friend, a neighbor, a *compadre* or *comadre* (co-parent) who was knowledgeable in a particular area of interest to me.

I had no preconceived plan or set number of people to be interviewed on a given topic, but from the outset I hoped that most of the interviewees would be able to address several topics. Most of them were quite knowledgeable about a fair number, as the chapters will attest, but some were stronger in certain areas.

I tape-recorded all interviews. Most took place in 1994, although a handful was conducted as recently as 1999. Given that the informants were all Spanish speakers, I conducted the interviews in that language. They were then transcribed, checked for accuracy, and catalogued. All taped interviews and their transcriptions constitute part of my collection of New Mexico's oral history compiled since 1968.

Like my previous publications on oral history, *Old Las Vegas: Hispanic Memories from the New Mexico Meadowlands* is presented in Spanish and English in a sustained effort to reach readers throughout the U.S. Southwest (i.e., Arizona, California, Colorado, New Mexico, and Texas). Many people in this part of the country have been interested in the Spanish language and culture of northern New Mexico for a long time. It is equally important to continue to attract those readers whose primary language is English, including Hispanics who have lost their native tongue but may retain some of their ancestors' culture.

The coexistence of Spanish and English in New Mexico emphasizes the state's bilingual vitality. In the nineteenth century American settlers came in contact with Hispanics whose cultural and linguistic legacy—the use of Spanish and indigenous languages—dated to the sixteenth century. This same bilingual spirit is increasingly prevalent today throughout the American Southwest, thanks in large measure to immigrants who continue to come to this region from Mexico and other Latin American countries.

Old Las Vegas: Hispanic Memories from the New Mexico Meadowlands is divided into chapters that range from life in the countryside to folk healing to supernaturalism to folk sayings and riddles. Each chapter is preceded by a short introduction addressing the subject at hand. The stories themselves, while ostensibly simple and straightforward, without fail mirror the narrators' profound thinking about and reflection on personal experiences. This is typical of *viejitos*, whose lucid and honest wisdom shines without preconditions or pretense.

In listening to these voices of the past, we come away appreciating the richness of a language that spans several centuries in New Mexico—from colonial archaisms (*mesmo* for *mismo*, *vide*, instead of *vi*, *trujo* in place of *trajo*, *or dende* versus *desde*) to today's Anglicisms (*fon*/fun or *cranque*/crank). Other linguistic influences, including indigenous words like *chíquete=chicle* from *Náhuatl*, plus New Mexico's own indigenous lexicon (*cunques* for coffee grounds, and *chimajá* for parsley, are two popular examples) have also modestly contributed to New Mexican Spanish.

An aggregate of words prevalent in northern New Mexico points to a number of common pronunciations heard in Spain (e.g., Andalucía) and Latin America. Here are a few examples: *agüelo = abuelo*, *güeno = bueno*, *golvieron = volvieron*, *nadien = nadie*, *acabao = acabado*, *naa = nada* and *muncho = mucho*. It is also not unusual to hear words like *daa(n)* for *daba(n)*, *teníanos* for *teníamos*, *cai* for *cae*, *aá* for *allá*, *ai* for *ahí*, *ea* for *ella*, *too* for *todo*, and a host of others (c/f the glossary) as part of the people's local dialect. Occasionally one can even hear somewhat peculiar pronunciations like *podío* for *podido*, although these are much less common both in New Mexico—and to my knowledge—in Spanish-speaking countries familiar to me.

The old-timers' local vocabulary is not only central to their lexical domain, but differs also in many respects from so-called standard or modern Spanish. The Spanish dialect they inherited and practice is their standard mode of communication and is characteristic of their sociocultural environment. For that reason, I have provided a glossary that juxtaposes the regional lexicon with modern usage. Said glossary will enable the student of Spanish not acquainted with New Mexican Spanish to observe and determine the differences in pronunciation, spelling, and application, or even dissimilarities in meaning that the local or regional register commands.

In deference to the interviewees and their language, I have made a sincere effort to transcribe the stories as accurately as possible so as to maintain the integrity of the local Spanish dialect. The same approach is reflected in the English versions, where I have tried not to sacrifice content and to remain mindful that meaning and intent must at times supersede a more literal translation because of the cultural nature of words, phrases, or expressions.

I have also undertaken to ensure the readability of the narratives by editing to avoid repetition, cacophony, or non-sequiturs without disrupting content or style. From time to time I have added or deleted a word or two to make a sentence more coherent and less cumbersome.

Furthermore, it is important to remember that the narrators are not professional storytellers. In spite of that, these old-timers by and large were capable of relating their experiences, regardless of scope or nature, in a clear and comprehensible way. In the main, they were quite forthcoming on subjects they were knowledgeable about, but reticent when they felt less competent or comfortable with the topic.

Irrespective of their abilities or shortcomings as raconteurs, of fundamental importance are their memories, which can help all of us comprehend a world that stretches from northern New Mexico to Spain via Mexico. The informants' enduring love of the Spanish language and culture is undeniable. This intertwined and inseparable dichotomy of language and culture becomes an avenue through which the interviewees provide lively and meaningful information about their modus vivendi of years gone by.

After all is said and done, language is the master key that unlocks a world of unlimited cultural dimensions and energy. These alone may also help clarify some people's misconceptions regarding the Hispanos' world in northern New Mexico. (The ubiquitous and convoluted use of Hispanic, Hispano, Mexican American, Mexicano, Spanish American, Spanish, Latino, and Chicano by my compatriots evokes and attests to this confusion and misunderstanding.)

But a look at the past of Hispanic old-timers may also broaden our knowledge of the travails and hardships they endured while striving to earn a living, oftentimes in a hostile and poverty-stricken environment. Their remembrances are neither sugarcoated nor vicarious; rather, they are lodged in realistic—not so pretty—impressions of life at the grass-roots level.

Acknowledgments

The true joy of putting together a book involving old-timers is the friendships that are born from getting to know wise and unassuming men and women with different personalities and levels of vitality. These people hold the key to success in reaching the goals of the investigator in oral history projects. Old-timers are a treasure trove of lore, as the present work demonstrates.

I would like to add a special note of thanks for their gracious willingness to be an integral part of this book. Coming in contact—as they did—with a total stranger who was interested in resurrecting their remote past was not always easy. Yet I was always greeted warmly and invited into their homes, a gesture that cannot be taken lightly. Nor will I ever forget being offered, without fail, a cup of coffee and something to munch on before leaving the kitchen following an interview. The kitchen, after all, is a special place in Hispanic homes, where friends and relatives congregate.

I also want to thank former students. The important role they played in putting me in contact with their grandparents, aunts, uncles, or in-laws cannot be overlooked.

A special note of thanks is due Nicolás Kanellos and his staff at the University of Houston for the research grant I was awarded under the auspices of the Recovering the U.S. Hispanic Literary Heritage Program. It was eminently helpful in carrying out portions of my fieldwork. During my tenure at New Mexico Highlands University, the Office of Research and Sponsored Projects, too, granted me research monies.

I especially wish to express my sincerest appreciation to Marc Simmons for reading portions of the manuscript. His perceptive and insightful suggestions always cast a special glow on one's work. A special note of thanks goes to Adrian Bustamante for clarifying the role of the *Penitentes* within the Catholic Church in northern New Mexico.

Last, but by no means of lesser consequence, I should like to thank the staff at Texas Tech University Press for their generous help throughout the publishing process. I especially wish to express my sincerest appreciation to Judith Keeling, editor-in-chief, for her genuine interest in my work. One would be hard-pressed to find a more enthusiastic supporter.

Old Las Vegas

Introduction

Old Las Vegas: Hispanic Memories from the New Mexico Meadowlands comprises Spanish and English oral accounts that take us back in time and space to both Las Vegas, New Mexico, and outlying villages in San Miguel County. Most of the *ancianos* featured in this work lived and eked out an existence in rural San Miguel County before abandoning their rural homes for Las Vegas—La Plaza, as they liked to call it. For them this was the "big city," where they once did their shopping but where they now spend their time among compatriots who were born and reared in Las Vegas. Although some informants were not born in Las Vegas, a number of them moved there fifty to seventy years ago and speak proudly of both the countryside and their adopted town.

This book was assembled for various reasons: first, to share the fast-disappearing old-timers' reminiscences with different ethnic groups across the Southwest; second, to shed light on the complexities of the Hispanos' culture in general and of northern New Mexico in particular as demographics change owing to emigration from Latin America; and, finally, to preserve an important slice of our cultural heritage for Hispanics and non-Hispanics to reflect on and enjoy.

Each time that a *viejito* or *viejita* dies, a portion of our cultural and linguistic soul is interred with that person. One day many of us will wake up and ask ourselves, "¿Qué pasó?" What happened? Where have our culture and language, two inseparable entities, gone? Countless answers will be offered and a litany of theories postulated, but they will render no satisfactory answer. Time and indifference will have taken their toll, and, alas, we shall cry out that something should have been done. But it will be too late.

Las Vegas, at 6,470 feet above sea level, is where the Sangre de Cristo Mountains meet the "Staked" Plains (Llano Estacado). With a population that hovers around seventeen thousand, it is predominantly a Hispanic community (70 percent to 75 percent) situated about sixty miles due east of Santa Fe, the state capital. People have variously referred to Las Vegas as a historical town (it was founded in 1835), a cow town, a sheep town, a railroad town, a college town, or a company town. Others, including natives and non-natives, privately have been less flattering in their characterization. Regardless of what label is pinned on Las Vegas, however, one would be hard-pressed to find a community in New Mexico with a more colorful and diverse history. To be sure, its past is replete with controversy, contradictions, contrasts, and paradoxes.

Today Las Vegas, as the Las Vegas–San Miguel Chamber of Commerce poignantly suggests, is "a land of castles and conquerors, ideas and icons, and it has carved for itself a proud and unique heritage. In its own way, Las Vegas has emerged as a symbol of the Western frontier. The unparalleled history of the community . . . has come to symbolize the birth of the Southwest."

Beginning in the first half of the sixteenth century and continuing until the start of the nineteenth century, Spanish expeditions traveled through the area en route to the plains and farther east. In 1541 the first Spanish explorer to visit this region, Francisco Vásquez de Coronado, searched in vain for the elusive Seven Cities of Cíbola. A plaque at the Gallinas River (actually, it is more of a creek) on Bridge Street commemorates his visit. Don Juan de Oñate, the first governor of New Mexico and its last conquistador, came through the area with his entourage sixty years later—in 1601—on his return from Kansas after searching fruitlessly for Quivira and its gold deposits. The Spanish adage "No todo lo que relumbra es oro" (Not all that glitters is gold) aptly applies to Coronado and Oñate. Kansas, to be sure, did not glisten with the richness they hoped for.

Their explorations produced gold for neither explorers nor adventurers. Unsuccessful efforts to open trade routes linking Texas and Missouri (part of the Spanish empire between 1763 and 1801) to Santa Fe suddenly changed overnight with the opening of the Santa

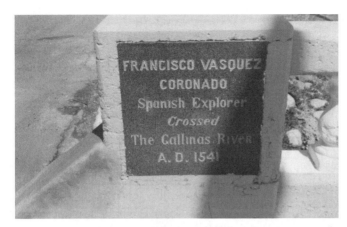

Francisco Vásquez de Coronado, Gallinas River Bridge, 2000

The Santa Fe Trail, A.D. 1821–1879, Gallinas River Bridge, 2000

Fe Trail in 1821. In 1996, the 175th anniversary of the Santa Fe Trail was celebrated. It was a rueful reminder not only of the quick passage of time but also of the rapidity with which history changes because of intervening and often unforeseen events such as the building of the railroad (more on this later). H. G. Wells writes in *The Outline of History,* "The earth on which we live is a spinning globe." Not only are the galaxies in constant motion, but people on this planet, too, are forever in search of ways to better their lot. The Santa Fe Trail, which preceded both the California and the Oregon trails, is a case in point.

What did the Santa Fe Trail mean to New Mexico and its citizenry? Specifically, what was its impact on Las Vegas? With Mexico's independence from Spain in 1821, northern New Spain, which included the Territory of New Mexico, became part of an independent country and remained so until the signing of the Treaty of Guadalupe Hidalgo with the United States in 1848.

Before 1821 the doors to trade in New Mexico were legally shut to outsiders such as trappers, traders, and foreign mountain men. But it was the Mexican government after independence that swung them open to commercialism destined to benefit both American and foreign investors alike beyond the use of the Santa Fe Trail. This spirit of cooperation between the two countries—for better or for worse—today is made manifest by the North American Free Trade Agreement (NAFTA) of 1994.

Let us examine briefly the genesis of the Santa Fe Trail and its commercial impact on Las Vegas and surrounding areas. Tales of the Seven Cities of Cíbola lured explorers to New Mexico, but it was now Santa Fe's turn. Unlike the Seven Cities of Cíbola, however, this seeming mirage in the desert was to become an economic boomtown. Stories of lucrative profits and potential wealth swirling around Santa Fe concocted by frontiersman William Becknell enticed many Missourians to head west in an attempt to "cash in" on whatever fortunes beckoned.

William Becknell, the so-called Father of the Santa Fe Trail, transformed it into the "super trail" of the era and a mecca for economic expansion. In 1821 he and a group of traders embarked on a risky journey that took them nine hundred miles into southeastern Colorado and northeastern New Mexico with Santa Fe as their final destination. Soon thereafter a multitude of adventurers and caravans loaded with all kinds of merchandise journeyed laboriously through treacherous and rugged terrain, flirted with death, confronted the elements, risked their health, and faced hostile Indian attacks. Even under ideal conditions, it took around sixty days, traveling at fifteen miles per day, from Franklin, Missouri, the beginning of the trail, to reach Santa Fe.

But these fortune seekers were resilient and tough; their endurance, tenacity, and dreams enabled them to survive the arduous journey. Courageous and ambitious efforts proved beneficial not only to them, the Americans from the States, but to New Mexico as well. As a result, they were able to pave the way for unprecedented commer-

cialism and entrepreneurship, which would turn the Land of Enchantment on its head. Becknell and his followers conducted their
first business transactions at San Miguel del Vado in the Pecos Valley
southeast of Santa Fe, a main stopover on the Santa Fe Trail. These
dealings jump-started the use of the Santa Fe Trail in New Mexico,
giving the territory an economic boost and putting countless local
citizens on the payroll, so to speak.

Owing to San Miguel del Vado's population growth in the 1830s,
many young San Miguelinos felt alienated and cut off from
landownership. Consequently, they began looking for a place to
resettle beyond the Pecos Valley. The fertile meadows (*vegas*), better
known as Las Vegas Grandes en el Río de las Gallinas, attracted them.

On March 23, 1835, Juan de Dios Maese, the first mayor of Las
Vegas (whose descendants still live in the community), along with
Miguel Archuleta, Manuel Durán, and Antonio Casa(d)os framed the
grant petition submitted to the local *ayuntamiento* (town council) in
San Miguel del Vado on March 20, 1835. Consisting of nearly a half
million acres, the grant was approved in Santa Fe. The name given
the settlement was Nuestra Señora de los Dolores de las Vegas
Grandes (Our Lady of Sorrows of the Large Meadows).

The grantees had to honor certain stipulations, to wit, land had to
be cultivated, a townsite with a plaza had to be built, and homes had
to be constructed around the plaza for security. Also sketched were
the irrigation ditches (*acequias*), including the Mother Ditch, la Ace-
quia Madre.

Throughout the 1840s, Las Vegas' economy prospered, thanks to
the Santa Fe Trail. The trend continued well into the 1870s, but
entrepreneurs did suffer periodic bumps and bruises. The *ricos*
(wealthy), both Mexican and New Mexican landowners in particular,
controlled economic development. Many proprietors formed
alliances with Americans from the States, which further strength-
ened their economic hand and monopoly on trade on the Santa Fe
Trail. Therefore, the rich got richer, and the common people (*el
pueblo*) found themselves struggling to make ends meet, at times
unable to purchase even the basic commodities. Many of them
relied, as has traditionally been true of rural Hispanos of northern
New Mexico, on the land (*la tierra*) for survival.

To make matters worse, in 1846 President James K. Polk declared war and ordered Colonel Stephen Watts Kearny to take over New Mexico. (Kearny remained a colonel until a courier reached him between Las Vegas and Santa Fe with news of his promotion to brigadier general.) This mandate, which in retrospect affected those of Mexican and Spanish descent more than anyone else, changed the whole course of history in the Southwest. Having marched in from the east leading the Army of the West, Kearny proceeded to the plaza in Las Vegas, where, on August 14, 1846, he proclaimed in dictatorial fashion that, effective immediately, the town, along with the Territory of New Mexico, was part of the United States. His vacuous rhetoric—"We come among you for your benefit, not for your injury"—to this day rings loudly and clearly for many Hispanos, especially Las Vegans. It is ironic that the building on whose rooftop Kearny stood to utter his now-famous (or infamous) words today houses Casa de Música, hardly music to the Hispanos' ears.

The Treaty of Guadalupe Hidalgo, which was signed two years later, is no less significant in its triviality and hyperbole. The cynic's point of view aside, it is well understood that the American government failed to protect the Hispanos' individual rights and reneged on assurances to safeguard their land grants (*mercedes*) from intruders or takeover. As a result, and further exacerbating the Hispanos' predicament and struggle for survival, they became the victims of unscrupulous land grabbers who used "by hook or by crook" tactics based on so-called legitimate and legal interpretations of the law to feather their own nests.

The coming of the railroad into Las Vegas, only three decades away, however, looked promising for the town. The Atchison, Topeka and Santa Fe Railroad (AT & SF), chartered by Cyrus K. Holliday in 1860, arrived in Las Vegas on July 4, 1879. This momentous event had at least a two-pronged effect on the community: first, it meant the death knell of the Santa Fe Trail; and, second, it was to create a second Las Vegas, a phenomenon that still haunts the community. Curiously, it was not the railroad that physically divided the town, as often occurs; rather, it was the Gallinas River that served as the line of demarcation. But the division between West and East Las Vegas, Old Town (La Plaza Vieja) and New Town, Hispano and Anglo, or adobe and fired brick came about as a result of the railroad being routed through the eastern

Locomotive, Mills Blvd., 2000

Old advertising sign, Bridge Street Building, 2000

part of town instead of through West Las Vegas, as most people had expected. (The railroad often missed established towns, e.g., Conejos-Antoñito, Colorado; Old Albuquerque–New Albuquerque.)

While the railroad brought Las Vegas prosperity, it likewise became a magnet for respectable and not-so-respectable people, particularly the latter. From professional businessmen to schoolteachers, church people, and cowboys, they all flocked to the frontier town. Among the undesirable element were barroom girls, prostitutes, gamblers, gunslingers, robbers, murderers, swindlers, and vagrants.

*Hanging windmill,
circa 1879–1880*
James N. Furlong,
courtesy Museum of
New Mexico. Negative
14386

These sleazy folks created an ambience that led to all kinds of violence and turpitude, making Las Vegas, as Howard Bryan says, "the Wildest of the Wild West."

Citizens, both locals and newcomers, took the law into their own hands and meted out their own brand of civil justice. Myriad hangings on the plaza at the "hanging windmill," for example, were carried out in full view of the general public, including children. Eventually, the windmill was removed because children started hanging dogs (some writers include cats) in imitation of the plaza lynchings.

Perhaps the most colorful of characters to invade Las Vegas during the railroad's peak were outlaws and lawmen. Household names in Western Americana such as Doc Holliday, Billy the Kid, Jesse James, Pat Garrett, Butch Cassidy, and Wyatt Earp top the list. Lesser known to the average person are such picturesque characters as Rattlesnake Sam, Hatchet Face Kit, Cock-Eyed Frank, Split Nose Mike, Beefsteak Mike, Harry the Dancehall Rustler, Bullshit Sam, and Hoodoo Brown.

Neither the affluence nor the depravity that came with the railroad was to last in Las Vegas, however. As the Atchison, Topeka and Santa Fe Railroad moved south to Albuquerque (on April 5, 1880), so too did business and commercial centers and the merchants who headed them. Businessmen like Charles Ilfeld, Jacob Gross, and H. W. Kelley also went to Albuquerque in pursuit of new business ventures.

By 1905 Las Vegas' railroad traffic and stature as the principal commercial center in the Land of Enchantment had begun to wane even more, with no evidence that the decline would be reversed. The town's economic future looked very uncertain. Nevertheless, rail activity, despite a reduction in freight loadings, was not dead. The AT & SF in 1909 continued to repair its steam locomotives at the roundhouse in Las Vegas (which still stands), but by 1921 the railroad finally began laying off workers, because few freight cars were being loaded in Las Vegas. The railroad's role, after forty years as an important cog in the wheel of the local economy, was now history.

To compound the economic problem, an agricultural depression hit the rural United States, including Las Vegas, in the 1920s. It created a deeper divide between survival and failure in a community whose economy had traditionally relied, to some extent, on farming. Even some banks had to close their doors during the 1920s. The Great Depression of the late 1920s and the early 1930s further exacerbated the town's economic dilemma. Moreover, a series of droughts in the late 1930s affected farmers and ranchers as well. Similar droughts followed during the 1950s and the 1980s.

Undaunted, Las Vegas' leaders launched initiatives to attract new industry and tourism in order to inject new life into the fragile economic base. Among those efforts were promoting rodeos, advertising the local climate to health seekers, proclaiming Las Vegas as the national capital of boxing (the famous bout between heavyweight champion Jack Johnson and challenger Jim Flynn took place in Las Vegas on July 4, 1912), and enticing movie producers to film in the community. The latter started with the Romaine Fielding and Tom Mix movies of the 1910s and continues to this day. Las Vegas even had a parachute factory on the plaza during World War II.

While the foregoing met with moderate success for a time, Las Vegas' strong economic foundation, aside from farming and the cat-

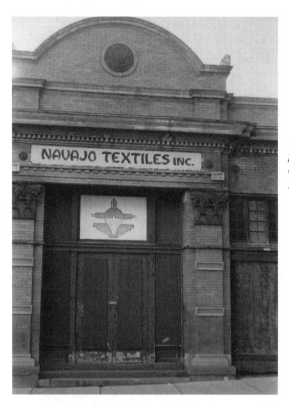

*World War II
parachute factory
on the plaza,
2000*

tle industry, has invariably been—and continues to be—government related. Governmental entities, among them the Las Vegas Medical Center (formerly the New Mexico State Hospital), New Mexico Highlands University, Luna Vocational-Technical Institute, the public schools, the State Highway Department, and city and county government employ the majority of people in the community. Utility companies, the Northeast Regional Hospital (at one time community owned), and a wide spectrum of small businesses and tourism also contribute to Las Vegas' current economy.

Las Vegas, like many other communities in New Mexico, has suffered a kind of economic hangover, typical of a boom-and-bust economy. Furthermore, there is a notable, if not eerie, feeling that Las Vegas, weary and lethargic from this episode, simply slumped into an economic depression of sorts. For eighty to ninety years after railroad business shifted to Albuquerque, Las Vegas saw little industrial development. More recent efforts to revitalize the economy go back to the early 1970s, with emphasis on companies geared toward technology and manufacturing being established at the Dee Bibb Industrial Park south of Las Vegas.

It was not until about 1986 that the town seemed to awaken from its prolonged economic stupor. Since then several businesses have moved in. For example, nationwide chain stores such as Walgreens and Wal-Mart now form part of the business community. Burger King and Taco Bell make up part of the local business mosaic as well, although outlets such as Long John Silver's have gone belly up. A small core of motels, among them the Comfort Inn and Motel 8, are more recent arrivals to the area. All of these establishments contribute in a significant way to employment and to the outflow of money to Santa Fe and Albuquerque.

Perhaps no area has undergone a more dramatic change than the Old Town Historic District. Bridge Street, which leads into the plaza—blessed with an assemblage of some of the most interesting historic buildings in town—has received a face-lift. Not only have many of the structures been refurbished, but Bridge Street itself has also been repaved. This fresh look, coupled with new retail stores in the renovated buildings, has begun to attract a fresh wave of tourists and local retail activity. A walk up and down Bridge Street leads into a time when life was simpler, but the visitor can step into an old antique shop full of yesterday's treasures or browse around a more modern gift shop while enjoying a cappuccino.

The Plaza Hotel, built in 1882, is the queen of historic edifices on the plaza. It underwent extensive renovation during the 1980s and today sits proudly in the midst of historic gems that embrace it affectionately, like grandchildren hugging their grandmother.

But the fascination for, and interest in, historic sites transcends the Old Town Historic District. As a matter of fact, there are five designated historic districts scattered throughout Las Vegas. Within each one, it is possible to see contrasting architectural styles unlike in any other New Mexican community. These run the gamut from adobe to Romanesque to Territorial to Queen Anne to Italianate, all except adobe imported from the East with the coming of the railroad. At the present time there are more than nine hundred buildings in the city listed on the National Register of Historic Places—a

*Bridge Street, May
4, 1970*
Bart Durham,
courtesy Museum of
New Mexico.
Negative 67374

number unequaled by any other city, town, community, or village in
the Land of Enchantment. For that reason Las Vegas has been
described as an "outdoor museum," a depiction it justly deserves in
terms of its architecture and as it relates to the community's historical and cultural façade.

Today leisurely strollers are awestruck to discover historic nuggets
here and there—four-digit telephone numbers inscribed on the side
of a building advertising a long-gone local business, or Spanish and
English signs still visible on buildings that date to the 1920s. Even
more picturesque evidence of the past may greet the casual pedes-
trian: "$5.00 FINE FOR COMMITING NUISANCE HERE," a Victorian
euphemism enjoining citizens not to urinate in public.

As the casual stroller abandons the Plaza and its environs and
ventures into side streets linking West with East Las Vegas, a few sur-
prises may be in store. Certain cultural practices brought to Las Vegas
over half a century ago still connect Hispanics to their rural roots in
places such as Cañada del Medio, Ojo del Venao, Ojo del Barro, Pina-

*Public warning
on side of build-
ing, 1997*

betoso, which do not even appear on the map or in books of place names. Finding religious shrines dedicated to the Virgen de Guadalupe or the Santo Niño de Atocha in front of homes, seeing families raise rabbits and chickens, or even spotting a harrow in a backyard also remind us of a people's way of staying in touch with their rural past.

Nor is it unusual to see car enthusiasts show off their immaculately rebuilt old cars on weekends or holidays, especially during the lively July 4th fiesta in the Plaza, in contrast with the Jaguars, BMWs, Mercedeses, and Land Rovers of the more affluent. This seeming contradiction is a reality that blends the past with the present to remind us of Las Vegas' glorious and engaging history, whatever the observer's roots.

Old Las Vegas: Hispanic Memories from the New Mexico Meadowlands, therefore, reflects a cultural past that takes us back to a world about which old-timers reminisce. Their memories in this modern technological age may come across as anachronistic and clash with our contemporary universe and values, but it is apparent that these proud and humble old-timers are open-minded, honest, compassionate, altruistic, reflective, independent, and, yes, philosophical, with a keen sense of humor. They harbor no ill will, demand nothing, make no apologies for their failures or seek recognition for their accomplishments. They live very much at peace with themselves as they look beyond their mortal existence.

1

La vida en el campo
Life in the Countryside

Introduction

Life in the countryside for the typical Hispano of northern Mexico, including San Miguel County, where Las Vegas is located, has always been a challenge. Yet the spacious but isolated world in which Hispanos have been able to maneuver and survive with relative freedom has conjured up a certain mystique among some writers and artists.

Absent has been a depiction of the hardships Hispano farmer-ranchers and their families faced sixty to seventy years ago in trying to carve out an existence on the land. At times even their *santos* (religious statues) seemed to ignore prayers for water for crops and livestock. Poverty, which has haunted the Hispano from time immemorial, is a fact of life, not fiction sketched in a short story.

The Hispanos' remote life on the plains (*llano*), in the desert, and in the sierras is neither unique nor unprecedented, nor is it different from that of other settlers on the frontier who came after them. The distinction is that many Hispanos still make their home in rural New Mexico and, while they are rich in real estate, their fight to make ends meet continues unabated. The land, traditionally the icon of self-sufficiency, has become more of an avocation and a symbol of past struggles and successes than a practical way of feeding a family.

Some Hispanos have even sold part of their land to outsiders to make ends meet.

In the countryside Hispanos learned to appreciate that the sun was their clock and domestic animals were vital if their families were to survive. The daily chores confronting them, whether it was herding sheep or taking care of the fields, were a source of pride and were carried out in stoic fashion, for, in their eyes, it was God's will (*la voluntad de Dios*) and hence their destiny.

Both men and women shared the workload, perhaps not equally because of certain cultural mores. Still, it was not uncommon for women to do men's work, whether it was milking cows, hoeing the fields, shoveling manure, or hitching up a team of horses. As Jesusita Aragón tells us, "We worked as hard as the men." Her pronouncement does not come as a great surprise to many of us who grew up on a farm or ranch in rural New Mexico. Both my paternal grandmother and my mother fit this pattern. For them there was hardly a "male" boundary they could not traverse. Like so many women I saw while growing up in my tiny village of Guadalupe (also known as Ojo del Padre) in the Río Puerco Valley, they were strong and resilient; at the same time, they could knit a handsome sweater or embroider the most beautiful dishtowels or pillowcases. Perhaps no generation of Hispanic men and women in the twentieth century was more capable of survival under the most adverse circumstances than old-timers such as my parents and grandparents or the elderly men and women featured in this book. Plain and simple, they were tough (*correosos*).

Although people worked hard, they also had time to kick up their heels. The *placita*, or village, and the church were central to all festive occasions. An assortment of activities usually followed Mass, provided a priest was available (he only came once a month to small communities). Entertainment included horse races and rooster pulls (*corridas del gallo*) for the young males and different games for the old-timers, such as *tejas* (similar to horseshoes), or *barajas* (cards). Saint Anne's Day was reserved for women to ride on horseback without male interference. Boys played marbles (*bolitas*), spun tops (*trompos*), or played with homemade toys. Girls were usually not allowed to play outdoors, but indoors they played with dolls or jacks.

Perhaps the most popular sport for young swaggerers was the so-called rooster pull—a misnomer at best. Virtually every Hispanic community participated in this sport, especially on Saint John's Day, June 24. Both Reynaldo Gonzales and Arsenio Montoya, Sr., offer us a good description of what typically constituted a rooster pull. While the young men engaged in the sport, held, by and large, in the afternoon, the women, older folks, and children observed. Invariably, the rooster racer (*gallero*) who lost had to sponsor a dance.

The festivities always culminated in an evening dance in the schoolhouse or dance hall. The latter was nothing fancy, and oftentimes it was no more than a place of modest size with dirt floors, so people raised a lot of dust, particularly when they danced polkas. Sprinkling water to settle the dust is something my cousins and I did as kids in my village of Ojo del Padre. We would soak the floor and the end result was pure mud by the time the dance ended. Some interviewees in this chapter relate similar accounts.

No one expresses the joy and jubilation of dances better than Cesaria Montoya in "Aclarábanos bailando." But liquor and the illegal brewing of moonshine added to the joyous occasion. Alfredo Trujillo, in "Muncho licor había," talks about brewing moonshine and how emotions incurred by liquor contributed to fistfights at the local dances. However, those involved in fights shook hands the next day and went back to their daily tasks on the farm or ranch without holding any grudges.

From time to time community dances included a special dance called the *chiquiao,* from the word *chiquearse/chiquiarse,* to be coaxed. In the absence of this formal dance, an exchange of *chiquiaos,* love quatrains, took place. A *chiquiao* is indigenous to New Mexico and reminiscent of the *piropo* (flirtatious remark made by a male and directed to a young lady in the streets) of rural Spain. It is a colorful and witty four-strophe stanza (sometimes with one or two more lines) that expresses themes such as love, affection, and infatuation, but at times can be sarcastic, piquant, and even risqué. Many men and women were adept at composing these love quatrains spontaneously on the dance floor. It was customary for dancing partners, primarily older couples—not husband and wife—to exchange *chiquiaos* while the *bastonero,* a kind of floor or dance hall manager, collected money from the men to pay the musicians or the owner of the dance hall. *Chiquiaos* were not as fashionable among young couples, although young men at times invoked the practice as a pretext for flirting.

The following is a *chiquiao* I learned from my maternal grandmother, Lucinda Atencio, when I was a small boy:

> *De la pera no comí,*
> From the pear I did not eat,
> *del vino bebí una gota*
> from the wine I took a few sips.
> *Del besito que te di,*
> From the small kiss I gave you,
> *dulce me quedó la boca.*
> my mouth turned sweet like your lips.

The male, whenever it was not a formal *chiquiao* dance, usually took the initiative in reciting these short verses, but quite frequently liquor loosened his tongue and impaired his judgment, so he said the wrong thing to the wrong woman, who responded in kind. An exchange of this kind quite often resulted in a heated argument and possibly even a fight that brought an abrupt end to the dance. Here is an example from Guadalupe Luján:

> MAN
> *Flor blanca,*
> White flower,
> *flor amarilla,*
> yellow flower,
> *ven a bailar,*
> come dance with me,
> *patas de horquilla.*
> you with legs like a hairpin.

> WOMAN
> *Alma mía de tu vida,*
> My dear beloved soul,
> *ojos de cuervo mechero,*
> shifty eyes like a crow,

espinazo de muy flaco,
with a weak backbone,
y costillas de carnero.
and ribs like a lamb.

With rare exceptions, the majority of old-timers featured in this and subsequent chapters long ago abandoned their ranches or farms in rural New Mexico. Having their way of life threatened by government-imposed restrictions on lands to which they once had free access, their culture devalued, and their power diminished, they moved to places like Las Vegas in the hope of providing a better life for their families. Their remembrances, packed with emotions that run the gamut from joy to despair and misfortune to blessing, are recorded in their own words and thus dramatize what used to be, but what is no longer, part of the northern New Mexican Hispanos' cultural tapestry.

Andrés Archuleta

El ranchero no usaba relo

El ranchero en Trujillo, no usaba reló. La luz del día. Dando su luz el sol, ya usté andaba trabajando, ¿sabe? Si iba a trabajar por otro, eran cincuenta centavos el día. No ocho horas como ora. El día completo, de sol a sol. ¿Sabe cómo? De moo es que no se necesitaba reló. Ésa era la vida del ranchero.

Güeno, en papá tuvo borregas. No munchas, pocas. Tamién tuvo vacas—y sembraba. Sembraba poco, porque no había material para sembrar como ahora. En un arado y a pie, de moo que no podía sembrar muy muncho. Pero sembraba lo que podía. Sembraba frijol, maíz y de too. Huertas de calabazas, melones, sandías y de too eso. Verduras.

Casi mi vida de joven de ranchero, pues era muy diferente a la vida de ora en esos tiempos. No había las oportunidades que hay ora para perdición del hombre. Le voy a dijir la verdá, porque pus no hay casi ganancia. ¿Sabe cómo? No había los modos, las facilidades que hay ora. Ora son tantas las facilidades que ya es por demás. En esos tiempos no había tal. En un burro no podía ir usté muy lejos. A pie tampoco, y casi más del tiempo lo hacía a pie.

Pos a mí se me hace que güeno no jui, porque yo no sé quién será güeno cuando está joven. No lo creye uno, pero ya pasó, porque tiene uno la cabeza llena de aigre, no de otra cosa. De modo es que asina es.

Le voy a cuentar una cosa que ójali hubiera sido diferente. No estuviéranos platicando yo y usté. Me gustaban las armas; me di un balazo solo. Güel, tenía yo como unos, pueda que dieciséis, diecisiete años, y me había regalao un pariente una pistola. Andaba monquiando con ea, queriendo matar tecolotes. Y era grande la pistola. Era una .44, de las de antes. Me la puse acá en un brazo y iba bajando una ladera, un lugar muy rofe, y se me cayó de allí. Ya cuando quise agarrala, ya se había disparao. Pero de mala suerte no me maté. [Risas] ¿Cómo la mira ahi?

Me pegó el balazo aquí en la rodilla junto lo más requiaso, y loo aquí, y se quedó la bala aquí arriba porque no pudo deshacer. El cuero estaa muy duro. No entró pa dentro. Se jue entremedio de las dos costillas, y se paró acá 'trás. Mi papá me trujo al dotor aquí en Las Vegas y él me quitó la bala. Y sané.

Pos, en papá, ¿qué podía decirme? Pues era un equívoco. Que me cuidara de no volverlo hacer. ¿Qué no? Ésa jue una mala suerte porque no me maté. [Risas]

The Rancher Didn't Go by the Clock

The rancher in Trujillo didn't go by the clock but by the light of day. Once the sun came up, you were already working, you understand? If you went to work for someone else, it was fifty cents a day. Not eight hours a day like now. A complete day, from sunrise to sunset. You understand? Therefore, you didn't need a clock. That's what the rancher's life was like.

Well, my father had sheep. Not many, a few. He also had cows—
and he planted. He planted a little, because there was no machinery
for planting like nowadays, with a plow and on foot, so he wasn't
able to plant a whole lot. But he planted whatever he could. He
planted pinto beans, corn, and everything. He had pumpkin fields,
melons, watermelons, and all of that stuff. Vegetables.

As far as my own life as a young rancher, well, life back then was
quite different from what it is today. The opportunities for leading a
man astray were simply not there. I'm going to level with you,
because you don't gain anything otherwise. You understand? The
ways and means were not there like now. Nowadays the easy-come
ways are so numerous that it's too, too much. Back in those days
they didn't exist. You couldn't go very far on a donkey. On foot,
either, and most of the time you went on foot.

Well, I don't believe that I can say that I was a good person,
because I don't know who's good when you're young. You don't take
no for an answer, but it's over and done with, because your head is
full of air, nothing else. So that's the way it is.

I'm going to tell you something that I wish had turned out different. We wouldn't be talking here. I liked guns; I wounded myself.
Well, I was about, maybe around sixteen, seventeen years of age, and
a relative of mine had given me a pistol. I was fooling around with it,
wanting to kill owls. And the pistol was big. It was a .44, the old
type. I strapped it around my shoulder and, going down a hill, a very
rough place, it slipped off my shoulder. By the time I tried to grab it,
it had gone off. But, unfortunately, I didn't kill myself. [Laughter]
How do you account for that?

The bullet struck my knee close to the thickest part, and then the
bullet ricocheted above my knee, because it didn't penetrate. The
skin was very thick and hard. The bullet didn't penetrate. It pierced
between two ribs and almost came out my back. My father brought
me to the doctor here in Las Vegas and he removed the bullet. And I
got well.

Well, what could my father say? It was just an accident. He told
me to be careful so that it wouldn't happen again. It was a misfortune because I didn't kill myself. [Laughter]

Cesaria Montoya

Trabajos de rancho

San Pablo, Nuevo México, onde yo nací está al oeste de Las Vegas. Ya no hay nadien. Ya ni ruinas no quedan de lo que había antes. Una sola casa está, que vive un americano. El camposanto está allí. ¡Oh, ya es muy viejo!

Pues todos los trabajos que tenían mis padres eran trabajos de rancho: sembrar y cosechar. Mi papá tenía vacas, tenía cabras. Tenía, oh, como trescientas cabras y luego tenía como diecisiete vacas. No eran ranchos grandes. *That's what you call a farm.* Me acuerdo que mi papá tenía tanto animal—tanta cabra, tanta vaca, tanta gallina, de todo. Y mi mamá ea le gustaba muncho empacar

de todo también: frijol, alberjón, maíz, calabaza, de todo. Tenían lo que le dicían "dispensas." Con *shelf all around* el cuarto. Y ahi tenía ella sus frascos empacaos.

Bueno, mi hermano y el muchacho que crió mi papá y mi mamá, los dos cuidaban las cabras. Venían y le robaban a mi mamá lo que empacaba. Le robaban un cabrito a mi papá y se iban a case unos vecinos que hacían mula. Les daban el cabrito o lo que le robaban a mi mamá [risas], por mula. De moo que había travesuras. Yo no me acuerdo si contaran que los llegaran a pescar borrachos, no. Pero sí los llegaron a pescar robando y hacelos decir por qué.

Pa hacer la lavada, había de la casa unas, yo no sé, pueda ser que cien yardas, pueda que poco más lejos, un riíto onde corría l'agua. Y tenía puestos mamá unos botes de cinco galones, botes en piedras, y les ponía lumbre y del arroyito ese traía agua pa calentar. En cajetes con lavadero, allí lavaba y loo colgaba la ropa en los encinos, en los *branches* que hubiera. Ahi colgaba la ropa que se secara. No había perchas. Bueno, ea podía haber tenido perchas pero las hubiera puesto en la casa. Y pa no jalar la ropa patrás y pa delante tanto, así la colgaba allá y loo ya no era más de doblala y traerla para la casa, ya lista pa plancharse.

Mi papá era un hombre muy grande y muy pesao. Yo tenía como unos, como unos nueve, diez años, y mamá me hacía lavar la ropa en el cajete, la ropa de mi papá. Usaa de aqueos *long johns*. ¡Tan pesaos! Mamá me hacía lavarlos a que quedaran tan bonitos como quedaban cuando ea los lavaba. Había veces que me daba mis güenos vaquetazos porque no los podía lavar como ella. Porecita.

Pa jabón usábamos de aquel *P and G* o *G*. Ése era el jabón que usaba mi mamá. Mi mamá usaba amole también. Ya no me acuerdo cómo lo usaba. Yo no sé si conforme lo traía nomás lo raspaba o lo limpiaba. No me acuerdo cabalmente.

Ranch Chores

San Pablo, New Mexico, where I was born, is west of Las Vegas. There's nobody there anymore. There's not even any ruins of what used to be. Only one house is standing, where an Anglo lives. The cemetery is there. Oh, it's really old!

Well, all of the tasks that my parents had were ranch chores: planting and harvesting. My father had cows; he had goats. He had, oh, about three hundred goats and about seventeen cows. They weren't big ranches. That's what you call a farm. I recall that my father had so many animals—lots of goats, lots of cows, lots of chickens, and everything. And my mother, she liked to can all kinds of stuff: beans, peas, corn, pumpkins. Everything! They had what they called "pantries," with shelves all around the room. That's where she had her canned goods [jars].

Okay. My brother and the boy my parents raised, both of them watched over the goats. They used to come and steal what my mother canned. And from my father they stole a baby goat, a kid, and they'd head for these neighbors who made moonshine. They would trade the baby goat or whatever they stole from my mother [laughter] for the moonshine. So you had those kinds of pranks. I don't recall if they were ever caught drunk or not. But they did get caught stealing and were asked to tell why they did it.

When it came to washing clothes, there was a little stream where the water ran about, I don't know, maybe one hundred yards, perhaps a bit more, from the house. And my mother had some five-gallon cans sitting on top of rocks, and she lit a fire underneath them and brought water to heat from that small stream. A tin tub and a washboard, that's where she washed clothes, and then she hung the clothing on the live oak trees, on the branches she could find. That's where she hung out the clothing to dry. There were no clotheslines. Well, she could have had clotheslines but she would have set them up at home. So in order not to haul the clothes back and forth, that's why she hung them over there [on the oak trees], and then it was only a matter of folding them and bringing them back to the house, ready to be ironed.

My father was a large man and very heavy. I must have been about, about nine, ten years old, and my mother made me wash his clothing in the tin tub. He wore those long johns. They were so heavy! Mother made me wash them so they would come out clean like when she washed them. There were times when she gave me a good whacking with the belt because I couldn't wash them like her. Poor mother.

For soap we used that P and G or G. That's the soap my mother used. My mother also used the amole plant for soap. I can't remember how she used it. I don't know if she scraped it just the way she got it or if she cleaned it. I can't recollect exactly.

Isabel Romero

Los borregueros pasaban buena vida

¿Trabajo? D'eso no me preguntes porque yo hacía de toa clas de trabajo, onde jallaba trabajo. Yo cuidaba borregas. Yo cuidaba vacas. Cuando yo estaba mediano, yo era cabrero. [Risas] Tenía en papá cabras, y ahi me tenía cuidando las cabras. Comiendo carne de cabrito. Cabras gordas, y por

ahi, pero cuidaba cabras. Muy a gusto. Y trabajaba en los ranchos. Yo era vaquero en el Bell Ranch por varios años cuando estaa joven. Ya luego despés estaa de por sí. Y así era.

Había munchas borregas en aqueos años. Pero los borregueros tenían partidos de borregas—quinientas o mil borregos o más. Ocupaban los dueños dos hombres y ponían campo ellos. Los tenían cuidando las borregas en el campo. Siempre tenían dos borregueros.

Luego pa los hijaderos ocupaban gente: muchachos y too pa hijar las borregas. Luego vinía el tiempo que tenían que trasquilar. Trasquilaban. Luego enpacaban en sacos grandes la lana, y la traiban aquí a Las Vegas a un almacén que estaa ahi de Ilfeld. Ahi traiban la lana. Ahi la dejaban.

Pues, eh, hubo un tiempo que no había precio por la lana ni por los borregos ni naa. La lana se estaba agonojando. Antonces cerraron ese almacén, y por muncho tiempo ya no hubo. No había. Loo pusieron borregas otra vez, otros, y así. Quinientas, conforme tenían de pasteo. Pero el sueldo en aqueos tiempos pal borreguero, pagaban catorce, quince pesos el mes. Ése era el sueldo de los borregueros. Sí le daban la comida al borreguero.

En los campos cuasi siempre traiban carpas. Vivían en carpas, porque en aqueos tiempos estaba too el mundo libre pa pasteo. ¡Libre! No como ora; ora no hay pastos libres. Antes sí. Dicían, "¡Allá llovió!" Mudaan el campo pallá. Lo que hacían los borregueros era buscar onde llovía pa irse con las borregas. Ése era el sistema antes.

Los borregueros mismos cociniaban. Eos comían carne. ¡Gorda! Mataban una borrega gorda o un carnero gordo o borregos. Comían suficiente carne. Los borregueros pasaban buena vida. Y buñelos, sopaipillas, pero eso ya vino después, porque hubo un tiempo que jue la depresión más grande que ha 'bido, que yo me acuerdo. En ese tiempo no había trabajo. La gente no trabajaa, muy poquito, pero los borregueros ponían campo. Ahi borreguiaban. Se peliaban los borregueros y los vaqueros por el pasteo en aqueos años.

¿Por qué? Porque estaba libre. Antonces no había un *branch* aquí y otro allá como ora. Antonces estaba libre, y por eso cada quien quería el pasteo. Por eso se peliaban. Dijían, "¡Quita! Aquí es mío. De aquí hasta aá es mío." No tenían nada. Estaba libre, pero se peliaban los borregueros y los vaqueros. Se daban golpes. Se golpiaban malamente. Yo taa muy joven pero oía, "Quítate de aquí. Vete paá. Aquí es mío." "No, que aquí es mío." "Mira. Aaá, aá está la esquina de mi terreno." No tenían nada. Alegando. Pues al fin que ni unos ganaban, porque se quedaban peliando, y toos usaan el terreno. Eso no jui yo. Yo nunca pelié. [Risas]

The Sheepherders Led a Good Life

Work? Don't ask me about that because I did all kinds of work, wherever I could find work. I herded sheep. I herded cows. When I was young, I was a goatherd. [Laughter] My father had goats, and there he had me herding goats. Eating baby goats [kids]. Fat goats and what have you, but I took care of goats. It was very nice. And I used to work on ranches. I was a cowboy at the Bell Ranch for several years when I was young. Later on I was on my own. That's the way it was.

Back then there were a lot of sheep. But the sheepherders participated in the *partido* system—five hundred or a thousand or more sheep. The owners hired two men and they set up camp. They had them taking care of the sheep in the countryside. They always had two sheepherders.

Then for lambing season they hired all kinds of people: boys and all for lambing. Then came the time for shearing. They sheared. Afterwards the wool was packed in large sacks, and they brought it here to a warehouse in Las Vegas that belonged to Ilfeld. That's where they brought the wool. That's where they left it.

Well, ah, there was a time when neither wool nor lambs nor anything brought any money. The wool was infested with weevils. That's when they closed that warehouse, and for a long time there was no wool. There just wasn't. Afterwards others started raising sheep again, and so forth. Five hundred, according to how much pasture there was. But the salary back in those days, what the sheepherder got paid was fourteen, fifteen dollars a month. That was the sheepherder's salary. Food was provided for him.

In the countryside they almost always had tents. They lived in tents, because back then the whole countryside was free to roam and pasture. Free! Not like now; now there are no free pasturelands. Long ago, yes. They would say, "It rained over there!" They moved the camp over there. What sheepherders did was to look for places to take the sheep where it rained. That was the way the system worked long ago.

The sheepherders themselves did the cooking. They ate meat. Fat meat! They would kill a fat sheep or a fat ram or lambs. They ate enough meat. The sheepherders led a good life. And fritters, fry bread, but that came later, because then came the depression, the biggest one there ever was, as far as I can recollect. At that time, there was no work. People weren't able to work, very little, but the sheep-herders set up camp. They herded sheep there. Sheepherders and cowboys fought over pasture back during those years.

Why? Because it was free. At that time there wasn't a branch [marker] here and another one over there, like now. Back then it was open territory, and for that reason everyone wanted pasture for himself. That's why they fought. They'd say, "Get out of here! This is mine. From here to there is mine." There were no boundaries. Every-thing was free, but the sheepherders and cowboys got into squab-bles. They'd beat each other up. They beat one another pretty bad. I was very young but I would hear: "Get out of here. Go over there. This is mine." "No, this is mine." "Listen. There, that's where the marker is to my land." They didn't own anything. Arguing. In the end neither one nor the other won, because they went on fighting while using the land. I was never one of them. I never fought. [Laughter]

Filimón Montoya

A papá le gustaba trasquilar ganao

Pus por la mayor parte del tiempo en papá era labrador de la tierra. No teníamos ran-cho grande. Eran pedazos de terreno onde se hacía su siembra.

Luego él buscaba trabajitos hacia afuera. A él le gustaba muncho en la primavera salir a onde iban a trasquilar ganao. ¡Oh! Él se llevaba el carro con sus caballos, con el tiro de caballos, y se estaa por semanas. Ponía una cobija, echaba su cama y se iba y ahi andaba de lugar en lugar onde había trasquilas de ganao. Ése era una de las clases de trabajos que él hacía afuera de la labor de la tierra.

También si le daban chanza, cuando ya estaa más joven, que estaa yo más chamaco, si lo comprendían para cuidar ovejas, usté sabe, borregas. También eso hacía. Era una buena ocupación, de cuidar borregas por otra gente, no de él mismo, de otra gente, y le pagaban sueldo. Así era como hacía su vida.

Yo no sé cuánto le pagarían. En esos días usaban muncho la medida del real. Dos reales, que son veinticinco centavos. Cuatro reales, cincuenta centavos. Seis reales, setenta y cinco centavos. Ocho reales, un peso. Doce reales, un peso y medio, y así iba. Pues sí. Creo que le pagarían pueda muy poco. Si lo contaban en pesos, pueda que unos diez, quince pesos al mes pa cuidar borregas. Cuanto más quince pesos, que eran cuatro reales al día.

Luego pa la trasquila le pagaban cinco centavos por cada oveja que trasquilaba. Pus de que yo me acuerdo, yo creo que si trasquilaba, no llegaba a las cien, porque ya no estaa joven. Pero yo creo que cuando estaa más joven sí, tal vez sí trasquilaría cien borregas al día. Ya cuando yo nací, ya era hombre grande él, pero trasquilaba sus cuarenta, cincuenta.

My Father Liked to Shear Sheep

Well, most of the time my father was a farmer who worked the land. We didn't have a large farm. They were just tracts of land where he had planted his fields.

Then he looked for small jobs elsewhere. During the spring he really liked to go where they were going to shear sheep. Oh! He'd take his horse-drawn wagon, with his team of horses, and he'd be gone for weeks. He would spread out a blanket, load up his bedroll, and take off and go from place to place where they were shearing sheep. Besides working his own land, that's one of the kinds of work that he did away from home.

Then if they gave him a chance when he was younger, when I was smaller, if they contacted him to look after sheep, to herd sheep, you know what I'm talking about, that's something that he did as well. Taking care of sheep for other people, not his, but those belonging to other people, was a good occupation, and they paid him a salary. That's how he earned his living.

I don't know how much they paid him. Back in those days they used the real. Two reals [bits] are equal to twenty-five cents. Four reals, fifty cents. Six reals, seventy-five cents. Eight reals, a dollar. Twelve reals, a dollar and a half, and so on and so forth. Why yes. I believe he got paid very little. If you count his salary in dollars, perhaps he earned some ten, fifteen dollars a month to take care of sheep. The most he got perhaps was fifteen dollars a month, which was fifty cents a day.

As far as shearing goes, he got paid five cents for every sheep that he sheared. Now, as best as I can recall, I don't believe that he even came close to one hundred head because he was no longer young. But I believe that when he was younger, yes, perhaps he did shear one hundred sheep per day. By the time I was born, he was already a grown man, but he was still able to shear his forty or fifty sheep.

Alfredo Ulibarrí

Yo tenía güenos caballos

Güeno, cuando me juntaba con otra plebe hacía mal. Pero no males a que pudiera ofender a la gente mayor. Males asina, no.

O quería ser más güeno que los otros munchas veces, porque yo tenía muy güenos caballos que me tenía mi papá, y siempre me tenía muy güenas sillas también. Una vez me escapó de echar un caballo pa entro de un carro de bestias. Yo lo había vendío el caballo ese. Güeno, lo había cambiao. Loo andaan unos muchachos allí conque no poemos subirnos en esta bestia que es muy mala y le traiban un saco de tierra y ensillao. Me dijeron que si por qué no me subía yo en él. Pus ya yo me había subío aá en el rancho y por eso lo cambié porque no me gustó el caballo.

—Sí, te cambeo, —les dije—. Sí, me subo. Sí, me subo en él, —les dije, —nomás déjenme echar la silla mía.

Le eché la silla mía y me subí en él y le clavé las espuelas pa reparar pero no me tiró. Me dio vergüenza que se jueran a rir. Ya me andaba agarrando que se jueran a rir de mí, pero me le prendí como chinche y no me tiró.

Después la plebe quería que anduviera too el tiempo y lo amanzara.

—No, —les dije, —nomás una vez lo hago y la otra vez no.

Pero pior con ése, porque era muy malo. Güenos caballos llegué a tener yo. Bonitos caballos y muy güenos pa la silla. Pa too eran muy güenos, pa lazar, pa too eran güenos.

Una vez me acuerdo que no podíanos yo y un hermano mío encerrar una vaca en el corral. La íbanos a herrar otro día, y me acuerdo que me dijo mi hermano,

—Curri laza esa vaca. Vamos a lazala y atríncala y métela pa entro el corral a huevo.

—Güeno. Vamos hacelo.

Pus ya se nos hizo brava, y loo jui y la lacé yo de aquí de los cuernos y él la lazó de las patas y la arrastramos pa entro el corral. Loo después cuando llegó en papá, estaa muy nojao él.

—¿Pa qué hicieron eso? —dijo—. ¿Por qué no la dejaron sola que se quedara aá juera del corral? Ora se va murir.

Jue cierto. Le hicimos tan nojar que se murió la vaca. Pero él tamién se nos nojó esa vez a nojotros, pero nojotros no la íbanos a dejar porque el becerro lo teníanos en el corral. De manera que si se nojaba una vaca muncho, se muere. Se muere.

I Had Good Horses

Okay, whenever I got together with other kids I did mean things. But nothing mean enough to offend adults. Bad things, no.

Or many times I wanted to be better than the other kids, because I had very good horses that my father had for me, and he always had good saddles for me too. One time a horse almost threw me inside a horse wagon. I had sold that horse. Okay, I had traded it. Then these boys were going around complaining that they couldn't mount the horse because it was meanspirited and they had it saddled, with a sack of sand on it. They asked if I wouldn't get on it. Well, I had already ridden him over at the ranch and that's the reason I traded him, because I didn't like the horse.

"Yes, I'll change horses with you," I said to them. "Yes, I'll get on it. Yes, I'll get on it. The only thing is, let me put on my own saddle."

I saddled it and I mounted the horse and I dug in my spurs so that he would buck but he didn't buck me off. I was afraid that they might laugh at me. I was scared no end that they might laugh at me, but I hung on like a bedbug and the horse didn't buck me off.

Afterwards the kids wanted me to ride him all the time so that I could break him in.

"No," I said to them, "I only did it once and not a second time."

But especially with that horse, because he was very mean. I had really good horses. Very beautiful horses and very good for riding. They were good in every way—roping, you name it.

I recall one time that a brother of mine and I couldn't get this cow into the corral. We were going to brand it the following day, and I remember my brother saying to me:

"Go and rope that cow. Let's lasso it and you corner it and put it in the corral whether it wants to or not."

"Okay. Let's do it."

Well, it turned angry on us, and then I went and roped it by the horns, and my brother roped its legs and we dragged it into the corral. Later when Dad got there, he was really furious.

"Why did you do that?" he said. "Why didn't you leave her alone so she would stay outside the corral? Now she's going to die."

Sure enough. We got the cow so angry that she died. But Dad also got mad at us that time, but we weren't going to leave the cow alone because we already had the calf in the corral. The fact is that if a cow gets mad enough, it dies. It dies.

Isabel Romero

Se iban de campo a matar cíbolos

En aqueos años, según l'historia, se juntaan munchos hombres, y se iban pallá pa Tejas, pal Llano Estacao que le dicen. Allá había munchos cíbolos, y los hombres se iban de campo a matar cíbolos pa secar la carne. Iban a caballo. No llevaan carros, pero llevaan ciertos caballos ligeros. Estos caballos no los manejaan con silla ni nada. En pelo. Con las puras piernas los guiaban los hombres. Pues esos hombres que iban, le rompían a un atajo de cíbolos. Pus ahi iban. Y les pegaban con una lanza. ¿Conoció usted las lanzas esas? Eran largas y tenían como esquinas, y le ponían un cabo de palo. Pus con ésa alcanzaban un cíbolo. Le clavaban la lanza esa aquí en las costillas y se caiba, y se embocaban al otro. Los caballos los manejaan con las puras rodillas.

Secaban carne allá en el Llano Estacao. Llevaan los ciboleros palos altos y cabrestos y ponían perchas pa secar carne. Hacían cecinas. Ahi en las noches andaan lucecitas aá en las perchas. Pus eran las mujeres de los cazadores [risas]; andaan viendo a ver ónde estaan los maridos. [Risas] Loo cuando volvían, les dijían a las otras mujeres [las esposas]. Eas volaan porque eran brujas. Éstas iban pa *warn* a las otras que ya los maridos venían, que se sosegaran. [Risas]

Las brujas se iban a ispiar a los maridos. Vían eos andar las luces aá, y pensaan qu'eran d'esas linternas. Hay un animalito que anda y da luz en la noche. Pensaan qu'eran linternas que andaban. Nada, pus eran las brujas que andaan aá en las perchas, viendo a ver ónde estaan los maridos. [Risas]

Otra cosa, de los cíbolos ablandaan el cuero. Luego los cosían y ahi enpacaan las cecinas. Traiban las cecinas. Tamién hacían maletas de los mismos cueros. Yo no vide. Eso jue hace munchos años. Mi agüelo era de los ciboleros. Él era desollador de los cíbolos, un viejito, y lo llevaan pallá pa los ciboleros de desollador. Los mataban, y él los desollaba, porque el cíbolo no se puee desollar como las vacas. No. El cíbolo tienen que desollalo por l'espinazo, porque son muy corcovaos. No pueen voltialo como las vacas. Echaos. Ahi por la corcova, por aquí por l'espinazo, les abrían y echaban el cuero par un lao y loo pal otro. Luego, como dije, en esos cueros, ahi enpacaban la carne, ya seca. Traiban los ciboleros enpaques de carne de cíbolo. Comían más carne ahi.

Ahi en el Llano Estacao era onde iban los cíbolos. Luego por último había unos tejanos o no sé qué eran. Había lagunas onde bebían agua los cíbolos. Había cíbolos en cantidá. Luego estos tejanos, lo que hicieron, envenenaron las aguas pa desollar [matar] los cíbolos. Pus, los cíbolos eos bebían agua. Se morían, y ahi los desollaban.

Tenían campos [los tejanos], y loo de ahi la enpacaban la carne seca. Comían carne seca y todo. Muy a gusto. Lego el gobierno dio orden de que esas lagunas no se usaran. Que las lagunas de las Salinas, que dijían, que no usaran agua de ahi, porque las habían envenenao pa matar los cíbolos pa quitales los cueros. Y los cueros los mandaan quién sabe par ónde. Los shipiaban. ¿Pus quién sabe par ónde los llevarían?

They Went Camping to Kill Buffaloes

Back then, so the story goes, all kinds of men got together and headed for Texas, the Llano Estacado, as it's called. There were lots of buffaloes, and the men went camping to kill buffaloes to dry the meat. They went on horseback. They didn't take wagons, but they took certain horses that were fast. These horses were not ridden using a saddle or anything. Bareback. The men guided them strictly with their legs. Well, the men who went buffalo hunting would take off after a herd of buffaloes. They went in pursuit and would spear them with a lance. Do you know what those lances look like? They were long and had like spines, with a wooden handle. Well, that's what they used to spear a buffalo. The hunters would stick the lance in the ribs and the buffalo would keel over, and they went on to the next one. The horses were controlled only with the knees.

They made jerky out in the Llano Estacado. The buffalo hunters took with them long poles and rope and put up something like clotheslines to dry the meat. They cut thin slices of meat. At night you could see tiny lights around the clotheslines. Well, they were the wives of the hunters [laughter]; they were looking to see what their husbands were up to. [Laughter] Then when they returned home, they would tell the other wives. They flew because they were witches. These women went back to warn the other wives that the husbands were already on their way home, so for them to calm down. [Laughter]

The witches went to spy on the husbands. The husbands would see the tiny lights moving about and thought that they were those fireflies. There's a little insect that flies and shines at night. The men thought they were like lanterns. No, why they were witches who were snooping around the clotheslines, seeing what the husbands were doing. [Laughter]

Another thing, the hunters softened the buffalo hides. Then they sewed them and that's where they packed the slices of jerky. That's where they carried them. They also made handbags from the hides. I didn't see all this. That was many years ago. My grandfather was one of the buffalo hunters. He was a buffalo skinner—a little old man— and the buffalo hunters took him along as the skinner. They killed the buffaloes, and he would skin them, because the buffalo can't be skinned like cows. No. The buffalo has to be skinned starting at the spine, because they're very hunchbacked. You can't turn them over like cows. Lying down. Starting at the hump, along the spine, the buffalo would be opened up and the hide pulled to one side and then the other. Then, as I said, in those hides, that's where the meat, which was already dried, was packed. The buffalo hunters brought back loads of buffalo meat. They ate more meat than all get-out.

There on the Llano Estacado was where the buffalo went. Then toward the end there were these Texans or I don't know what they were. There were several lakes where the buffaloes drank water. There were large numbers of buffaloes. Then these Texans, what they did, they went and poisoned the water to kill the buffaloes. Well, the buffaloes would drink the water and die, and that's where the Texans skinned them.

The Texans had camps set up, and that's where they packed the dried meat. They ate jerky and all. Very nice. Then the government gave orders for those lakes not to be used. For water in the Salinas Lakes, as they were called, not to be used, because it had been poisoned to kill the buffaloes just for the sake of getting their hides. And the hides were sent who knows where. They were shipped. Who knows where they were taken?

Jesusita Aragón

Trabajábanos como los hombres

Yo me crié en Trujillo en un rancho. La mujer era trabajadora. Trabajábanos como los hombres, en las labores, tresquilando borregas, porque mi agüelito jue un hombre que tuvo dos mil borregas, quinientas cabras, y pocas vacas. Él era más borreguero que vaquero. Ahi me crié yo lo mismo que un hombre, muy a gusto, muy contenta, trabajando duro, sufriendo lluvias de día y de noche, porque cuando uno tiene animales, entra en la casa cuando se desocupa a medianoche. Pero yo viví muy contenta con mi agüelito, porque quedamos güérfanas muy chiquitas. En 1908 murió mi mamá. Quedamos todas medianitas. Éranos ocho hermanitas. Nomás yo vivo. Soy la mayor.

Hacían unas fiestas muy hermosas en Trujillo. Hacían rodeo, hacían *barbeque,* hacían baile. Muy lindo. Muy bonitos los bailes. Cuando íbanos al baile, nos llevaba mi tío Isidro o mi papá. Mi papá era un hombre muy gustoso.

—No me vayan a desaigriar a naiden, porque si desaigran me las traigo pa la casa.

Y luego, como quien dice, desde que se metía el sol comenzaba el baile, hasta que ya vinía rayando el sol en la madrugada.

Llegábanos a la casa. Yo llegaba cantando, chiflando, muy alegre. Me dicía mi agüelita,

—¿Qué no te acabalates, Jesusita?

—No! Qué bonito estuvo, agüelita!

Nos quitábanos la ropa, nos poníanos la ropa del rancho. Mis hermanas hacer la comida, y yo al corral a mamantar borregos, a ordeñar vacas, y a ordeñar cabras y al almorzar. Marchar y atajando borregas. Yo cuidaba esas dos mil borregas. Bien contenta, ni sueño

34

ni nada. Ora dígame. Van al baile hasta las diez o las once de la noche y duermen todo el día, y antes no.

Yo comencé de doce años a cuidar las borregas; hasta la edá de veinte y seis años cuidé borregas. Se murió mi agüelito y no me quiso mi tío dar ninguna herencia. Les dije,

—Güeno. De hoy pa delante se acabó la borreguera, —porque mi agüelito lo merecía. Ese hombre era güeno con nosotras. ¡Muy güeno! Porque cuando enviudó mi padre, se jue a trabajar lejos. Sí vinía a vernos, pero mi agüelita y mi agüelito nos acabaron de criar. Nada nos faltaba.

We Worked as Hard as the Men

I grew up on a ranch in Trujillo. The life of a woman was very difficult. We worked as hard as the men, in the fields, shearing sheep, because my grandpa had two thousand head of sheep, five hundred goats, and a few cows. He was more of a sheepherder than a cowboy. I grew up just like a man, but very comfortable, very happy, working hard, suffering from the rainstorms, day and night, because when you have animals, you go home late at night. But I lived very happily with my grandpa, because my sisters and I were very small when we were left without a mother. My mom died in 1908. We were all very small. There were eight of us. I'm the only one alive. I'm the oldest.

People used to have some beautiful fiestas in Trujillo. They had rodeos, barbecues, and dances. It was very nice. The dances were beautiful. Whenever we went to the dances, my uncle Isidro or my father would take us. My father was a happy-go-lucky man.

"Don't go turn down anyone who asks you to dance, because if you do, I'll take you home."

The dance went on from sunset until early next morning when the sun was coming out.

We'd get home. I'd be singing, whistling, very happy. My grandma would say to me, "Didn't you have enough dancing, Jesusita?"

"Boy. It was so beautiful, Grandma!"

We'd take off our nice clothes and we'd put on our work clothes. My sisters would start cooking, and I'd go nurse the lambs in the corral, milk the cows, the goats, and back for breakfast. Moving and keeping the sheep together. I used to take care of those two thousand sheep. I'd be very happy, not sleepy or anything. Nowadays, look. Kids go to a dance till 10 or 11 o'clock and then they sleep all day long. That wasn't true a long time ago.

I started herding sheep when I was twelve years old. I took care of sheep until I was twenty-six. When my grandpa died my uncle refused to give me any inheritance. So I told everyone, "Okay. From now on there's no more shepherdess."

My grandpa deserved better than that. He was a good man with us granddaughters. He was very good to us! Because when my father became a widower, he went to work far away. He'd come and visit us, sure, but it was my grandma and my grandpa who raised us. We always had everything we needed.

Cruzita Vigil

Ya yo andaba a caballo

Yo nací en el lugar que le dicían el Corazón. Ése queda como pa esos rumbos, bajo de la mesa de Trujillo, pa bajo. Cerca de Trementina. Jui casada. Con Féliques Vigil. Nos casamos en 1919 en el Chaperito, Noo México. En Corazón vivimos hasta el año cincuenta. Nos vinimos pacá pa Las Vegas porque él era muy enfermo. Y pa estar aquí junto el dotor nos vinimos por eso. Que de esa enfermedá murió al fin. Él ya ora hace como veintinueve años que está muerto.

En papá mío no era más de que cuidaba sus borregas que él tenía. Y mi mamá no era más de la casa. Era too. Pero en papá cuidaba los bienes que teníamos. Tenía como cerca de 190 borregas. De ahi vivíanos. Vendía los borregos, y de ahi vivíanos nojotros. Porque él, su trabajo dél, no era más de eso, de cuidar los bienes que él tenía. Era too.

Y los hijaderos vinían en abril. Antonces era cuando vinían los borregos. Y en junio era cuando se vendían los borregos. Ya cuando estaan de tantos meses, se vendían. D'ese dinero pos vinía pa mantener a nojotros.

Sí hacíanos siembras, pero él no las atendía. Yo las atendía. Cuando ya tenía yo dieciséis años, yo era la que sembraba. Yo era la que cosechaba lo que sembrábanos y too.

La vida de nojotras las mujeres más antes tamién era que teníanos que acarriar l'agua pa la casa. Si íbanos a lavar teníanos que calentala ajuera, en un tanque. Y loo llenala en un cajete pa lavar en lavaderos. Se usaban lavaderos. Asina la lavábanos nojotras.

Además de cociniar, yo tamién vía de los animales que teníanos, vacas que teníanos. Yo tenía un caballo ensillao pa hacer de toos mis negocios. Ya yo pa cuando me casé, andaba a caballo; sabía manejar muy bien los caballos.

Tavía que me casé yo con mi esposo, él no estaba en la casa más del miércoles y el jueves. Él corría el correo de Corazón a Chaperito. A caballo. Por munchos años anduvo en caballo, y por un año en un boguecito que teníanos. Pero ya después de un año en un boguecito compró un carro. Que no duramos muncho más en Corazón; ya cuando más seis meses nomás. Loo ya se enfermó muncho y nos vinimos. Compramos aquí y nos mudamos pacá pa Las Vegas.

I Was Already Riding Horseback

I was born in a place they called Corazón. It's situated in the direction of the mesa down below Trujillo, close to Trementina. I was married to Féliques Vigil. We got married in 1919 in Chaperito, New Mexico. We lived in Corazón until 1950. We moved to Las Vegas because he was very sick. And to be near the doctor, that's why we came here. In fact, he finally died from that illness. He's now been dead for almost twenty-nine years.

My father, all he did was to take care of the sheep he had. And my mother, all she did was to tend to the household. That was all. But Dad took care of all the goods and property that we owned. He had about 190 sheep. That's how we made our living. He would sell the lambs, and that's how we lived. Because for him, his own work, that was it, taking care of the goods and property. That's all.

And the lambing season was in April. That's when the lambs were born. And in June is when the lambs were sold. By the time they were so many months old, that's when they were sold. That money is what he used to support us.

We also planted fields, but he didn't tend to them. I'm the one who took care of them. By the time I was sixteen years old, I was the one who did the planting. I was the one who harvested whatever we planted and all.

The life of us women long ago also had to do with carrying water to the house. If we were going to wash clothing we had to heat up the water outside, in a tank. And then we filled up a tin tub to wash on a washboard. Washboards are what we used. That's how we did the washing.

Besides cooking, I also looked after the animals that we had, such as cows. I had a saddle horse to do all of my farm chores. By the time I got married, I was already riding horseback. I knew how to handle horses very well.

Even when I married my husband, he was home only on Wednesdays and Thursdays. He delivered the mail from Corazón to Chaperito. On horseback. He delivered the mail on horseback for many years, and for a year in a small horse carriage that we owned. But after a year with the carriage, he bought a car. We didn't last much longer in Corazón after that, at the very least six months, that's all. Then he became quite ill and so we moved. We bought a house here and moved to Las Vegas.

Arsenio Montoya, Sr.

No quedó más que un toro grandote

Yo trabajé con el Corn Jackson. Tenía ranchos de vacas. El trabajo mío era de ver que tuvieran aguas los tanques pa las vacas. Tenía catorce papalotes que tenía que chequiar en el día. Comenzaba aquí [en Las Vegas] y iba cuasi a voltiar por allá por cerca de Wagon Mound. Muy grandes llanos esos.

Y si estaba un ala desconpuesta, pus afijala o de ver que estuvieran bien la fajas y too.

Una vez estaba componiendo un papalote allá arriba y loo llegaron toas las vacas a beber agua y había un bonchi de esos *brown steers,* y bebieron agua y se jueron toas las demás. Que ya no se vía niuna. No quedó más que un toro grandote. Cada rato vía parriba. Y yo me quería bajar y no, no podía, pus, no se iba. No me daba chanza de que me abajara.

El patrón era Chelly Hayes. Él vivía aquí en la Calle Siete allá en Las Vegas arriba junto el Storrie Lake. Ya que vido que no caiba de las nueve, las diez pa delante, dijo,

—¿Pus qué pasará con el Archie que no viene?

Él isque con la pena. No. Se jue. Le dio güelta a los abanicos en el Jeep. Al fin llegó allá onde estaba yo, en Onava. Ahi estaba el papalote ese. Cuando llegó me dijo,

—¿Pus qué pasó? ·

—No— le dije— pus estaa el torote ahi.

Y él no podía arrimársele ni con el Jeep. Se lo levantaba parriba el Jeep asina.

—Ehhh— dijo—. Con razón no bajabas.

No, pus, ¿cómo me iba apiar? Sei, me dio güen espanto el toro ese y no me hubiera apiao en toa la noche, ¿pus qué? ¿Pa qué me iba a apiar? Me mataba allá. Al fin lo espantó Corn Jackson.

Yo tenía que cambiar tres caballos pa dar la güelta a los catorce papalotes, porque ya los caballos sabían. Ya cuando llegaba al otro tanque, el caballo que usaba allá, ya él sabía. Ya estaba allí parao. Entienden los animales. Quitaba la silla de uno y se la echaba al otro y dejaba lotro que descansara. Muy suave le hacía uno al trabajo.

The Only One Left Was a Huge Bull

I worked for Corn Jackson. He was a cattle rancher. My job was to see to it that the tanks had water for the cattle. There were fourteen windmills I had to check daily. I started here in Las Vegas and went all the way until I turned back near Wagon Mound. Very wide open plains. And if a blade was loose, well, I had to tighten it or see that the belts were okay and everything.

One time I was fixing a windmill way up on top and then all of the cows came there to drink water. There was a bunch of those brown

Cattle drive near Las Vegas, 1920
Negative 1558.
Courtesy of the Citizens' Committee for Historic Preservation, Las Vegas, NM.

steers and they drank water and left. Not one could be seen. The only thing left was a huge bull. Every once in a while he'd look up where I was. And I wanted to get down, but no, I couldn't, because he wouldn't leave. He wouldn't give me a chance to get down.

The foreman was Chelly Hayes. He lived up here in Las Vegas on Seventh Street close to Storrie Lake. Once he saw that I hadn't shown up from nine, ten o'clock on, he said, "I wonder what's wrong with Archie that he's not back?" I understand he was worried. So he took off. He made the rounds of the windmills in his Jeep. Finally he got to where I was over in Onava. That's where that windmill was. When he arrived he said to me, "Well, what happened?"

"Why, that huge bull is there," I said to him.

And not even he could get close to it with the Jeep. The bull would lift up the Jeep like so.

"Ha," he said, "no wonder you wouldn't come down."

Why, no, how was I going to get down? Yes, that bull gave me quite a scare and if I hadn't gotten down all night long, so what? Why was I going to come down? He would have killed me right there. Corn Jackson finally scared it away.

I used to have to change horses three times to make the rounds of the fourteen windmills, and the horses already knew. By the time I reached the other tank, the horse that I used there already knew. It was there waiting for me. Animals are intelligent. I would remove the saddle from one horse, leave it to rest, and I'd put the saddle on another one. It was a nice way of doing your job.

Munchas víboras en el rancho de mi abuelita

Yo too lo que me acuerdo de mediano es que en el rancho de mi abuelita había munchas víboras. Llegábanos a ver una víbora que se tragaa los conejitos, y los ligaa, ¿ves? Si tú miras un conejito y le tiras una piedra y no se mueve, es que está ligao de la víbora. Sí, los liga a los conejitos. Y cuando los liga la víbora, se los traga.

Y loo estos escupiones, ¿sabes lo que son escupiones? Como un sapito. Yo no sé cómo se llaman en inglés. Nojotros les dijíanos "escupiones." Tamién ese escupión sirve porque esos matan a la víbora. Va brinco y brinco y brinco y loo la víbora se queda viéndolo y la víbora no sabe ni lo qué es, pero abre la boca la víbora y loo brinca él pa dentro y se emboca pa dentro. Y adentro enpieza a caminale patrás y pa delante hasta que la raja por el medio y la mata.

Lo que vimos nojotros tamién matar víboras son esos *roadrunners*. Siempre procuran andar de a dos, ¿ves? Onde jallan una víbora uno le da aquí con las alas, y loo el otro le pica la cabeza hasta que la matan tamién a la víbora. La pura cabeza. Están livianos esos *roadrunners*. Paisanos.

Nojotros tamién íbanos al venao, porque en ese tiempo no había licencias. Tamién llegábanos a matar josos en el rancho de mi abuelita. Mataron uno en el camino de l'Agua Zarca. En ese tiempo le dijían el Ojito del Capulín, le dijían el Ojo del Venao, y el Ojo del Burro. Había como cuatro ojitos que corrían de la sierra, y loo abajo ya se hacían combinación. Era l'agua que pasaba en l'Agua Zarca. Ahi en l'Agua Zarca pasaban los josos. Tamién toos los carros de caballos paraban a dar agua.

Lots of Snakes at My Grandma's Ranch

The only thing I remember as a kid is that at my grandmother's ranch there were lots of snakes. We got to see a type of snake that swallowed rabbits, and it would put them in a trance, you see? If you see a little rabbit and toss a rock at it and the rabbit doesn't move, that means that it's in a trance. Yes, the snake puts the rabbits in a trance, and once it puts them in a trance, it swallows them.

And then there were these yellowish lizards. Do you know what these lizards are? They're like a small frog. I don't know what you call them in English. We used to call them lizards. A lizard like that also does some good because it kills the snake. The lizard jumps up and down, up and down and then the snake just looks at it and the snake doesn't even know what it is, but the snake will open its mouth, and then the lizard goes way inside. Once inside, the lizard begins to go backwards and forward until it slices the snake down the middle and kills it.

What we saw kill snakes also is those roadrunners. They always try to travel in pairs, you see? Wherever they find a snake, one of them will beat the snake with its wings, and then the other one will peck at its head until they kill the snake. They peck only at the head. Those roadrunners are quick. They're called *paisanos*.

We also used to go deer hunting, because back then you didn't need a permit. We also killed bears at my grandmother's ranch. Someone killed one on the road to Agua Zarca. Long ago they used to call it Ojito del Capulín, Ojo del Venao, and Ojo del Burro. There were about four springs that ran from the mountain, and then down below they came together. That was the water that ran into Agua Zarca. There in Agua Zarca is where the bears went to drink water. People in horse-drawn wagons also stopped there to water their horses.

Alfredo Trujillo

Escondía el dinero en botijas

Lo que oí que me dijo un hombre es de una persona que vivía en el Cañoncito. Él escondía el dinero en botijas grandes, porque él tenía máquina de rajar, y rajaba madera. Quizás hacía muncho dinero él, pero escondió diuna vez el dinero en las botijas, por allí cerquita de la casa. No sé ónde.

Loo pus en esos años caiba muncha lluvia, ve, y llegó una lluvia muy juerte hasta allá onde tenía él escondidas las boteas. Pus se las llevó. Se llevó toas las boteas con dinero, porque después estaan las señas onde estaan las botijas. L'agua se llevó too el dinero, de moo es que yo creo que se quedó enterrao ahi. Quién sabe ónde se quedaría, porque eran tinajas grandes. Estará enterrao por ahi en algún lugar, porque no sé si habría bancos antonces o no habría.

He Would Hide His Money in Earthen Jugs

What I heard from a man once is about this person who lived in Cañoncito. He would hide his money in large earthen jugs, because he had a machine for splitting wood, and he split lumber. I guess he made a lot of money, but right away he would hide his money in those earthen jugs, right close to his house. I don't know where.

Burros transporting wood, 1900
Negative 2301. Courtesy of the Citizens' Committee for Historic Preservation, Las Vegas, NM.

Then during those years it rained a lot, you see, and a heavy rainfall came that hit the place where he had his earthen jugs hidden. Well, the rain washed them away. It washed away all of the jugs with the money in them, because later on you could see where the jugs were buried. The rain washed all the money away, so it must still be buried there. Who knows where the money ended up, because they were large earthen jugs. It must be buried someplace, because I don't know if there were any banks back then or not.

José Nataleo Montoya

Se los robaron los indios

Ésta es una historia diun tío. Éste era hermano de mi bisagüelo. Se llamaa Andrés Martínez. Andaba cuidando unas chivas en Mineral Hill onde estaa l'escuela, y se los robaron los indios, a él y un Santillanas. Éstos se lo robaron los apaches. Por aquí [Las Vegas] los pasaron. Isque por ahi pasaron de la Laguna de Piedra, que le dicen, iyendo pal rumbo de Trujillo. Ahi lo mataron a este Santillanas porque iba llorando muncho. Que lo agarraron de los talones y le dieron con una piedra y lo mataron. El tío este tamién lloraa, pero cuitió de llorar. No volvió a llorar él. Se anduvo con los apaches hasta que hizo un robo. Por aquí en el Tecolote, ahi se robó una mula blanca, que ya platicaba él, porque él volvió pacá [Las Vegas]. Le hacían busla los indios, pero pasando tiempo jueron pal rumbo de Tejas.

Ahi estaan los kiowas. Andaan los kiowas y los apaches en un río. Andaba un cautivo, un tejano, y el tejano este le dijo a este Andrés, que se juera con eos, qu'eran mejores indios los kiowas. Trataban mejor que los apaches. Pus planiaron eos; hicieron sus planes. Quién sabe cómo haría de poderse escapar él en la noche y aqueos [los kiowas] lo esperaban allá al otro lao del río. Isque durmía este Andrés con su agüelo. Asina le dijía al indio. Quizás un indio viejo ya; ése era el agüelo. Con ése durmía. Pus en la noche cuando se jue a salir Andrés, lo sintió y lo jaló patrás. No pudo escaparse esa noche, pero en la segunda noche, sí. Se le peló. Isque peliaron por él los apaches y los kiowas.

Güeno, pasó tiempo. Hasta se casó allá. Pero, con tiempo, la india le pagó mal a este tío Andrés. Antonces le daban escoger a la india, que si qué quería mejor, que la mataran, o le mocharan las narices.

Que ea pidió que la mataran, pero él no pudo matala. No pudo. Pero otro sí la mató.

   Yo conocí a un hermano d'ese Andrés. Florencio, que vino aquí en Las Vegas. En el sesenta estuvo. Vivía en Santa Fe. Ya viejo vino con un tío de mi esposa, con tío Franque. Eos se venían siendo medios parientes. Tenía unas orejas muy largas el señor ese [Florencio]. ¡Y muy grande! ¿Quién sabe qué clas de sangre tendría?

The Indians Kidnapped Them

This is the story of an uncle of mine. He was my great-grandfather's brother. His name was Andrés Martínez. He was looking after some goats in Mineral Hill where the school is, and the Indians kidnapped him and a man named Santillanes. They were stolen by the Apaches and passed through here in Las Vegas. I understand they passed by Laguna de Piedra, as it's called, on the way to Trujillo. That's where they killed Santillanes because he was crying a lot. The Apaches dragged him by the heels and struck him with a rock and killed him. My uncle was also crying, but he quit. He didn't cry anymore. He roamed around with the Apaches until a robbery took place. Around here in Tecolote, that's where he stole a white mule, as he told the story, because he returned to Las Vegas. The Indians made fun of him, but in time they headed toward Texas.

   That's where the Kiowas were. The Kiowas and Apaches hung around this river, and the Kiowas had a captive, a Texan, and this Texan told Andrés to go with them, because the Kiowas were better Indians. They treated you better than the Apaches. Well, they— Andrés and the Texan—mapped out a plan; they made their plans. I don't know how [my uncle] managed to escape at night, and the Kiowas waited for him on the other side of the river. I understand Andrés slept with his grandfather. That's what he called the Indian. I guess he was an old man already; that was his so-called grandfather. That's who he slept with. Well, at night when Andrés started to leave, the Indian heard him and pulled him back. He couldn't escape that night, but on the second night, yes. He escaped from the grandfather. The Apaches and Kiowas supposedly fought over him.

   Okay. Time passed. He even got married over there. But, in time, his Indian wife deceived my uncle Andrés. Then she was given a choice, whether to be killed or to have her nose cut off. She chose to be killed, but he couldn't make himself kill her. He just couldn't. But someone else did kill her.

I knew a brother of this Andrés. Florencio was his name, and he came here to Las Vegas. That was in 1960. He lived in Santa Fe. He was already old when he came with one of my wife's uncles, Uncle Frank. They were related more or less. That man Florencio had very long ears. And he was huge! Who knows what blood mixture he had?

Carmelita Gómez

Mató a la viejita

Yo le voy a platicar de la Guerra de Valverde. El marido de mi mamá, Cilia, mi agüelito, se llamaba Rodrigos García, y ése le baliaron una pierna. De manera es que iban los soldaos; eran de aquí de Las Vegas. Se sentaban en el suelo, dicía este don Hilario Romero, y estaban los indios abajo bailando caballería. De ahi los mataron, los mexicanos a los indios. Isque le dijo una indita a mi compadre, —No me mates. Mira mi hijito, —pero la mató. La mató a la viejita, a la mujer, ve. Y le baliaron aquí al lao. Dicía él que le había castigao Dios.

No lo conocí yo pero, pero dicían asina. Me platicaba mi papá toas esas historias. Te voy a platicar. En la Liendre, se llamaba un lugar que le dicían Márquez. Ahi vivía su bisagüelo de mi papá. Se llamaba Julián. Y su hermana se llamaba Petra. Isque le dijo,

—Papá, están los indios arriba la mesa.

—Sí, sí.

—Quién sabe si nos vengan a matar.

¿Se acuerda que hacían unas casitas chiquitas? Eos tenían una casita chiquita con ventanita, y vino y calentó mi tía tizones de esos de fierros. Isque le dijo el indio, "Fuu fuu." Vino Petra y le picó los ojos y lo mató. Loo vino otro y le echó una taza de agua jirviendo. Se jueron los otros indios, y ahi se quedó el indio dándose güelta. No se lo llevaron, no.

Loo te voy a platicar de un tío mío. Ésos eran Gonzales. Estos iban pa Antón Chico. Siempre caminaban muncho pa Antón Chico. Ahi se llamaba la Chupaina. En la Chupaina llegaron los indios y mataron un güey y le hicieron teguas a las mujeres. Pero a mi tío y a mi tía los mataron.

Loo llegó un viejito. Se llamaba José de las Casas. Era muy músico. Tocaba el violín. Estaa sentao en unas piedras cuando llegaron los indios, y les tocó la caballería de los indios, la pieza. Enredondo de anduvieron, pero no lo mataron. Era [José de las Casas] de aquí de los Valles. Ahi en los Valles isque había munchas brujas. Dicen. Yo no sé. Pero dicían. Pero a él no lo mataron los indios. Lo salvaron.

¿Ve cómo le digo? Too eso platicaban diantes. Yo no supe, pero en papá platicaba. Eso sí supe yo.

He Killed the Little Old Lady

I'm going to tell you about the War of Valverde. My grandma, Cilia's, husband was named Rodrigos García, and he was wounded in the leg. The story has it that the soldiers were on the road; they were from here in Las Vegas. They would sit on the ground, according to this man Hilario Romero, and the Indians were down below doing a horse dance. From where they were sitting, that's where the Mexicans killed the Indians. I understand a little old Indian woman begged my compadre not to kill her. "Don't kill me. Look at my child," but he killed her. He killed the little old lady, the woman, you see. And he himself was wounded in the side. He used to say that God punished him.

I didn't know him, but that's what people said. My father used to tell me all of those stories. I'm going to tell you something. Near La Liendre, there was a place that people called Márquez. That's where my father's great-grandfather lived. His name was Julián, and his sister's name was Petra. They say that she told him, "Dad, the Indians are up on top of the mesa."

"Yes, yes."

"Who knows but what they may come to kill us."

Do you remember how they used to build small houses? They had a small house with a tiny window, and my aunt went and heated some of those smoldering branding irons. The Indian presumably said to her, "Fuu fuu." She then poked his eyes and killed him. Then another Indian came and she poured a cup of boiling water on him. The rest of the Indians took off, and that Indian stayed behind, going in circles. They didn't take him with them.

I'm going to tell you about an uncle of mine. He was one of those Gonzaleses. They were on their way to Antón Chico. They traveled a lot to Antón Chico. It used to be called Chupaina. A group of Indians came to Chupaina and killed an ox and made leather sandals for the women. But my uncle and my aunt were killed.

Then a little old man showed up. His name was José de las Casas. He was a musician. He played the violin. He was sitting on some rocks when the Indians showed up, and he played the Indian horse dance for them. They danced around, but they didn't kill him. José de las Casas was from around Los Valles. There were many witches in Los Valles, so they say. I don't know, but that's according to gossip. But the Indians didn't kill him. They spared his life.

Do you understand what I'm telling you? Those are the stories of yesteryear. I didn't see any of that stuff, but Dad used to talk about it.

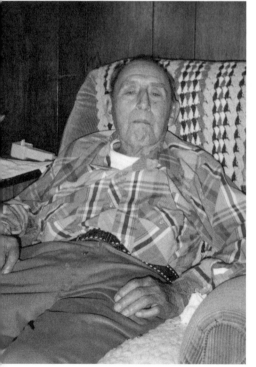

Reynaldo Gonzales

Jallé un indio muerto

Yo estaa muy chiquito. En papá me enseñó onde habían matao a su agüelo dél los indios. Me llevaba a enseñar allá onde pusieron sus hermanos una marca en el monte. Luego eos sacaron un rancho pa bajo de un cañón—él y su papá dél y un hermano o dos hermanos. Ahi se criaron eos, porque no eran de ahi tampoco. Eran de aá onde le dicen el Corazón. De ahi del Corazón paá bajo, un lugar que le dicen el Saladito. De aá eran eos. Pero se jueron viniendo pacá arriba, y se quedaron en San Agustín.

Lo mataron [los indios al abuelo] y lo

llevaron eos, en papá y sus hermanos, paá bajo pa San Agustín onde vivían. Lo mataron por unos caballos. Luego con los años, onde sacaron el rancho eos [mi papá y sus hermanos], ahi que tenían su *homestead.* Yo iba con mi papá mío. Iba yo y hay un ojo de agua. No se seca l'agua nunca.

Ahi hicieron su casa eos. Hace una cueva grandota cerca, y andaba jugando yo. Onde andaba jugando yo, jallé un indio adentro la cueva, muerto. Yo tenía puea que como unos diez años. De aá me vine juyendo a dicile a en papá que aá estaa un dijunto. Él se jue paá y se lo enseñé. Había tierra muy blandita dentro la cueva con las piedras. Escarbó con las piedras en la tierra y tapó los huesos. Ahi estaan los huesos toos. ¡Toos, toos los huesos! No le faltaba más de un diente. Los demás estaan toos ahi. Ahi lo dejamos.

Luego cuando eos vendieron el rancho por otro rancho, comencé yo a trabajar por uno de estos tejanos que compró ahi. Yo ya estaa grande. Comenzábanos a platicar, eos su historia y yo la mía, y les dije yo, por ver si eran muy hombres,

—A ver —les dije—. ¿Ustedes les tienen miedo a los dijuntos?

—No —dijo uno.

—Quién sabe si, si —dijo lotro, porque eran dos.

Nos apiamos de los caballos y nos bajamos a beber agua de un ojo, porque hace un ojo grande. Tiene yo creo como treinta pies pa bajo la tierra. Caiba agua de arriba del voladero pa bajo. Luego de ahi juimos a sentarnos aá dentro la cueva. Nos pusimos a mintir yo y los gringos que andaban conmigo. Eran Reynolds eos. Les dije yo de que si no le tenían miedo a los dijuntos. El mero Reynolds dijo que no, que él no. Y lotro dijo,

—Quién sabe si, sí.

Pus les dije yo,

—Vengan pacá.

Quité las piedras que había puesto en papá. Saqué la tierra, la ladié y saqué los huesos del indio. Se los enseñé. Todo. Antonces el Reynolds este, él era veterano de la guerra, era un hombre muy rico, estaa muy valiente. Le mandó al otro gringo. Era su trabajador lotro, como yo trabajaba por eos. Pero al otro mandó, y le dijo,

—Saca esos huesos bien pacá.

Los linpió bien y los puso otra vez adentro la cueva, arriba de unas piedras. Allí puso toos los huesos. Nos juimos pal rancho. Había como unas cinco millas pa bajo onde estaa el rancho. Toavía está el rancho ese. Antonces mandó a ese trabajador dél de aá que viniera por los huesos, y me mandó a mí que viniera con él. Echamos los huesos toos en un saco. Los llevamos. Par ónde los llevarían, nomás eos saben. Ya están muertos. Se llevaron los huesos. Pus eran indios, seguro.

Cuando en papá vino a esos lugares, estaa mediano él. Eos [mi papá y mi abuelo] siempre tuvieron cabras y vacas. De too tenían. Isque una vez bajaron las cabras al ojo, a beber agua en l'ojo, y oyeron una voz que les dijo a las cabras,

—¡Chivas, cabronas! ¡Retírense de ahi!

Arrancaron a juir las cabras, y arrancaron a juir eos tamién. Pus no vieron a naiden. Nunca supieron quién era. Pero era el indio que estaa muerto aá dentro la cueva, ése era. Seguro que se murió ahi. Ése eran los huesos.

La historia de los viejos que oía yo era asina. Cuando se llegaban muy viejos los indios que ya no los podía ver naiden, los llevaan a un lugar y los ponían solos aá. Le llevaban comida hasta que se murían. Y agua, pus allí tenían l'ojo. Ya cuando no podían bajar a beber agua o comer, pus tenían que murir.

I Found an Indian Dead

I was very small. My father showed me where the Indians had killed his grandfather. He would take me to show me where he and his brothers put a cross on the mountain. Then they established a ranch down below the canyon—he and his father and a brother or two. That's where he and his brothers grew up, because they also were not from there. They were from a place called Corazón. Down below Corazón, at a place called Saladito. That's where they were from. But they kept making their way up north, and finally ended up in San Agustín.

The Indians killed the grandfather; then my father and his brothers took him down to San Agustín, where they lived, to have him buried. The Indians killed him for some horses they wanted. Then many years later, where my father and his brothers had established the ranch, they applied for homestead. I used to go with my father. There's a spring that never goes dry.

That's where they built a house. There's a great big cave close by, and I was playing around. Where I was playing, I found an Indian inside the cave, dead. I must have been about ten years old. From there I came running to tell my father about a dead person in the cave. He went with me, and I showed it to him. There was very soft dirt in the cave with some rocks. He dug up the rocks and covered the bones with dirt. All the bones were there. All, all of the bones! All he was missing was a tooth. He had all the others. We left him there.

Then when they sold the ranch for another one, I started working for one of these Texans who bought the place. I was already grown up. We started talking, they with their story and I with mine, and I said to them, just to see how brave they were:

"Let's see," I said to them. "Are you afraid of dead people?"

"No," said one of them.

"Perhaps we are," said the other, because there were two of them.

We dismounted to drink some water from a spring, because there's a large spring. It must be about thirty feet deep. Water cascaded down from the precipice. From there we went to sit down inside the cave. The Anglos [Texans] who were with me and I started to tell whopping lies. They were named Reynolds. I asked them if they were afraid of dead people. The real Reynolds, the owner, said no, he wasn't afraid. And the other one said, "Maybe we are."

Then I said to them, "Come here."

I removed the rocks that Dad had arranged. I dug the dirt, moved it to the side, and took out the Indian's bones. I showed them to them. Then this Reynolds, the owner, he was a war veteran. He was a very rich man and very brave. He told the other Anglo who was his worker, just as I worked for them, he said to him, "Take out those bones and put them over here."

He cleaned them real good and he put them back into the cave, on top of some rocks. That's where he put all of the bones. We headed back to the ranch. The ranch was about five miles below the cave. That ranch is still there. Then he told that worker of his to go after the bones, and he asked me to go with him. We put all of the bones in a sack. We brought them back. Where they took them, only they know. They're already dead. They took the bones with them. For sure, they were Indian bones.

When my father settled in those places, he was young. They [my father and grandfather] always had goats and cows. They had everything. The story has it that one time the goats went down to the spring to drink water, and they heard a voice that said to them, "Damn you, goats! Get the hell out of there!" The goats took off, and my father and grandfather took off as well. They never saw anyone. They never found out who it was. But the Indian who was dead inside the cave, that's who it was. Surely that's where he died. Those were his bones.

The story I heard from old-timers was exactly the same. When the Indians got very old and nobody could care for them, they were taken to a secluded place and left there alone. They took them food to eat until they died. As for water, well, there was the spring. When the time came and they couldn't drink water or eat, they had no choice but to die.

Teresina Ulibarrí

A mi papá lo mató una centea

A mi papá lo mató una centea en 1938. Se había ido a cuidar las borregas pal Pinabetoso. Y luego, como a las dos de la tarde, lo mató la centea, porque vinía la lluvia, una nube muy estrendosa. Él no cayó. Mi papá no vino.

Juimos yo y mi hermanito y teníanos que cruzar la Cañada de los Martinitos. Ahi así iba como la Cañada de los Martinitos y el Río del Tecolote, y jallamos las borregas, en la Cañada esa, pero poco retirao del río, onde pasaba el camino en el Pinabetoso del lugar de nosotros.

Luego nos descalzamos y cruzamos paquel lao del arroyo. Teníanos nosotros una borrega que le llamábanos la Merlinda, porque si nosotros las queríanos echar pa juera del corral, ea era la primera. Era muy adelantada. Y dijo mi hermanito,

—¡Vamos a cruzala!

Cuando estáanos grito y grito por en papá arriba del bordo vimos un hombre con un farol. Echamos nojotros las borregas, y nomás brincó la Merlinda, se siguieron toas las demás y agarraron güelo pa la casa. Antonces vimos al hombre parao arriba del bordo, y pensamos que era en papá, pero era don Petrolino, un vecino. A mí se me jue un zapato en la creciente, porque yo los llevaa en brazos, y mi hermanito me llevaa de la mano. Él era menor que yo. Cuando cruzamos le dijíanos de aá nojotros al hombre, porque ya estaa muy escuro, era una escurana y estaa lloviendo, que no se vía uno ni la palma de la mano, y le dijimos a don Petrolino, loo que vimos que no era en papá, le preguntamos que nos llevara. No nos quiso llevar a casa. No nos quiso prestar el farol. Él quería que nos quedáranos a durmir en su casa. Y le dijimos nojotros,

—No, mamá está con la pena de nosotros.

Mamá estaba esperando. Llegaron las borregas pero no llegáanos nosotros.

Ahi íbanos caindo y levantando pero sabíanos el rumbo y llegamos a la casa. Cuando llegamos a la casa no había en papá. Llegamos y dijimos que no lo habíanos jallao. De modo que estaba el Arroyo del Tecolote ahi ende vivemos, y no había naiden más d'este hombre. Se llamaba Santiago Padilla. Era un hombre pelao, y doña Cipriana, su esposa. Ése era el hombre que estaba ahi. Estaba otro señor que se llamaba, *I can't remember his name.* Diuna vez vinieron toos los vecinos. Don Santiago y doña Cipriana vinieron pa mi casa tamién. Y estaba este otro señor, y jue avisales a mis otros parientes, a mis otros primos hermanos de mi papá, al Chupadero. Pero ese Arroyo del Tecolote estaba bien crecido, y pasó por las canovas, porque hay unas canovas que cruzan pallá, y llamó a mi tío Anacleto, a mi tía Ana, y a mi tío Bencés, y vinieron a buscalo [al papá]. Salían los hombres y vinían toos bien mojaos buscando a mi papá. No lo jallaban.

Al fin mi tío Bencés dijo,

—Voy a cruzar y llamar, —al hermano de mi papá. Se llamaba Alvires Martínez. Él vivía en otro lugar. Pal Valle. Y le dijieron,

—¿Cómo vas a cruzar? Hay muncha creciente.

Les dijo,

—Voy yo con el farol. Voy ir con el farol, —y cruzó allá en la madrugada.

Ya se había bajao poco la creciente, y jue y llamó a mi tío Alvires, y vinieron y se jueron a buscalo. Mi papá traiba un perro con él. Ese perro se llamaba Shepherd, y lo vido caido mi tío Alvires a en papá, porque [mi papá] caminaba y le traiba su lonchera, o su maleta del lonche. Él caminaba siempre asina. Pero cuando le dio la centea, que se iba a repechar de l'agua, quizás cayó boca arriba. Mi tío Alvires se hincó a velo, a ver qué pasaba. Antonces le rompió el perro.

Lo jallaron a en papá en la mañana aclarando. Luego no lo pudieron levantar ni nada. Tuvieron que aguardar que juera el dotor y el jurao coronario pa podelo levantar. Y lo llevaron, ya en la tarde, en un carro de bestias. Su hermano, mi tío Alvires, lo jalló. Alvires Martínez.

En ese tiempo mató a mi papá ese verano una centea. El siguiente [verano] mató una muchacha joven, una centea, y el siguiente verano mató otro muchacho joven y loo el siguiente verano mató otro ahi en Bernal. Dos en Bernal y uno en el Empedrao. Casi cerquita.

My Father Was Killed by Lightning

In 1938 lightning killed my father. He had gone to take care of the sheep over by Pinabetoso. And then, about two o'clock in the afternoon, lightning killed him, I believe, because the rain was coming down, a very strong cloud. He didn't show up. My father didn't come home.

My little brother and I went and we had to cross the Cañada de los Martinitos. There where the Cañada de los Martinitos was, the Tecolote River ran, and we found the sheep in a ravine, but a good distance from the river, where the road was in El Pinabetoso, where our place was.

Then we took off our shoes and crossed to the other side of the arroyo. We had a sheep we called Merlinda, because if we wanted to get the sheep out of the corral, she was the first one to go. She was very aggressive. And my brother said, "Let's cross the arroyo!"

As we were hollering and hollering for Dad from the top of the hill, we saw a man with a lantern. We chased the sheep away, and as soon as Merlinda jumped, the rest followed and they took off for home. Then we saw the man standing on top of the hill, and we thought that it was Dad, but it was Don Petrolino, a neighbor. I lost a shoe in the current, because I was carrying them in my arms, and my little brother was holding on to me with his hand. He was younger than me. When we crossed, it was already very dark; it was pitch dark, and raining so much that you couldn't see the palm of your hand. And we asked Don Petrolino, once we saw that he wasn't our father, we asked him to take us home. He refused. He wanted us to stay and sleep at his house. And we told him, "No, Mother is going to be worried about us." Mother was waiting for us. The sheep got home but there was no sign of us.

There we were falling down and getting up, but we knew the way and we got home. When we arrived home there was no father. We said that we hadn't found him. Fact is that where we lived there was the Arroyo Tecolote, and there was only this man. His name was Santiago Padilla, and Doña Cipriana, his wife. He was bald-headed. That's the man who lived there. There was another man. I can't remember his name. Right away all of the neighbors came. Don Santiago and Doña Cipriana came to my house also. And there was this other man, and he went to inform my other relatives, my father's other cousins who lived in Chupadero. But that Arroyo Tecolote was running high, and he crossed using the canoes, because there's some canoes that go to the other side, and he called my uncle Anacleto, my aunt Ana, and my uncle Bencés, and they came to look for my father. The men would go out and come back soaked from looking for my father. They couldn't find him.

Finally my uncle Bencés said, "I'm going to cross and go for help," referring to my father's brother. His name was Alvires Martínez. He lived on the other side of the arroyo. Toward El Valle. And they told him, "How are you going to cross? The current is very strong." He said to them, "I'll take the lantern along with me. I'll take the lantern," and he crossed in the early morning.

The current had already gone down by then, and he went and asked my uncle Alvires for help, and they came to go look for Dad. My father had a dog with him. That dog's name was Shepherd, and my uncle Alvires saw my father down on the ground, because he always carried a lunch bucket, or his lunch bag. That was always his way. But when he was struck by lightning, when he was going to take cover from the rain, I guess he must have fallen face up. My uncle knelt down to look at him, to see what was wrong. About that time the dog lunged at him.

They found my father at dawn. Then they couldn't pick him up or anything. They had to wait until the doctor and coroner showed up to be able to pick him up. And they did so, well into the afternoon, in a horse-drawn wagon. His brother, my uncle Alvires, found him. Alvires Martínez.

During that time, that summer, lightning killed my father. The following summer lightning killed a young girl, and the next summer it killed a young boy, and then the summer after that it killed another one in Bernal. Two in Bernal and one in El Empedrado. Very close to each other.

Reynaldo Gonzales

Sacaban el gallo

Pasáanos trabajos, pero tamién teníanos güen tiempo. Pal día de San Agustín hacían una comida pa mediodía. Primero daban la misa y loo pasaban toos en fiesta, too el día la gente junta. Comían toos. Iban a comer aá a case los mayordomos, porque la daban [la comida] los mayordomos.

Loo en la noche, antes de que se hiciera escuro, los hombres prendían un enbolansa que tenían, con dos caballos. Salía toa la placita a andar, como hacen aquí en los *parades*. Iban tocando los músicos. Tocaban el violín y la guitarra, en veces l'acordión y ahi iban. Ahi iban los músicos, invitando toa la gente al baile. Invitaban a toos. En la noche se juntaan toos al baile. Se ponían a bailar toa la noche. Contentos. No como ora. Ora se pelean. Se enborrachan.

Después, ya cuando yo nací, cuando ya yo crecí, nojotros enterrábanos un gallo en la tierra y lo sacábanos corriendo el caballo. Nos colgábanos de la cabeza [de la silla] y lo sacábanos con la mano izquierda, corriendo. Si no podían alcanzarte los galleros, se quedaa uno con el gallo. Era de nojotros. En veces comprábanos un pollo ahi de cualesquier gente, a jugar el gallo—no nomás ahi en San Agustín. En toas esas placitas.

Luego ya enpezamos ir aá onde era la Liendre. La gente en la Liendre era muy cicatera. ¡Muy cicatera! No daban una gallina pa naa, ni naa. Eos no daban ni querían vender ni una gallina. Loo llegó uno con un gatito chiquitito, d'esos que tenían dinero en la Liendre. Enterró el gatito con las patitas amarraas parriba, y lo sacáanos yo y Fermín. Hacíanos los caballos corriendo y lo levantáanos. Vide yo varios d'esos de la Liendre. Sus caballos de eos no sabían. Se iban agachar y se ponían a reparar los caballos con eos. Pero los de nojotros sí sabían. Nojotros jugáanos toos los días de fiesta. Pus era el juego de nojotros [de correr gallo].

They Pulled the Rooster

We had our hardships, but we also had a good time. For Saint Augustine's Day a noon meal was prepared. First Mass was celebrated and then everyone joined in the fiesta; all day long people were together. Everybody ate. They went to eat over at the home of the mayordomos because they sponsored the meal.

Then at night, before it got dark, the men hitched a carriage to two horses. All of the villagers walked, as they do nowadays in parades. The musicians played. They played the violin and guitar, at times, the accordion, and there they went. As the musicians played, they invited all of the people to the dance. Everybody was invited. At night everyone gathered for the dance. They danced all night long. They were happy. Not like now. Nowadays they get into fights. They get drunk.

Later on, after I was born, when I grew up, we used to bury the rooster in the ground and we'd pluck it up while riding horseback. We would hang on to the saddle horn with our right hand and pull it with our left hand as the horse was galloping. If the rooster racers could not catch you, then you kept the rooster. It was yours to keep. At times we'd buy a small chicken from just anybody to play rooster—not just in Saint Augustine—in all of those small villages.

Then we started going over to La Liendre. The people in La Liendre were very stingy. Very tight! They wouldn't even donate a chicken for anything. Nothing! They neither gave nor even sold you one. Then somebody showed up with a small cat, one of those individuals who had money in La Liendre. He buried the cat with its legs tied and sticking up, and Fermín and I were able to scoop it up. We had the horses take off running and we'd grab it. I saw several men from La Liendre. Their horses weren't trained for rooster racing and all that. When they went to lean down to scoop up the rooster, the horses would start bucking. But ours knew what to do. We had rooster races [pulls] every feast day. Rooster racing was our sport.

Arsenio Montoya, Sr.

Corría uno gallo

Güeno, había fiesta como pa los días de santos: el día de Santiago, y día de San Lorenzo. Ésas eran fiestas pa los hombres que corrían a caballo, que corrían gallo [los galleros]. Corría uno gallo. Lo enterraban en la tierra y lo sacaban. Esta corrida de gallo iba de una placita a otra, y a ver quién se llevaba el gallo, quién traiba mejor caballo.

Yo tenía un tío, mi tío Antonio Salas; era hermano de mi mamá. Ese hombre no hubo quién le ganara a correr gallos. Tenía caballos muy aguantadores y loo tenían muy güena rienda, ¿ves? Si uno de los galleros l'iban pescando, pus se detenía y se pasaban los otros, y ahi los traiba nomás güeltas y güeltas.

Yo tenía una yegüita muy ligera pero nomás por un ratito. La tenía inpuesta que brincara cercos. Ya nomás era que viera yo que los demás me iban pescando, y la metía a que brincara el cerco, y se quedaban viendo.

—¡No se vale asina Montoya!

—No, pus síganme —les dijía yo.

No me podían siguir porque los caballos d'eos no brincaban cercos, ¿ves? Me dijían que no valía asina. Allá iba caindo en casa con un atajo de gallos. Me dijía en papá,

—¡Llévate esos gallos! ¿Qué vamos hacer con tanto gallerío aquí?

Apostaba uno. Apostaban bailes los galleros hacer un baile. Munchas veces tamién apostaban una misa y un baile. Hacían la misa ese día y loo la siguiente noche se hacía el baile.

Güeno, pal gallo, lo entierran como onde está amplio el camino. Se paran los caballos poco patrás, y éste que va a sacar el gallo, tiene que irse galopiando y agacharse, porque lo tienen poco trampao con tierra. Munchos lo amarraban duro, que cuando lo agarrabas te tiraba del caballo. ¡Taa peligroso! Uno siempre se arriesgaba muncho. A mí me llegaron a cortar el cincho de la silla. Despés ya yo no usaba silla pa correr gallo. Ya andaba a puro pelo como los indios. Y tenía uno muncho fon, pero ya de que había peleas, las había, porque se agarraan los galleros allá por el gallo. El que lo llevaa no quería entregárselo a otro. Se agarraan a puros jalones. Al fin mataban el probe gallo.

Era el único juego que había aquí en los Vigiles, ahi en Montezuma. Aquí en Tecolote tamién enterraban gallo. Ahi corrían muncho gallo tamién, y son muy feas lomas ahi. Nomás que había munchos güenos caballos en ese tiempo, ¿ves?

Eran bonitos tiempos. No había más en que entretenerse uno. De moo que too el tiempo estaba la gente junta. No había carros de automoviles ni naa. Se entretenía uno nomás en puro caballo.

We Had Rooster Races

Okay. There were fiestas for saints' days: Saint James' Day and Saint Lawrence's Day. They were fiestas for men who had horse races and competed in rooster racing [pulls]. We used to rooster race. They would bury the rooster in the ground and scoop it up. This so-called rooster racing went from village to village, to see who would grab the rooster and who had the best horse.

I had an uncle, Uncle Antonio Salas; he was my mother's brother. There was no one who could beat him at rooster racing. He had very good horses with stamina in addition to being very well trained, you see? If one of the rooster racers was about to catch up with him, he'd slow down and the others would pass on by. He had them going in circles.

I had a very fast little mare, but she was only good for a short spell. I had her trained so she could jump fences. As soon as I saw that they were about to catch up with me, I'd dig my spurs into her to jump a fence, and the rest were left with their mouths open.

"That's not fair, Montoya!"

"Why not? Just come after me," I'd tell them.

They couldn't follow me because their horses didn't jump fences, you see? They complained that my way wasn't fair. I'd show up at home with a whole bunch of roosters. My father would say to me, "Get out of here with those roosters! What are we going to do with so many roosters?"

We used to place bets. The rooster racers' bet was to sponsor a dance. Many times they also wagered a Mass and a dance. The Mass was then said that day, and the following night they had the dance.

Now, as for the rooster, they bury it where the road is wide. The riders then line up their horses, back a ways, and the one who's going to attempt to pluck up the rooster, he has to take off galloping and then stoop down, because the rooster racers have the bird pretty well packed into the ground. Many of them packed the dirt real hard, so that when you leaned down from the horse to grab it, the horse would throw you off. It was dangerous! You always took a lot of chances. I had the cinch on my saddle cut many times. Afterwards, I didn't use a saddle for rooster racing. I only rode bareback like the Indians. And I used to have a lot of fun, but as far as fights were concerned, they did occur, because rooster racers would get into it on account of the rooster. The one with the rooster—the one who had plucked it up—didn't want to share it with anyone else. Then they'd get into a tug-of-war. They finally ended up killing the poor rooster.

It was the only game or sport here in Los Vigiles and Montezuma. They also buried roosters in Tecolote. That's where they had lots of rooster races, and there are some pretty ugly hills around there. Good thing there were lots of good horses back in those days, you see?

Those were good times. That's the only thing we had to entertain ourselves with. As a result, people were always together. There were no automobiles or anything. All you had was your horse for whiling away time.

Cesaria Montoya

Aclarábanos bailando

Había bailes sí. Había bastonero, y reguroso. Nomás los que el bastonero nombraba a bailar, nomás ésos bailaban. Los músicos eran un guitarrero, un violinista. Era total. Pero en esos tiempos era muy lindo. ¡Oh, muy lindo! Ora, ni que les digan a la plebe que va haber música de guitarra y violín. Tiene que ser *rock and roll or whatever.* Pero en esos tiempos, no. Bailábanos desde las nueve. Había veces que aclarábanos bailando el siguiente día, y en suelos de tierra. No había hule, no había *tile,* no había nada. Suelos de tierra. ¡Unos polvaerones! [Risas] Echaban agua pa que se humeciera que no se levantara tanto polvo. Bailaban una pieza y loo ahi andan echándole agua al suelo. [Risas] Cuando no había polvo, había zoquete. [Risas] Tamién había chiquiaos. Había lo que le dicen el redondo, polcas, cuadrillas, chotises, la vaquera y la raspa. Todas ésas bailadas había. ¿Chiquiao? Pus andaban la gente bailando, y cuando dicían, "el chiqueo," pus el par que estaba más cerquita donde tenían puesto el asiento [la silla], se paraba. La señora o la señorita se sentaba, y el hombre tenía que darle, echarle un versito. Y si la mujer era poco caprichosa, no se paraba con ese verso. [Risas] Ahi lo podía tener toa la noche contándole versos.

Había mula. *Moonshine.* Eso era lo que tomaban más los hombres. Oh, eran unas borracheras buenas. Pero no se peliaban ni borrachos. Oh, alguna vez algunos cabezudos se daban sus trompazos, pero el siguiente día andaban contentos. Ora, Dios nos libre que no se vuelven hablar si se pelean. Y si se van hablar, se van hablar con una pistola. En esos tiempos, no, que yo me acuerde, no. No, no nomás moquetes, cadenazos se daban también, pero que se mataran, yo no me acuerdo haber oído decir que se matara nadien.

Yo me acuerdo haber visto una pelea onde estos hombres, se me hacía a mí, pueda que no juera tan cruel así. ¡Oh, qué golpes se daban! Zumba, sonaban, parecía que le estaban pegando a un tambor. ¡Tras, tras, tras! y encuerados. Se quitaban la ropa y le entraban al moquete. Sonaban aqueos porrazos. Pero no se hacían nada, quizás, porque siguía el baile. [Risas]

¿Las mujeres? No, oh no, no se agarraan. No faltaba quien las quitara. Algún papá del chonguito las quitaba del medio. [Risas] Yo me acuerdo una vez que teníamos un baile, y tenía yo este muchacho, que isque era mi novio. Estáanos medianos, dieciséis, diecisiete años, y andábamos bailando y andábamos platicando. Vino mi papá y me agarró; traía yo rizos. ¿Sabe lo qué son rizos? Así largos. De un rizo me sacó y me llevó pa la casa; ya no me dejaron más en el baile. [Risas]

Los padres eran muy estritos. No podía uno platicar con los muchachos si andaba uno bailando. No importa qué baile hubiera. Tenía que llorar yo como por dos semanas pa que me dijieran que sí me iban a llevar otra vez. [Risas] Pero me llevaban, pero me llevaban a los bailes.

Mi mamá era más cruel. Me sentaba junto de ea. Venían [los muchachos] a sacarme a bailar, un pelizco. ¡Silencia y silencia! Pus ya cuando nos íbanos del baile, ya iba con las piernas todas moretiadas [risas] de tanto pelizco. Ora no le podía decir que me sacara pal escusao. No le podía uno decir nada. Ea era muy calladita, pero güena pal pelizco. En misa, si íbamos a misa, y nomás que nos moviéramos, ahi estaa el pelizco. Tenía uno que estar nomás orando. [Risas]

Oh, ora cuasi no ni necesitaban de pegarle a uno. Si miraban algo que no les gustaba, con los puros ojos. Nomás conque miraran a uno. Se acabó. Pero el baile era muy bonito; era muy bonito. ¡A pesar de tanto pelizco! [Risas]

We Danced till Dawn

There were dances, of course. There was a dance manager—and strict. Only the persons the dance manager selected, only those danced. The musicians were a guitarist and a violinist. That's all. But long ago it was very beautiful. Oh, very beautiful!

Nowadays, don't even think of telling the young kids that there's going to be guitar and violin music. It has to be rock and roll or whatever. But a long time ago, not so. We danced starting at nine o'clock. At times we danced till dawn the next day, and on dirt floors. There was no linoleum, no tile, no nothing. Dirt floors. Huge clouds of dust! [Laughter] People used to sprinkle water to wet the floor in order not to raise so much dust. They would dance a number and then they'd sprinkle water. [Laughter] Whenever there wasn't dust, you had mud. [Laughter]

People also danced what's called *chiquiaos*. They had what's called *redondo*, polkas, *cuadrillas,* schottische, the *vaquera,* and the *raspa.* For the *chiquiao?* Well, people would be dancing, and when somebody hollered *chiqueo,* then the couple who was closest to the chair that was on the floor for that purpose would stop. The lady or young girl would sit down, and the man had to recite a short verse. And if the woman was a bit stubborn, she wouldn't stand up after just one poem. [Laughter] She could have him reciting verses all night long.

There was moonshine. That's what men drank more than anything. Oh, you saw some real drunken sprees. But men didn't get into fights even when drunk. Oh, once in a while some pigheaded men beat each other up, but next day they were friends again. Nowadays, God save us if they speak to each other after they get into a fight. And if they're going to talk to one another, they're going to do it using a pistol. Back then that wasn't the case, not that I can recall. No. Only fistfights, or they'd hit each other with chains also, but as far as killing one another, I don't remember having heard of anyone getting killed.

I recollect having seen a fight in which these men, it seemed to me, perhaps it wasn't as cruel as I saw it, boy, did they beat each other up! Boom, bang, it sounded like they were beating on a drum. Whack, whack, whack! and without their shirts on. They took off their shirts and the punches started flying. The blows sounded loud. But they didn't hurt each other, I guess, because the dance continued. [Laughter]

The women? No. Oh no, they didn't get into it. There was always someone who would pull them back. Someone's father would grab them by their pigtails. [Laughter] I recall once, we were having a dance, and I had this friend, supposedly my boyfriend. We were kids, sixteen, seventeen years old, and we were dancing and talking. My father came and grabbed me. I had pincurls. Do you know what pincurls are? He grabbed me by a pincurl and took me home; that was the end of the dance for me. [Laughter]

Parents were very strict. You couldn't talk with the boys while you were dancing. It didn't matter what type of dance celebration was going on. I had to cry for about two weeks for them to tell me that they were going to take me to a dance once again. [Laughter] But they did take me back to the dances.

My mom was very mean. She would sit me next to her. The boys would come to ask me to dance, and here comes a pinch. I just kept quiet! Well, by the time we left the dance, my legs were purple from all the pinching. Why, you couldn't even ask her to take you to the outhouse [bathroom]. You couldn't tell her anything. She was very quiet, but good at pinching you. In church, if we went to Mass, all you had to do was move, and here comes a pinch. You had to be doing nothing but praying. [Laughter]

Oh, they hardly had to spank you. If they saw something they didn't like, they disciplined you with their eyes. All they had to do was to stare at you. That was it. But dances were very pretty; very nice. In spite of the pinching! [Laughter]

José Nataleo Montoya

Había suelos de tierra

Bueno, los bailes eran en un cuartito, con una lámpara, un violín y una guitarra. Bailaban hasta que salía el sol. ¡Y todos! Había suelos d'estos de tierra en esos tiempos, en algunos lugares, y salía uno con toas las narices llenas de zoquete. [Risas]

Los bailes eran alegres en ese tiempo. Había algunos que tenían buena música y era muy alegre la música de violín y guitarra. Era too lo que se acostumbraba en ese tiempo.

Pero siempre ya despúes había reborujitos en el baile. De un pueblito a otro siempre, había diferencias unos con otros y se pelia-ban. Una vez, era pa acabarse el baile, y estáanos nosotros medianos, pero no me acuerdo por qué jue que comenzó el motivo ese, y se peliaron algunos tomaos. Se dieron sus güenos agarrones, pero no a lastimarse, quizás.

En algunas veces, sí, como más atrás d'eso en un casorio, cuando se casó la hermana d'este Genoveo Gómez. Había un tío de mi esposa, y él tenía un modo muy, muy diferente a los demás. Siempre si vía venir alguien, no lo topaba. Siempre se le escondía y lo cuidaba, mientras que pasaba, ¿ve? Y en esta vez estaa éste, que tamién se lla-maa José Montoya [como yo], y Miguel Crespín. Estaan retiraos del baile, como unas cien yardas, yo creo que, así o si más. Taba el camino y había un encino, y ahi estaan eos sentaos tomando mula. Éste se llamaba Reyes, Reyes Aragón [tío de mi esposa]. Se vino de aá este Reyes que iba pa la casa, y llegó onde estaban eos y le dijo a este José que se ladiara, pa pasar. Y le dijo él [José] que no, que no se ladi-aba que pallá estaba el camino que pasara por allá. Pero jue pa comenzar el motivo nomás. Ahi se dieron y este José, qu'era un chap-arrito, yo no lo conocí, isque cada golpe que le daba saltaba una muela.

Lego el hijo dél [Reyes] se llamaba Miguel. Él era el bastonero. En ese tiempo ponían un bastonero [en bailes] como un *security guard* más o menos a ora. Tamién ahi andaban [José Montoya y Miguel Crespín], y a ése pobre le quebraron las narices. Estaa muy pequeño yo. Pero no sé si se acabaría el baile o qué pasaría. Pero sí, tamién resultó sin muelas el hombre ese.

The Dance Floors Were Dirt

Well, the dances were held in a small room, with an oil lamp, a violinist and a guitarist. They danced until the sun came out. Everyone! Back then the floors in some places were made of dirt, and you came out with your nose full of mud. [Laughter]

The dances in those days were quite joyous. There were some that had good music, and the music with violin and guitar was cheerful. Those were the instruments that were popular at the time.

There were always differences between villagers, and they got into fights. One time, the dance was about to end, and we were young, but I can't recollect why these drunks got into it. They beat each other up pretty good, but not enough to get hurt, I guess.

At times, yes, like, for example, some time back in a wedding, when the sister of this Genoveo Gómez got married. There was an uncle of my wife's, and he had a very different way about him. Every time he saw someone coming, he wouldn't greet him. He would always hide and watch him until he passed by, you see? And this one time there was this man, whose name was also like mine, José Montoya, and Miguel Crespín. They were quite a distance from the dance hall, about one hundred yards, I believe, more or less. There was a road and a live oak tree, and that's where they were sitting drinking moonshine. My wife's uncle's name was Reyes Aragón. This Reyes, who was headed home, approached the two [José Montoya and Miguel Crespín], and he told José to step aside so he could pass. And José said no, that he wasn't about to move and for him to go the other way where the road was. It was just an excuse to start an argument. They got into it, and this José, who was very short, and I didn't know him, but I understand every time he hit Reyes, a tooth would fly out.

Then Reyes' son, whose name was Miguel, he was a floor manager. Back in those days they had a floor manager at dances like a security guard nowadays. José Montoya and Miguel Crespín were present, and they broke that poor Miguel's nose. I was very small at the time. But I don't know if the dance ended or not. But, yes, he [Reyes's son Miguel] also ended up without any teeth.

Reynaldo Gonzales

Aprendí hacer mula

En esos años que yo estaa mediano, se habían cerrao las cantinas. No había cantinas. Allá en mi casa mía, en papá y mamá tenían una botea o dos boteas de licor en la casa, pero lo usaan nomás pa meecina. No era licor muy juerte quizás, porque eos le dijían *brandy.*

Pos no era mula. Era güen licor ese. Quién sabe de qué lo haría la gente. Luego en esos años crecí yo poquito más. En papá tenía un rancho que se daba muncha cirgüela. Durazno. Que yo quisiera ver esos años. Corría una cequia por el terreno onde estaan los cirgüelares esos. La cirgüela onde caiban de madura se hacía atarque.

Cayó un hombre. Muy amigo d'en papá se hizo. Le dijo que si le daba la cirgüela a él pa hacer mula. Antonces jue cuando comencé yo a ver la mula blanca. Le dijo en papá que sí, que se la daba a medias. Tenía unas casas en papá aá en la puerta de un cañón. Muy güenas casas estaan esas. No techo de tierras como eran las otras casas. Ahi tenía los barriles lo mismo que ves esos jarros ahi. Bien atrincaditos uno al otro onde tenía el negocio pa hacer la mula. Loo tenía otro cuarto aá onde hacían la comida, pa comer. Pus yo comía con eos. Ahi me estaa yo. Me mandaba en papá de aá de lotro rancho. Me dijía,

—¡Anda! Da la güelta paá arriba, a que no vayan a bajar las cabras a la alfalfa.

Tenía terreno de alfalfa. Me vinía yo y daba la güelta toa la mesa que no bajaran las cabras. Las cabras andaan aá en la mesa.

Loo yo me iba paá pa la casa onde tenían la mula. Ahi me comencé yo a juntar con un muchacho. Se llamaba Abelino. Este Abelino nació quebrao. Estaa de l'edá mía. Me dijía,

—Vamos a bañarnos al río.

Pus nos íbanos a bañar. Él se vinía de allá donde estaa el negocio de la mula, y yo, pus, andaa suelto. Yo no andaa más de cuidando las cabras. Era too. Ya yo comencé a crecer poquito más, más, y más y más. Yo notaba la vida de eos como era. Después dije yo,

—¿Por qué diablos no poo hacela yo la mula, en igual de que esté dando en papá esta cirgüela y too? Yo puedo hacer mula. Yo la puedo hacer licor.

Pus yo aprendí hacela. Cuando ya se jue el hombre ese [de la mula], le dije yo a en papá que yo iba hacer mula, y me dijo él,

—Tienes que cuidarte, pendejo, —porque era su dicho d'en papá, "pendejo." —Tienes que cuidarte. Te pescan [las autoridades].

Antes se lo llevaan a uno lo mismo que llevar un prisionero diuna vez a la prisión. Pus ahi andaa escondido yo en casas viejas, pero aprendí hacer mula.

I Learned How to Make Moonshine

During those years when I was a kid, the bars had closed. There were no bars. Over at my house my father and mother had a bottle or two of liquor, but they used it only as a medicine. I guess it wasn't very strong liquor, because they called it brandy.

It wasn't moonshine, for sure. The liquor they had was good. Who knows what people used to make it from? Then as I got a little older, my dad had a ranch that yielded lots of plums and peaches. I wish those years would come back. A ditch ran through the land where the plum trees were planted. The plums were so plentiful that when they ripened and fell to the ground they dammed up the ditch.

A man showed up. He became a very good friend of my father. He asked him if he would give him the plums so he could make moonshine. That's when I saw white moonshine [white lightning] for the first time. Dad said yes, that he would go halves [the plums for half the moonshine]. He had several houses as you entered this canyon. They were very good houses. They didn't have flat roofs [dirt roofs] like the rest of the homes. That's where he had the barrels just like those tin cans that you see there. The barrels were lined up very close together where he had his moonshine still. Then he had another room where he and this man prepared food for eating. I ate right along with them. I would spend some time at that place. My father used to send me there from the other ranch. He'd say, "Come on! Go take a look on up there [on the mesa]. Don't let the goats get into the alfalfa patch."

He had alfalfa fields. So I'd take off and make the rounds all over the mesa to make sure the goats didn't come down to the alfalfa fields. The goats were on top of the mesa.

I would then go over to the house where they had the moonshine. That's where I started hanging around with this fellow. His name was Abelino. This Abelino was born poor. He was my age. He'd say to me, "Let's go swimming in the river."

Okay, we'd take off to go swimming. He would leave the place where they brewed moonshine, and I, well, I was free to roam. All I was doing was taking care of the goats. That's all. As I started growing up more and more and more, I began noticing their way of life. Afterwards I said to myself, "Why in the devil can't I make moonshine, instead of having my father give away the plums? I can make moonshine. I am capable of making that liquor." Sure enough! I learned how to make it. When that man who brewed moonshine disappeared, I told my father that I was going to make moonshine. And he said to me, "You have to be careful, stupid," because that was my father's favorite word, "stupid." "You have to be careful. They'll [the authorities] catch you."

Back then they'd take you to prison just like taking a prisoner. Well, I would take turns hiding in those old houses, but I learned how to make moonshine.

Alfredo Trujillo

Muncho licor había

¡Oh, sí! Muncho licor había. Mula. Yo trabajé en esa mula. Yo trabajé en esa mula con este hombre, Nazario Quintana. Él tenía unos chantes; le dijían chantes, aá escondíos en el monte. Tenía ocho barriles trabajando. Los llenaa. ¡Grandotes barriles! Les echaba maiz. Treinta y cinco libras de maiz. Dos libras de levadura. Y treinta y cinco libras de azúcar a cada barril. Maiz quebrao. Ahi trabajaa por los ocho días, casi. A los siete días comenzaa uno. Conforme se iba poniendo el barril, lo estilaba uno, porque ése estaa jirbiendo asina con la levadura. Ya cuando estaa güena pa estilala, la mula, se abajaa el maiz pa bajo, porque ése estaa jirbiendo con la levadura. Se asentaa. Ya no trabajaa. Antonces tenía que estilala. Yo hice ese trabajo. Me pagaban un peso el barril a mí por estilalo. Un barril d'esos se tardaba uno algo estilándolo. Yo creo que se tardaba algo porque salía el chorro muy, muy, muy despacito, ¿ve? Ponía l'estiladora Nazario Quintana como en unas piedras altas parriba, y loo le echaba la lumbre abajo al bote ese de cobre. Pero era un barril grande, grandote. Ahi estilaba la mula, y loo el cañute de aquí de l'estiladora estaa pallá onde está la infriadora. Otro barril con el cañute que va abajo, ése tenía que tener agua fría, hielo, hasta que saliera el licor, porque estaa saliendo vapor. Logo allá abajo ya ponía uno otro barrilito pa juntar el licor, y loo se ponía en barriles. Unos barriles mire de cinco galones o de diez galones. Estos barriles ya al último estaan quemaos. Al primero no, no estaan quemaos. Los tiñía con azúcar quemaa; los tiñía tamién el licor. Ya estaan quemaos adentro. Loo parecía que ya hacía años que estaa ese licor hecho. Parecía que años y años, porque agarraba el sabor del barril.

En esos años vendía la mula Nazario Quintana por cuatro pesos el galón. ¡Cuatro pesos el galón! Y la dejábanos *a hundred and ten proof,* porque yo la hacía. Tenía testiadores. Unos grandes, otros medianitos. La echábanos en un cajete, y ahi la testiábamos. Y tenía conforme quería uno dejala. Ciento diez grados la dejáanos en veces. Un licor pero muy güeno era. Sabía muy suave, pero estaa muy fuerte.

¡Oh, ese hombre vendía muncho licor, porque estaa güen licor! Ese hombre era el único que hacía güen licor. Muncha gente hacía ahi en la cañaa. Casi toos hacían. Pero no lo hacían güeno. Ese hombre sí sabía hacelo. Él me dijía cómo lo hiciera. En veces le echaa al barril una bandeja de pasas molidas. Pues trabajaan también como l'azúcar.

Con el tiempo se acabó el licor porque ya empezaban a venir d'estos deitetivos del gobierno. Quizás los ponía el gobierno. Iban allá a buscar la gente que estaa haciendo licor, y los agarraban y los llevaan a la pinta. Allá los multaban y tenían que pagar la multa encerraos. Si no podían pagar la multa, se quedaan encerraos. No munchos jueron a la pinta. En primo Nazario no jue, porque él pagó el dinero. Él tenía con que pagar. Lo agarraron al fin los deitetivos. Le quebraron toas las estiladoras y los barriles y too. Con un'hacha se los quebraron, y las estiladoras se las apachurraron toas tamién. Hicieron horrores. Yo creo que no se soponía hacer eso pero yo creo que tenían orden seguro por el gobierno o por la ley. Yo no sé.

There Was Lots of Liquor

Oh, yes! There was lots of liquor. Moonshine. I worked that moonshine. I worked that moonshine with this man, Nazario Quintana. He had these shanties—they called them shanties—hidden in the mountains. He had eight barrels going. He'd fill them up. Large barrels! He used to pour corn in them. Thirty-five pounds of corn. Two pounds of yeast. And thirty-five pounds of sugar in each barrel. Mashed corn. It would brew for almost eight days. On the seventh day is when you started the brewing process. As the ingredients in the barrel began fermenting, you would tend to the corn, because it was boiling with the yeast. By the time the moonshine was ready to distill, the corn would settle at the bottom of the barrel. It settled and didn't ferment anymore. Then it was time to distill the moonshine.

I did that kind of work. I used to get paid one dollar per barrel. It took quite a bit of time to distill one of those barrels. I guess it took a while because the drip was very, very, very slow, you see? Nazario Quintana used to set the distilling apparatus like on some high rocks, and then he would build a fire underneath a copper container. But it was a large, very large barrel. That's where he distilled the moonshine, and then the tubing from the distilling machine ran to where the cooling system was situated. Another barrel with a pipe that goes underneath, that one had to have cold water, until the liquor came out, because steam was coming out. Then underneath I would put a small barrel to catch the liquor, and then it went into barrels. Listen, the barrels were five or ten gallons. As time went on, the barrels were already burned. At first, they were not burned. The barrels turned dark with the burned sugar; the liquor also made them dark. They were burned inside. Then it looked like years since the liquor had been made. It seemed like years and years, because the moonshine took on the taste of the barrel.

During those years Nazario Quintana sold the moonshine for four dollars per gallon. Four dollars per gallon! And we left it at 110 proof, because I'm the one who made it. We had different testers—some were large, others small. We would put the moonshine in tin tubs, and that's where we had it tested, depending on how strong you wanted to make it. At times we left it at 110 proof. It was really good liquor. It tasted real smooth, but it was very strong.

Oh, that man used to sell a lot of liquor, because it was good liquor! He's the only man who made good liquor. A lot of people made moonshine there in the ravine. Just about everybody made it, but it wasn't good. That man really knew how. He taught me how to make it. There were times when I would toss a pan of chopped-up raisins in the barrel. They worked just like sugar.

As time passed there was no more liquor because these government detectives [agents] started coming around. I guess the government hired them. They'd go looking for people who were making moonshine and they'd catch them and take them to the penitentiary. Here they were fined and had to pay the fine while they were locked up. If they couldn't pay the fine, they were kept locked up. Not many went to prison. My cousin Nazario didn't go, because he paid the fine. He had the money to pay with. The detectives finally caught him. They destroyed all of his distilling equipment and the barrels and everything. They used an ax to destroy the barrels and smash the equipment. They did horrible things. I don't think they were supposed to do that, but I believe they must have had orders from the government so they were just following the law. I don't know.

José Nataleo Montoya

Se volaba toda la cerveza

Pus en ese tiempo mío rifaa muncho la mula. *Moonshine.* Cuasi todos la hacían. Que un tío mío la hacía, porque a él siempre le gustó muncho el licor. Pero se cuidaban muncho, porque si los pescaban, les iba mal. Asina era que cuasi toos los que tomaan, tomaan mula, porque no había otra clas de licor, porque cerveza, de este *home brew,* alguno que otro hacía. Taa en mis tiempos yo llegué hacer cerveza.

Güeno, tenía un barril de unos cinco galones, y había un *malt.* Oh, traiba como unas treinta, cuarenta onzas d'este *malt.* Y ese *malt* se lo echaba uno a l'agua, y le echaba azúcar. Como unas cinco libras de azúcar y luego le echaba, ya sea papas o arroz, pa que agarrara más alcol. Loo ponía todo onde estuviera caliente, y ahi estaba jirviendo hasta que se asentaba y antonces estaba listo pa empacalo en boteas. Había unas empacadoras que, güeno, semejante a las que tenían corchos. Las tapas eran la misma cosa que estos corchos de las boteas que había antes con *soda,* la misma cosa. Con esa la sellaba. Pero tenía la cerveza que echale una poca de azúcar a cada botea, porque si no, cuando la abrías, se volaba toda la cerveza. Se salía. Cuasi la mitá se perdía si no le echabas azúcar en la botella. L'azúcar era pa 'paciguala.

The Beer Would All Blow Up

Well, during my day, moonshine was king. Moonshine. Just about everybody made it. I even had an uncle who made it, because he always liked liquor a lot. But he was very cautious, because if you got caught, you paid the price. As a result of all the moonshine, just about everyone who drank liquor, drank moonshine, since there was no other kind of liquor, because beer, what you call home brew, only a few made it. During my time, I made beer.

Well, I had a barrel that held about five gallons, and there's what you called malt. Oh, I'd buy about thirty or forty ounces of malt. And you added that malt to water, and you poured in sugar. You poured in about five pounds of sugar and then you added either potatoes or rice, so that the alcohol content came out stronger. Then I would put the whole thing where it was hot, and it would boil there until it settled and then it was ready to put it in bottles. You had these bottling machines that were, well, similar to those that used cork. The caps were the same as corks that you had long time ago in soda pop bottles, the same thing. That's the machine that I used to cap the beer. But I had to pour a little bit of sugar in each bottle, because if I didn't, when you opened it, the beer would all blow up. It would spill. About half of it would be lost if you didn't put sugar into the bottle. The sugar was used to "calm" the beer.

Filiberto Esquibel

Celebraba un vecino con otro

Pa fiestas en mi ranchito, los qu'eran de religión, iban a misa. Loo iban a jugar gallo, a correr carreras. Celebraba un vecino con lotro. Una comunidá con lotra ya juera con un baile. Hoy en día ya no se junta tanta gente como más antes, pero tavía se miran los muchitos el día de Santana. El día de Santiago. Día de San Juan, y tavía tienen los mismos valores que tenían más antes. Puea que no se junten tantos en l'iglesia, pero tavía tienen los mismos valores que más antes.

Más antes hacían baile. Había oportunidá pa juntarse los vecinos. Ya bien platicaban de la labor a más de la religión. Iban a misa y allá se platicaban, cambiaban ideas y asina. Eran muy, muy cerca un vecino del otro. Casi toos tenían la misma moralidá. Se ayudaban uno con lotro. Hacían fiestas. Éste trujo unos cabros. El otro trujo algotra cosa del rancho, y hacían fiesta y no había conque, "Yo puse más que tú." Ése traiba lo que podía, lo que tenía. Y si no tenías naa, naa traibas. Pero de toas maneras que tenían basilón.

One Neighbor Celebrated alongside Another

For feast days at my small ranch, those who were religious went to Mass. Then they went to play rooster, to run races. One neighbor celebrated alongside another. One community with another, whether it was a dance or not. Nowadays people don't get together the way they used to, but you can still see little boys and girls for Saint Anne's Day, for Saint James' Day. Or Saint John's, and people still have the same values as long ago. Perhaps not as many people gather in church, but the same principles are still there.

July 4th celebration, 1925
Negative 2583.
Courtesy of the
Citizens' Committee
for Historic
Preservation, Las
Vegas, NM.

Long ago they used to have dances. There was an opportunity for neighbors to mingle. They talked about their crops in addition to religion. They'd go to Mass and they chatted; they exchanged ideas and so forth. The neighbors enjoyed a very, very close relationship. Just about everyone had the same moral standards. They helped one another. They organized parties. This one brought a goat or two. The other brought something or other from the ranch, and they had a party, and there wasn't the matter of "I put in more than you." Each one brought what he could, whatever he had. And if he didn't have anything, he didn't bring anything. But in any case, they had a blast.

2

El valor de la educación

The Value of Education

Introduction

From time to time one hears, and even reads published accounts, about Hispanics in rural New Mexico lacking interest in education. That may have been true to some extent seventy or eighty years ago, and it may still be somewhat true, but the same thing could be said of any segment of the population. We can stack or shuffle the cards any way we desire in order to justify an argument. Our inability at times to view things in an objective and unbiased fashion is as much a part of the human condition in general as it is a human frailty in particular.

If we listen carefully to what our elders have to say about education and the barriers that confronted them, it is a wonder they attended school at all. Critics have to look beyond the veneer of seeming lack of interest and probe more deeply to better understand why pursuing an education was more a luxury than a necessity for the old folks.

Let us consider for a moment some important factors. Public schooling did not become a reality in New Mexico until the 1890s. Still, the debate on public education and the need to educate all of New Mexico's children outside of the Catholic, Presbyterian, and

Methodist churches, which began setting up schools in the 1860s, started in earnest during the 1840s.

When public education did come to the forefront of public discussion, ironically, it was the Hispanic governor Donaciano Vigil (1847–1848) and Félix Martínez, Democratic territorial legislator, among others, who grappled with the issue and with their colleagues in the legislature. Vigil brought the issue before the Legislative Assembly in 1847; even so, it took over forty years before a public school system began to be put into place after the approval of the public school law of 1891.

Since the grease slated to make the wheels of public education run smoothly was predicated on monies appropriated from taxes, it became clear that Hispanics in rural New Mexico, most of whom were surviving on subsistence farming, would suffer in comparison to people in the more affluent school districts. The poorer the county, the less revenue schools received, a phenomenon that holds true to this day. (In rural areas of New Mexico a large percentage of Hispanic children are the poorest in the United States, an issue critics contend is ignored for political reasons.)

To begin with, not only were educational facilities in Hispanic school districts inferior and barely conducive to learning, but there was also a scarcity of books and school materials. School libraries, as such, were a luxury. Top-notch teachers were scarce in rural villages as well, because salaries were lower than in the larger cities or communities. Those teachers who were attracted to rural schools often were ill prepared. As Andrés Archuleta told me, "The first teacher I ever had taught only in Spanish because he didn't know English. How was I going to learn it?"

If education appears to have been a low priority for the Hispano, particularly if one examines statistics on the high dropout rate, the conclusion is somewhat valid. On the other hand, if we look at the time period during which most old-timers in this chapter attended school (approximately 1910–1925), mitigating factors come into play, some of which, until recently, were still a bone of contention in political and pedagogical circles. In the first place, Hispano children went from a cultural environment uniquely their own to an educational setting that was, at best, alien. For instance, pursuing an education was not something their parents did during the Territory

(1850–1912). Therefore, the children lacked any understanding of its importance and benefits, other than the fact that the law required it. To confound them further, switching from their home language, Spanish, to English did little to help them in the transition unless they were fortunate to have a teacher who was bilingual and empathetic. (I know how this feels because I started school in the Río Puerco Valley in a one-room schoolhouse and did not know one word of English.)

Despite the obstacles that faced schoolchildren, most parents favored sending their sons and daughters to school. Next to the local priest or the scribe (*escribano*), who wrote letters for the community, the teacher (*el m[a]estro, la m[a]estra*) was the most revered person in the community, respected as the "master" of his or her trade and a person who could do no wrong as far as the parents were concerned. Teachers had a free hand in enforcing discipline; in more serious cases corporal punishment was even administered. Unfortunately, some teachers abused their charges, with few if any repercussions from the parents. A small number of teachers were ruthless in their treatment of students. Others could be rather ingenious in disciplining their pupils. Jesusita Aragón recalled a teacher named Jacobo Durán. "That man," she says, "didn't spank anybody. Whenever he had to discipline the kids, he had these caps with rabbit ears, and he'd sit them facing the class." Regardless of the punishment meted out, it did little to motivate some students, and it discouraged others from continuing their studies.

Further evidence that education was not necessarily a low priority for the parents was the fact that children walked miles to school, even in the dead of winter and during inclement weather. If it snowed, the father hitched up the horse-drawn wagon (not always a covered wagon), bundled up the children, and took them to school. At times, even at a very young age, children rode alone to school on horseback or on donkeys, as my father did when he was in the first and second grades. Once in school, they did not have the luxury of a cafeteria, so everyone took a lunch, which usually consisted of beans, chile, and tortillas, but nobody was embarrassed because of the food they packed.

Notwithstanding the best of intentions on the part of the parents, when the choice was between putting food on the table or attending school, the latter was deemed a lower priority. Harvest time is a case in point. Harvesting crops to store for the winter for human and animal consumption was considered much more important than reading, writing, or arithmetic, and children were expected to lend a helping hand. Other chores, for example, canning, fell into the same category. There were times when a young boy would have to quit school to work as a cowhand or at some other job to earn money to help support the family. Even daughters who had learned to sew from their grandmothers were forced to leave school to make clothing for the rest of the family. Certain matters simply took precedence over education; this was the rule, not the exception.

So parents were invariably faced with having their children miss school or even quit to help the family. When survival was at stake, the decision to keep their children out of school became clear and unequivocal.

With rare exception, virtually all the accounts in this chapter underscore certain commonalities among Hispanos vis-à-vis their educational experience. We learn of their positive attitude toward education, although some of the interviewees adhered to the notion that a woman's place was in the kitchen. Regardless of this feeling and ill-prepared teachers, and however daunting the task of getting children to school, most parents encouraged both sons and daughters to attend school.

Elba C. de Baca, who was a public school teacher for many years and who is featured in this chapter, is proof that girls could get an education if properly motivated and it was economically feasible. Unfortunately, parents' good intentions for most kids fizzled in time. Emphasis on education began with a capital E, but as children grew older and family needs became more urgent, it shrank to a lowercase "e."

Arsenio Montoya, Sr.

Lo exigían a uno que juera a l'escuela

Yo jui a l'escuela nomás hasta el libro tercero. Lo exigían a uno que juera a l'escuela. Yo lo poco que aprendí, lo aprendí ahi nomás hablando con los gringos. Y sé sacar cuentas, sé escribir en inglés y en mexicano, pero yo creo que lo que sé se aprende.

Yo agarré munchos trabajos de mayordomo, maquinarias. En Portales yo corría los *gins* del algodón. En Bernalillo yo corría la máquina de las planas esas pa trabajar madera. Yo era el maquinista; tenía que setiar las máquinas al tamaño de la madera que iban hacer. En los *peanut mills* del Borden's y toos ésos, yo los corría tamién toos.

Pus tamién tengo recuerdos pero muy feos. Vine a l'escuela aquí a los Vigiles, yo y mi hermanita y, pa pasar el río, teníanos que pasar una tabla como de catorce pulgadas de ancha y como unos dieciocho, veinte pies de larga, ¿ves? Y nomás íbanos en la mitá del río, enpezaban a balanciarla éstos de los Vigiles hasta que cáibanos yo y la hermanita pa entro l'agua. No había más chanza. Les dijíanos a en papá y mamá pero no, quizás no reportaban ni naa. Se pasaba la misma cosa. Nos maltrataban [los de los Vigiles] algo a mí y a mi hermanita como con el cuento que éranos del rancho. Yo lloraba y too y les dijía,

—Algún día cre, crezco.

—¡Crece pronto! —me dijían.

Y sí, gracias a Dios que sí. Después me desquité con eos. Y ya pa que mires tú, ya toos ésos, ya están muertos toos. ¿Pa desquitarme? Pus nomás pegales cuando ya sabía que podía pegales. Güeno, pus estaa enpuesto, estaa más macizo yo que eos porque yo hacía leña con l'acha y estaa enpuesto agarrar leños gruesos, pero lo que ahi es que si le pegaba a uno, me brincaban toos los demás.

Hechos agua a l'escuela, hechos agua, llegábanos yo y mi hermanita. Lo mesmo cuando viníanos de allá pacá. Mamá dijía,

—Pus no podemos hacer naa, hijito.

Yo no sé. Era muy tímida la gente de antes. No les gustaa andar yo creo en bromas.

—¡Quién sabe si ustedes se caírían solos o vendrían ahi corriendo! —como que no le creían a uno lo que era la verdá.

Había veces que ya como que arreglábanos, y pasaba yo bien el río, ¿ves? Pus ya éranos amigos.

—Vamos a bañarnos, Montoya.

Y yo creido que ya éranos amigos. ¡Naa! Ahi onde andábanos bañándonos, porque éranos unas truchas pa naar, alguno de eos iba y me escondía la ropa a mí. Cuando repicaba la campana, pus toos se

iban y yo a buscar la ropa. ¡Naa ropa! No iba en too el día a l'escuela.
Ahi me quedaba too el día en l'agua. Toos ésos eran malos castigos.
Está feo pa acordarme de eso yo. Loo si no iba a l'escuela, ni pre-
guntaba la mestra,

—¿Ónde está Arsenio?

Ea se quedaba dormida ahi. Y era de éstas muy conocidas, se llamaba *Miss* Baca, de estas Bacas, y iba con unas *miniskirts.* Táanos aquí
en el Montezuma antonces, de aquel lao de Montezuma. Ahi estaa
una escuela grande junto el *swimming pool.* Y iba y se levantaba las
naguas y se sentaba a ver. Una vez jui, ¿usté sabe esa hierba de
hormiga? que dicen que hay hierba de la hormiga, una hierbita
verdecita que pica, y le dije a la plebe,

—Yo le voy a echar hierba a la silleta.

—¡A que no!

—Sí la hago —era muy entrao yo.

Era atroz tamién. Y agarré de esa hierbita bien seca y la molí y le
eché a la silleta y entró y se sentó. Al ratito enpezó . . . tuvo que
salirse. No aguantó.

—Güeno, y loo se están calladitos. Orita güelvo.

No, pus no volvió por tres días. ¡Tres días no jue porque eché
hierba de hormiga al asiento! Era medio travieso yo.

Loo otro, José Gómez, pescó un ratón. Era una mestra [la señorita
Baca] que se durmía asina pa bajo y dejaba los tacones pa juera, de
los zapatos. Jue aquel y pescó un ratoncito y luego al ratito jue y
trujo otro y le echó uno en cada pie [zapato]. Loo agarró un gra,
grande. Era pior este José Gómez. Ahi vivía en Romeroville, y agarró
un grande. *"Hey teacher. There's a mice!"* Y lo vido y párase muy recio
y cuando se paró, reviéntansele los dos ratones en los zapatos. ¡Jiii
esa mujer! Y no pudo hacer naa porque ea no supo que alguien se los
echó. Ella pensó que ahi se le habían metido. Despúes ya no se quedaba dormida.

Ese José Gómez era más atroz que toos nojotros juntos. El otro día
quedó viudo. ¡Probecito!

You Were Required to Go to School

I only attended school till I was in the third grade. You were required
to go to school. And what little I did learn, I learned speaking with
the Anglos. I know how to solve math problems, I know how to

write in English and in Spanish, but I believe that what I know is simply because of personal desire to learn.

I got a lot of jobs as manager, and operating heavy machinery. In Portales I ran the cotton gins. In Bernalillo I ran those leveling lumber machines. I was the machinist. I had to set the machines according to the size of the lumber or boards. I also ran the peanut mills and all of that belonging to Borden's.

Well, I also have very unpleasant memories. I came to school here in Los Vigiles [north of Las Vegas], I along with my little sister, and, in order to cross the river, we had to walk across a board about fourteen inches wide and about eighteen, twenty feet long, you see? And just about the time that we'd be about halfway, these guys from Los Vigiles would start to rock the board until my little sister and I fell into the water. There was nothing we could do about it. We used to tell Dad and Mom, but I guess they didn't report it or anything. The same thing would happen time and again. Those kids from los Vigiles used to mistreat my little sister and me just because we came from a ranch. I would cry and everything and I would say to them, "Someday I'm going, going to grow up."

"Grow up quick!" they'd say to me.

And yes, thank God, I did grow up. Later on I got even with them. And just to show you how the tables can turn, all of them are already dead. What did I do to avenge myself? Well, all I did was to beat them up when I got old enough to do so. You see, I was much more muscular than they were because I would chop wood and I was used to handling large pieces of wood, but the thing is that if I beat one of them up, the rest of them would jump me.

We [my sister and I] got to school soaking, soaking wet. The same thing would happen on the way back, on the way home. Mom would say to us, "Well, we just can't do anything, my son."

I don't know. People long ago were very timid. I guess they just didn't like to get involved in difficulties.

"Who knows but what you didn't fall into the water by yourselves or because you were running and messing around!" like they [my parents] didn't believe what you were saying.

There were times like when we and those kids from Los Vigiles had a truce, so I would cross the river all right, you see? We were now supposedly friends.

"Let's go swimming, Montoya."

I was under the impression that they were really friends. Nothing doing! There where we were swimming, because we were like trout when it came to swimming, and one of them would go and hide my clothes. When the bell rang, why, everyone took off and there I'd be looking for my clothing. No clothes whatsoever! I wouldn't go to school the entire day. I'd stay in the water all day long. Those things were nothing but mean acts of humiliation. It's very hard for me to look back on all of that, but I had to put up with it all the time. And to make matters worse, if I didn't return to school the teacher wouldn't even ask, "Where's Arsenio?"

There she'd be falling asleep. And she was well known one, of these Bacas. Her name was Miss Baca, and she used to wear these miniskirts. We were in Montezuma at the time, on the other side of Montezuma. There was a large school next to the swimming pool, and she would go and raise her skirt and sit down to watch. One time I went and, you know what ant weed is, right? People call it ant weed; it's a tiny green herb that makes you itch, and so I told the kids, "I'm going to sprinkle some of that little ant weed on her chair."

"I bet you don't!"

"Yes, I will." I was very daring.

I was also very mischievous. And so I got some of that very dry little weed and I ground it up and sprinkled it on the chair and she [Miss Baca] came in and sat down. A little while later she started . . . she had to leave. She couldn't stand the itching.

"Okay. I want you to be very quiet. I'll be back in a little while."

No, way. The truth is she didn't return for three days. For three days she didn't return just because I sprinkled ant weed on her chair! I was a bit prankish.

Then there was another kid, José Gómez, he went and caught a mouse. Miss Baca was the kind of teacher who would fall asleep with her head down and the heels of her shoes would be sticking out. So he went and caught a mouse and then a little while later he brought another one and put one in each shoe. Then he grabbed a large one [a rat]. José Gómez was worse than me. He lived there in Romeroville, and so he grabbed a large rat. "Hey, teacher. There's a mice!" She saw it and quickly stood up and when she did, she squashed the two little mice in her shoes. Boy, you should have seen that woman! And she couldn't do anything because she never suspected that someone had put the mice in her shoes. She thought the mice had gotten into her shoes by themselves. After that she never fell asleep.

That José Gómez was more of a cutup than all of us put together. Just the other day he became a widower. Poor thing!

Elba C. de Baca

Empezando l'escuela

Hace munchos años los niños empezaban l'escuela a la edá de siete años. Cada pueblito tenía su escuelita de un cuarto. En las ciudades y los pueblitos había escuelas públicas como también religiosas. En Las Vegas, Nuevo México, las Hermanas de Loretto estaban en cargo de l'Escuela de Nuestra Señora de los Dolores. Había estudiantes del primer libro hasta el ocho que iban a l'escuela todos los días. Otros vivían en l'escuela misma. También había dos escuelas públicas: North Public y South Public.

En lo que se llamaba New Town, estaba la Escuela de la Imaculada Concepción, la cual estaba bajo el encargo de las Hermanas de Loretto. L'escuela tenía del libro uno hasta el doce. Además, estaban Las Vegas High School, Normal University, y dos otras escuelas públicas. En un tiempo había un colegio en la Plaza Vieja que tenían los jesuitas.

Un niño cuando le daban sus libros en l'escuela, escribía las siguientes palabras:

> Si este libro se perdiera,
> como suele suceder,
> le suplico al que lo hallara,

que lo sepa devolver.
Y si fuera de uñas largas,
y de poco entendimiento,
le suplico que se acuerde,
del séptimo mandamiento [No robarás].

Si un niño hallaba alguna cosa, dijía,

Una cosa me he encontrado,
cuatro veces lo diré.
Si su dueño no aparece,
con ella me quedaré.

North Public School, 1912 Negative 3616. Courtesy of the Citizens' Committee for Historic Preservation, Las Vegas, NM.

Starting School

Years ago children started school at the age of seven. Each village had its own one-room schoolhouse. In the cities and towns there were public as well as religious schools. In Las Vegas, the Sisters of Loretto ran Our Lady of Sorrows School. They had both boarders and day students from first through eighth grades. There were also two public schools: North Public and South Public.

In New Town, there was the Immaculate Conception School, which was also run by the Sisters of Loretto. The school had grades one through twelve. In addition, there was Las Vegas High School, two other public schools, and the Normal University. At one time the Jesuits ran a college in Old Town [1877–1888].

When a child received his school books, he would write the following:

> If this book gets lost,
> as is apt to happen,
> I beg the person who finds it,
> to return it to its rightful owner.
> Or, if the finder happens
> to be light-fingered
> and rather unscrupulous,
> I beg him to remember,
> the seventh commandment [Thou shall not steal].

When a child found something, he would say the following:

> If I find something,
> I'll repeat it four times.
> If the owner doesn't come forward,
> I'll keep it for my own!

Jesusita Aragón

Me gustaba la escuela muncho

Yo comencé la escuela de seis años. Asina la comenzaba uno antes. Viníanos a pie de allá de casa. Tres millas estábanos de la escuela, porque estaba la iglesia y todo cerquita en Trujillo. Viníanos a pie. Muy contentos todos, los vecinos y nojotros, y tráibanos lonche a la escuela. No ponían cocinas antes, ni boses ni nada. Cuando se ponía nevoso, prendía mi papá el carro de caballos y nos traiba.

Nosotros teníanos un mestro, muy güeno, Jacobo Durán. Un hombre fino, mestro tan güeno. Lo queríanos todos. Ese hombre no le pegaba a naiden cuando tenía que ejecutalos a los muchachos. Tenía unas gorras con orejas de conejo, y los sentaba con la cara pa la clas. ¿Y sabe qué? Bajaban el libro en veces ellos y se sonreían, ¿ve?

No les daba recreo ni nada. ¡Nada! Asina los ejecutaba. Muy güen mestro. Muy güeno. Yo lo quise muncho. Ese hombre sí era vivo.

Oh. Munchas veces había mestros muy malos. Les pegaban con una jara a los escueleros. Eso hacían, y no se nojaban los papases. A mí nunca me pegaron, no.

A mí me gustaba la escuela muncho. Si había habido estos programas que hay ora, yo hubiera acabao mi escuela, porque a mí si me gustaba. Lo primero que hubiera estudiao era aprender bien inglés.

I Liked School a Lot

I started school when I was six years old. That's the age one started a long time ago. We used to go to school on foot. We were three miles from school, because the church and everything else was close together in Trujillo. We were all very happy, the neighbors, us, and everyone else, and we'd bring our lunch to school. They didn't have cafeterias back then, or buses or anything. Whenever it got snowy, my father would hitch up the team of horses and he'd take us.

We had a teacher, a very good one, Jacobo Durán. He was a fine man, such a good teacher. We all liked him very much. That man didn't spank anybody. Whenever he had to discipline the kids, he had these caps with rabbit ears, and he'd sit them facing the class. And do you know what? There were times when the kids would put the book in front of their face and they'd snicker, you see? Then the teacher wouldn't let them go out for recess. Nothing! That's how he punished them. A very good teacher. I liked him very much. That man was really intelligent.

Oh, let me tell you. There were times when we had some very mean teachers. They would spank the schoolchildren with a kind of thin twig or a sandbar willow. That's what the teachers used to do, and the parents never got mad. I never got whipped, thank goodness.

I liked school a lot. If we had had today's programs, I would have finished school, because I liked it. The first thing I would have done was to learn English.

Severa Archuleta

Un cuarto tenía nomás l'escuela

Sí. Sí, fui a l'escuela, ahi en Trujillo. Oh, hasta el libro quinto yo creo nomás. Estudiábanos. Salíanos al *recess*. Jugábanos un rato. Y lego nos metían otra vez.

Y antes si estaba cerca iba uno a pie a l'escuela. No había boses; no había nada. O los [nos] llevaba en papá en el carro de caballos.

Un cuarto nomás tenía l'escuela, y una mestra. Ora es un atajo de cuartos y de mestras. Antes sí llevaba uno lonche y todo. Oh, pus ya bien le echaban a uno en la casa *biscuits* y todo eso. Le echaban a uno en la casa. No como ora, voy y compro lonche. No. De la casa todo a los muchachos, a las muchachas. También lo que hacía ea [mamá] en la casa, papas. Nos hacía *sandwich* o los [nos] echaba las papas.

Pus, yo les echaba a mis hijos lonche. Les echaba lo que tenía en la casa, ya bien papas. Carne. Y duce. Pus *jelly*. Les hacía *sandwich*, con *peanut butter*. En tortilla. Pa beber, agua. Agua tenían en l'escuela.

Algunos mestros eran algo estritos. Algunos, no. Otros pues los [nos] paraban en un rincón. Voltiaos pa la pader. [Risas] O les daban avisos a los padres. Y lego, pus el papá y la mamá regañaban a uno. Ora no puede hacer eso usté, porque le echan los chotas.

Bueno, pus a mí no me castigaron asina. Munchas mestras tenían una rula pa dales en las manos. Ése era el castigo que había. Diuna jara no me acuerdo. Pero una rula, sí. Sí me acuerdo. En las manos nos pegaban. En la palma de la mano. No, no duele. O ya bien no dejaban salir a uno al *recess*. Lo dejaban adentro. Ése era el castigo también.

The School Had Only One Room

Yes. Yes, I went to school, there in Trujillo. Oh, I guess I only went to the fifth grade. We'd study. We'd go out for recess. We'd play a while. And then they'd get us back in school once again

And a long time ago if the school was close by you went on foot. There were no buses; there was nothing. Or perhaps my dad would take us in a horse-drawn wagon.

The school had only one room—and one teacher. Nowadays,

there's a whole bunch of rooms and teachers. A long time ago you took your lunch and all. Well, they were likely to pack biscuits and that sort of thing. It was all prepared at home. Not like now, I can go and buy lunch. No. Everything came from the house, not only for the boys but also for the girls. Whatever Mom made at home. Potatoes. She'd make us potato sandwiches.

Well, I used to fix lunches for my children. I'd pack whatever I had at home, possibly potatoes. Meat. And dessert. Or jelly. I'd make them a peanut butter sandwich. Rolled up in a tortilla. As for drinking, water. Water is something they had at school.

Some teachers were somewhat strict. Some, not. Others, well, they'd stand us in the corner. Turned toward the wall. [Laughter] Or they would inform the parents. And then the father and the mother would scold you. Now you can't even do that because they'll get the sheriff after you.

Well. As for me, they never punished me that way. Many teachers had a ruler to hit your hands. That was the punishment back then. I don't remember a willowlike whip being used. But a ruler, yes. That I remember. The teacher would hit us on the palms of our hands. No, it doesn't hurt. Or perhaps you weren't allowed to go for recess as punishment. You were kept inside. That was another means of punishing you.

Katarina Montoya

Íbanos en una chalupa

Yo tenía muncha anbición de acabar l'escuela, pero en antes no había oportunidades de vinir al colegio. Cuando uno acababa el *high school*, ahi se acababa too. Si agarraba un trabajo, eso quería dijir que había hecho muy bien. Y si no, pus, la otra cosa era casarse, yo creo.

Comencé l'escuela en Gusdorf [al este de Taos], pero no iba más de algunos días. A mí me gustaba muncho l'escuela. Tenían muy güenas mestras, a lo que yo me acuerdo. Le digo a mi esposo que pa contar tenían una cosa con cuentas de diferentes colores. El primero era un marco con alambres y ahi estaan las cuentas. Había de uno hasta veinticinco, y ahi podía uno aprender a contar hasta veinticinco en esa cosa. A mí me entusiasmó porque era muy, muy interesante. Y loo tenían los *charts* grandes conque se voltiaban las hojas. Ahi estaban las diferentes letras, que yo me tenía más entusiasmo en aprenderlas porque se me hacía que aprendía más pronto a leer si sabía las letras de los nombres de toas estas cosas que tenían en el *chart*.

Y juimos a l'escuela a pie antonces, pero loo nos hicieron una chalupa que la jalaban los caballos. Íbanos en una chalupa. En eso era lo que me gustaa de ir a l'escuela, la chalupa. Tenían los caballos allá en l'escuela. Los amarraban hasta en la tarde que nos viníanos. Porque allá caiba muncha nieve, no como ora. Tavía en la primavera estaa la nieve. No se vía cuando íbanos en la chalupa.

Una chalupa era una, ¿cómo le dijiera? No tenía ruedas. Tenía un ráfete hecho voltiao parriba, como un *sleigh*. Nomás qu'era hecho de tabla. Mi hermano mayor, él arriaba los caballos. Él iba a l'escuela tamién. Toos mis hermanos comenzaron l'escuela allá [en Gusdorf].

La mestra que yo tuve antonces no me acuerdo naa de ea. No me acuerdo quién sería la mestra cuando estáanos iyendo ahi. Nada, nada de ella, nada me imprentó en mi mente.

Nos castigaban con una *ruler.* [Risas] Y lego yo volví par esa escuela cuando mi hermana enseñó. Ya vivíanos allá en Gusdorf, y íba en el libro segundo. Yo y mi hermanito nos juimos con ea pahi. Era muy estrita, porque era mi hermana. Ea me enseñó a leyer. Éste era ya en el *second grade.* Cuando yo acabé ese año, ya yo sabía los cuarenta y ocho estaos y sus capitolios. Y ea me dijía,

—Tienes que saber porque, si no, los otros no van a querer aprender.

So, yo tenía que ser el ejemplo par eos. Y aprendían. Loo me enseñó las tablas de multiplicar. De uno hasta doce. Yo las sabía. Ya cuando jui a los otros grados, a mí se me hizo nada. Ya yo sabía todo eso, porque ea tomaba tiempo en la noche pa enseñarme y me explicaba lo que estaa pasando.

Y una vez dijo,

—El que traiga chíquite pa l'escuela y lo masque, se lo voy a poner en las narices.

Uno de mis mismos primos hermanos dijo que yo traiba chíquite y yo no traiba chíquite. Pero ea no me pudo perdonar porque él había dicho que traiba chíquete. Yo traiba chíquite, pero antes de que se comenzara l'escuela lo puse abajo el banco. Ahi estaba el chíquite, pero me lo pegó en las narices. Oh, yo estaba tan, ah, ¡me lastimó tanto! ¡Que delante de toos ésos estaba yo! Y yo dije, le prometí a mi primo hermano, que si yo podía con él, yo le iba hacer algo pero nunca pude porque *he lied*. Pero mi hermana me castigó. Cuando llegamos a la casa estaa muy triste, y loo me explicó y dijo mi hermana,

—Yo no quería hacelo pero pus él dijo una mentira, pero es su mentira dél. A él lo va a castigar Dios, no a ti, —con eso me conformé.

We Went to School on a Rig

I had aspirations of finishing school, but long ago there were no opportunities to go to college. Whenever you finished high school, that was the end of everything. If you got a job, that meant that you did well. And if not, well, the only other thing was to get married, I guess.

I started school in Gusdorf east of Taos, but I attended only on certain days. I liked school very much. I had very good teachers, as far as I can recall. I tell my husband that for counting they had a thing with different-colored beads [an abacus]. The first color was a wire frame and that's where the beads were. You went from one to twenty-five, and so you were able to count up to twenty-five on that thing. I got very enthused because it was very, very interesting. And then they had the large flip charts. There you had the different letters, which I was more enthused about learning, because it seemed to me that I could learn to read quicker if I knew the letters of all the things that appeared on the chart.

And we went to school on foot, but later on they built a rig that was pulled by horses. We went to school on that rig. That's what I liked to go to school on—that contraption. The horses were kept at school. They'd tie them up till the afternoon when it was time to come home. Because it used to snow a lot, not like now. There was snow even in the spring. You couldn't see a thing when we rode the rig.

A *chalupa* was, how do you say? It didn't have wheels. It had runners pointing up like a sleigh. The only thing is that it was made of wood. My older brother, he's the one who drove the horses. He also went to school. All of my brothers and sisters started school over in Gusdorf.

The teacher that I had at the time, I don't recall anything about her. I don't remember who the teacher could have been when we were going to school there. Nothing. Nothing stands out in my mind about her.

The teachers used to punish us with a ruler. [Laughter] Then later on I returned to that same school when my sister taught there. We were already living in Gusdorf. I was in the second grade. My little brother and I went to live with her. She was very strict because she was my sister. She taught me how to read. That was in the second grade. When I finished that year, I already knew the forty-eight states and their capitals. And she used to say to me, "You have to know because if you don't, the other kids aren't going to want to learn."

I had to set an example for them. And they used to learn. Then she taught me the multiplication tables. From one to twelve. I knew them. By the time I got into the other grades, it was a snap for me. I already knew all of that, because she took the time at night to teach me and she explained to me what was going on.

One time she said, "Anyone who brings gum to school and is caught chewing it, I'm going to stick it on your nose."

One of my cousins accused me of chewing gum, and I didn't have any. But she couldn't forgive me because he had said that I was chewing gum. I was chewing gum, but before school started I stuck it to the bottom of the desk. That's where the gum was, but she stuck it on my nose. Oh, I was so, ah, it hurt me a lot! There I was in front of everyone! And I said to myself, I promised my cousin, that if I ever had a chance, I was going to get even, but I never could. But my sister punished me. When we got home I was very sad. Then my sister explained to me, "I didn't want to do it, but he told a lie, but it's his lie. God is going to punish him, not you." That made me feel good.

Reynaldo Gonzales

Yo iba a l'escuela en un carro de burros

Pus yo iba a l'escuela dos millas y más—en un carro de burros, en un carrito de burros. Tamién con un caballo que tenía en papá. Mañoso. Le tiraba pataas al bogue, y con nojotros, yo y mis dos hermanas y mis otros dos hermanos. Yo era el más chiquito. Había otros más chiquitos pero a eos no les tocó. Tenía el bogue un barandal. Era de garra, con fierros. El caballo ese me acuerdo yo que rompía ese tapolio, cuando nos tiraba pataas. ¡Oh! Yo pasé toos esos trabajos.

Ya cuando yo jui a l'escuela, nos castigaban con una rula. Le pegaban a uno. A mí no me pegó niuna [maestra]. ¡Niuna! Pero había unos dos muchachos ya grandes, ya estaan grandes. Eran muy atroces, y vino un mestro. No hace munchos años que se murió. Eos [los muchachos] eran tan traviesos, que no los podía tener quietos. Sacaba uno de los muchachos y lo paraba en una esquina de l'escuela. Era grandota. Ya ora la tiraron. Y lotro con una piedra que detuviera aquí en las manos parriba. Aquí tenía que tener la piedra. Las manos parriba. Con eso los castigaba. Pero eran tan atroces, que nomás se descuidaba el mestro, bajaba la piedra y se ponía hacele monerías al otro. Hacían rir a la demás plebe. Muchachos muy atroces. Eran bárbaros. Güeno, era su vida de eos.

En munchas escuelas isque les ponían *tape* en la boca o no sé qué. Pero ahi onde estuve yo no, nunca. Yo aprendí. Sabía escribir bien español. Cuasi no enseñaban en inglés nada. Cuasi naa, naa en inglés. Too enseñaan en español. Después comenzó el inglés poquito. Yo comencé hablar inglés, aprendelo, trabajando por éste y por lotro. Yo el inglés no lo aprendí con los mestros.

I Went to School in a Donkey Wagon

Well, I traveled two miles and more to school—in a donkey wagon, in a little donkey wagon. We also used a horse that Dad had. It was quite vicious. It would kick the buggy, with us aboard, my two sisters and me and my other brothers. I was the youngest. There were others who followed me, but they didn't get to ride the horse-drawn buggy. The buggy had a railing with iron bars covered with cloth [tarpaulin]. I remember that horse tearing up the tarpaulin whenever it kicked at us. Oh! I experienced all those hard times.

Well, by the time I started school, they punished us with a ruler. No teacher ever spanked me. Not one! But there were some older kids; they were already much older. They were terrible, and a new teacher showed up. He died not too many years ago. They [the boys] were so mischievous that he couldn't keep them quiet. He would pick one of the boys and stand him in the corner. The school was huge. It's been demolished. And the other kid had to hold a rock and stand with his hands up in the air. That's the way he had to hold the rock. With his hands up in the air. That's how the teacher punished them. But they were so terrible. As soon as the teacher turned his back on them, the kid with the rock would lower the rock and start cutting up. He made all of the other kids in class laugh. The kids were awful. They were terrible. Well, that was their pastime.

I understand that in many schools they [the schoolteachers] would put tape on their mouth or I don't know what. But there where I was, not so. Never. I learned. I knew how to write well in Spanish. They hardly taught you anything in English. Almost nothing, nothing in English. Everything was in Spanish. Later on English was taught a little bit. I started to speak English, to learn it, working for this guy or the other. English is something I didn't learn from my teachers.

Katarina Montoya

Pa Crismes tenían un pograma en l'escuela

Pa Crismes tenían un pograma en l'escuela. Tenían del libro primero hasta el libro ocho. Mi tío decoraba el árbol. Un árbol grande. Tenían dulces y loo ponían un pograma. Y otro tío, el más joven del lao d'en papá, él traducía los *plays* de inglés a mexicano. Los ponía en mexicano porque toos entendieran. D'eso me acuerdo bien, porque me gustaba muncho. Mi tío decoraba el árbol con unos pajaritos muy delicaos. Con unas colitas. Cuando se acababa too nos daba un pajarito a cada quien. Pero eran tan delicaos que cuando llegáanos a la casa ya estaa quebrao el pajarito. Bueno, eran como vidrio, pero era tan delicao que cualesquier cosita más que uno los cuidara, se que-braban. Eran tan bonitos. Se abrían y loo prendían el árbol y se quedaba parao el pajarito. Pero pa nojotros era una cosa muy linda. Loo mi tío nos daba dulces y cacahuates y cosas asina.

For Christmas They Had a Program at School

For Christmas they had a program at school. The grades went from first to eighth. My uncle decorated the tree. A large tree. They had candy and then they would put on a program. And another uncle, the youngest on my father's side, he translated the plays from English into Spanish. He'd put them into Spanish so everyone would understand. I remember all of that because I liked it very much. My uncle would decorate the Christmas tree with these very delicate birds. They had tiny tails. When everything was over with, he would give each one of us a little bird. But they were so fragile that by the time we got home, the tiny bird was already broken. Well, the birds were made from something like glass, but they were so delicate that however careful you were with them, they seem to break anyway. They were so beautiful. They would open up and then the tree would be lighted up and each little bird stood up. But for us children it was a very pretty thing. Then my uncle would give us candy and peanuts and things like that.

Alfredo Ulibarrí

Eran muy güenos los mestros

Aquí en Las Vegas, le diré la verdá que eran muy güenos los mestros. Muy güenos eran con nojotros. A lo menos yo onde comencé, comencé en el Castle. Unos que otros teníanos una mestra que se enojaa con nojotros cuando la teníanos en el libro cuarto. La hacíanos nojar, y tú sabes se enojaa tanto que al fin hasta ea se caiba en el suelo y la sacáanos nojotros pa juera que le diera el viento, porque ya la teníanos cansada. ¡Si, era la misma cosa que lo de ora! Pero no la matábanos.

Lotro día me estaa acordando de ea. Estaa una muchacha plati-

Castle School, 1939
Fritz Broeske, courtesy
Museum of New
Mexico. Negative
120972.

cando tocante la mestra en el libro cuarto. Pero lo que jue del libro
primero al libro segundo, libro tercero, yo la pasé muy a gusto. Eran
muy güenas mestras. Pero del libro cuarto sí batallé. Pus esa mestrita
era muy mala. Y loo ya en ese tiempo, comenzaban a dale examina-
ciones a uno, cada mes, o cada cuatro meses le daban a uno una
examinación, a ver cómo iba caminando uno, y loo de ahi siguía más
adelante y loo aá más nos daan otra examinación.

Tamién nos castigaban—con una tripa. Yo jui el que agarró una
tripa una vez, porque brinqué una ventana pa juera. Ya estaa en el
libro cuarto con la Tammy, y brincamos yo y este File Esquibel. Andaba conmigo tamién, pero no me acuerdo si él brincó, pero se me
hace que sí. Pero yo y el Daniel sí brincamos pa juera de la ventana.
Loo que brincamos la ventana, pus otro día, supo mi papá y mi
mamá. Me dieron una frega, y loo después le dijo [a la maestra] que
nos tuvieran amarraos otra vez, *after school, you know.* Y a mí me
amarraron de esta pata aquí asina de la pata de la mesa de la mestra.
A los dos, a mí y a Daniel, ahi nos tuvieron como por tres, cuatro
días. Nos tenían amarraos, pero nos daan disciplina; nos daan con
una tabla o nos daan con una tripa. Teníanos miedo también, porque
ya después no lo golvíanos hacer. O le juíanos a juir. Que el que era
atroz, pus, era atroz como ora yo. Yo era muy atroz en l'iscuela.

Una vez tamién íbanos yo y su hermano de ea [mi esposa] de l'iscuela, porque esa vez vino de aá del rancho. Iba entrar a l'iscuela aquí al libro siete. Estáanos ya los dos en el libro siete. Luego iba una mestra. Yo no sé por qué esa mestra nos habíanos nojao yo y ea. O que nos había quitao de unos *swings* que tenían, y nos nojamos con ea y logo viníanos toos too el camino. Logo esa mestra, pus, iba delante de nojotros. Y loo dijo su hermano de ea [mi esposa],

—Ésa es la mestra que nos quitó de los *swings*. Vamos a agarrar hierba de esa piedra de los hormigueros y tirale.

Iba con unas cuatro, cinco muchachas ea, adelantito de nojotros, puea que iría como de aquí a la puerta. Cada quien agarró un puño d'esas piedritas de los hormigueros y tiramos y le pegamos aquí atrás, y nójase y otra vez me puso otra frega bien dada en papá a mí. Que a su hermano de ea [mi esposa], no le hicieron naa. Pero, *anyway,* que a mí sí me pegaron porque a mí me jue el que le echaron la culpa más. Me pegaron una frega bien dada.

The Teachers Were Very Good

Here in Las Vegas, I'll tell you the truth, the teachers were very good. They were very good to us. At least where I started, which was at Castle. From time to time a teacher in the fourth grade would get mad at us. We made her mad, and do you know that she got so angry that she even fainted on the floor and so we had to carry her outside for her to get some fresh air, because she was already fed up with us. Why it was the same thing as nowadays! But we didn't kill her.

The other day I was thinking about her. There was a girl talking about a fourth-grade teacher. But when it came to the first and second and third grades, I had it real good. The teachers were very good. But I did have a rough time in the fourth grade. That little teacher was very mean. And about that time, they started giving you exams every month, or every four months, to see how you were doing, and later on another exam.

They also punished us—with a rubber hose. I'm one who ended up one time at the wrong end of the hose, because I jumped out a window. I was already in the fourth grade with Miss Tammy, and this Phil Esquibel and I jumped out the window. He was with me, but I can't recall if he jumped or not, but it seems to me that he did. But Daniel and I did jump out the window. Then after we jumped, well, next my mom and dad found out. They gave me quite a beating, and then later on they told the teacher to tie us up once more after school. And they tied me from this leg [the right leg], like, of the teacher's desk. The two of us, Daniel and me, were tied there for three or four days. They had us tied down, but they disciplined us. They punished us with a piece of wood or they whipped us with a rubber hose. We got scared, because later on we didn't repeat our mischief. Or we avoided punishment. And as for the one who was atrocious, well, he was just like me. I misbehaved terribly in school.

One time [my wife's] brother and I were headed home from school, because that one time he came from the ranch. He was going to start the seventh grade. We had both passed to the seventh grade. Then there was this teacher walking along. I don't know why that teacher had made me mad. Or she had removed us from some swings, and we got mad at her. Then there we were walking along the road. The teacher was walking right in front of us. Then my wife's brother said to me, "That's the teacher that took us off the swings. Let's get some rocks from the anthills and throw them at her."

She was walking along with four or five girls right in front of us, no more than from here to the door [about five feet]. Each one of us got a handful of those little pebbles from an anthill and threw and hit her in the back and, bingo, she got mad. Once again I got a good whipping from my dad. As for [my wife's] brother, they didn't do anything. But anyway, I got a beating because I was the one who got blamed. I got a real good whipping.

Cesaria Montoya

Los maestros eran estritos

Creo que a la edad de once años ya tenía mi primer novio. Isque era mi novio. Una vez me dio un nicle, y lo llevé y le dije a mi mamá que lo había jallao y me lo quitó. [Risas] Me quitó mi nicle. Lloré más por ese nicle. Ora le digo a mi esposo,

—Yo tengo ganas de ver a ese hombre a ver ora de hombre qué parece.

Era en el cuarenta y tres, cuarenta y dos, por allá.

Pero los maestros eran estritos. Eran estritos. A mí me cuartiaron con una jara.

¿Sabe lo qué es jara? *Willow.* Verde. Me pintaron cuatro, cinco verdugos aquí en las canillas una vez porque nos peliamos yo y un primo mío. Ya los dos pariaditos nos paró en el cuarto [el maestro]. Pus dolió muncho pero no pasó más. Ya antonces no se bañaba la gente todos los días como nos bañamos ora. Antonces era una vez a la semana. Los sábados eran días de baño. [Risas] Cuando me jue que me desvistió mi mamá pa bañarme, pus estaa medianita, me vido los moretones.

—¿Qué pasó ahi?

—Yo no sé qué pasaría.

—Pus ora vas a saber —me dijo—. ¿Me dices qué pasó?

Pus, ya le tuve que decir. Agarró una jarita también ea y me dio otra frega. [Risas]

—Pa que no vuelvas —dijo.

No. Ahi tenía uno la culpa. Sí, uno era el de la culpa.

Miedo, miedo más que respeto. Yo creo que el miedo viene siendo el respeto. Ése era el respeto que había—el miedo. A todos les daban sus varejonazos. Nomás la jara usaban. Que yo me acuerde nomás la jara. ¡Oh! Nos paraban allá en un rincón. Ahi nos tenían. Por cinco, diez, quince minutos. Si tenía uno la chancita de que la mestra no estuviera viendo pallá, se voltiaba uno haceles musarañas a la otra plebe [risas], pa que los castigaran a todos.

Oh, y loo me acuerdo que pal tiempo de Crismes, las catequistas, las monjas, iban a enseñar catecismo allá en los ranchos. Ellas eran tamién las que ponían programas pa Crismes. ¡Muy bonito! Una vez me acuerdo que tuvimos afuera, en un llanito que estaa rodeao de monte, a San José y María Santísima, la misma plebe, y el ángel. Como te digo, yo era el ángel. Tavía soy, ¿no? [Risas]

The Teachers Were Strict

I believe that by the time I was eleven years old, I already had my first boyfriend. I understand he was my boyfriend. One time he gave me a nickel, and I took it and told my mother that I had found it, and she took it away from me.[Laughter]. She took my nickel away from me. I cried for that nickel. Now I tell my husband, "I'd like to see that man, to see what he looks like now that he's a man." That was in 1943, or 1942, thereabouts.

But the teachers were strict. They were strict. I got whipped with a slender twig. Do you know what a twig is? A willow. It's green. One time I got four or five welts on my shins because I got into a fight with a cousin of mine. The teacher stood both of us up in the middle of the room. Well, it hurt a lot but nothing happened. At that time you didn't take a bath every day the way we do now. Back then you bathed once a week. Saturday was bath day.[Laughter] When my mother undressed me to bathe me, because I was very young, she saw the black and blue marks.

"What happened here?"

"I don't know what happened."

"Well, you're going to find out," she said to me. "Are you going to tell me what happened?"

Well, I had to tell her. She grabbed a small twig herself and let me have it. [Laughter]

"That's so you stay out of trouble next time," she said.

No question about it. You were to blame. You were the one at fault.

It was fear, fear more than respect. I guess that respect comes from fear. That was the respect back then—fear. Everyone got their twig whippings. That green twig is all that was used for spanking you. As far as I can remember, that's all that was used. Oh! They used to stand us in the corner. There you were, for five, ten, fifteen minutes. If you had a chance and the teacher wasn't looking over where you were, you turned around to make faces at the kids [laughter], so that everyone would get punished.

Oh, and I also remember that at Christmastime, the catechists, the nuns, used to go teach catechism over at the ranches. They were also the ones who put on programs at Christmas. Very beautiful! I recall one time putting on a play outside, in a small plain field, surrounded by trees, with Saint Joseph and the Blessed Virgin Mary, the kids, and an angel. As I say, I was the angel. And still am, right? [Laughter]

Alfredo Trujillo

Eran muy crueles antes los mestros

Yo me acuerdo del mestro Rafel. Pienso qu'ese jue mi primero. Rafel de aá de Mora era él. Aá en el Terromote estaa l'escuela. Y iba yo pus a l'escuela. Él me trataa muy bien a mí porque yo me daba a respetar muy bien pa que no me jueran a pegar. Eran muy crueles antes los mestros. Castigaban a la plebe. ¡Y les pegaban! Pues les daban con una jara. Un jarazo les daban. Eran malos.

Yo tenía un mestro—no jue el mestro Rafel. Jue lotro. Juan Sánchez se llamaba. Yo creo que estaa poco mal del sentido, de algún modo, porque una vez estáanos sentaos ahi en los bancos—tenían unos bancos muy largos—y estáanos yo y este Pol Silva sentaos. Él era mure risueño, por cualquier cosa se ría. Que le dijía yo alguna cosa, se ría, y el mestro estaa sentao aá en la mesita, en una silleta. Pues le dije yo no sé qué a él [a Pol], y se soltó riéndose. Pus vino el mestro y agárralo y levántalo parriba, y estréalo en el suelo. Era malo. Pus lo agarró y lo sacó del banco y lo estrelló en el suelo. A mí no me dijo naa porque yo estaa pa lotro lao, y yo no me estaa riendo tanto asina. Él [Pol] era el que estaa riéndose. Eran malos los mestros; eran malos.

Yo creo que muy pocos, muy pocos hijos se educaban. Eos [los padres] tampoco no sabían naa. Casi nada. Pero pus como a mí, yo no me eduqué porque a mí me sacaban a trabajar. A mí me ponían a trabajar con este hombre, con lotro, con toos esos rancheros que estaan ahi. Yo no jui a l'escuela más de hasta el libro seis. Comencé el libro seis y ya no jui más, porque me metieron [mis padres] a trabajar.

Yo creo que pa vivir. Era muncha pobreza, ¿ve? Muncha pobreza había. No había dinero; no había nada. Yo creo que yo trabajaba porque iba aá por lo que me pagaban a mí, seguro, que pa trae comida. Por eso yo no agarré educación, casi nada. Lo poco que aprendí yo de inglés, lo aprendí iyendo pa Colorao a trabajar con gabachos allá y toa esa gente. Asina jui aprendiendo yo.

The Teachers Used to Be Very Cruel

I recall the teacher named Rafael. I believe he was my first teacher. He was from over in Mora. The school was over in a place called Terromote. That's where I used to go to school. He treated me very well because I was very respectful so that I wouldn't get whipped. The teachers used to be very cruel. They punished the kids. And they whipped them! Why, they used to spank them with a twig. They'd swat you with a twig. They were mean.

I had a teacher once—it wasn't Rafael. It was someone else. Juan Sánchez was his name. I believe he was a bit off his rocker, because one time we were sitting there on these benches—they had these long benches—this Pol Silva and I. He was a real laugher, who would laugh at any little thing. Every time I said something to him, he'd laugh, and the teacher was sitting over at a small table in a chair. Well, I said I don't know what it was to Pol, and he started laughing. Well, here comes the teacher and picks him up in the air and slams him against the floor. He was mean. Why, he just picked him up from the bench and slammed him against the floor. He didn't say anything to me because I was at the other end of the bench, and I

J. H. Stearns grocery wagon, circa 1900
Courtesy Museum of New Mexico. Negative 9472.

wasn't laughing all that much. It was Polo who was laughing. The teachers were mean; they were mean.

I believe that very, very few sons and daughters ever got an education. The parents also didn't get an education. Almost nothing. Take me, I never got an education because I had to go out and work. I had to work with this man or the other, with all of those ranchers who were around. I only went to the sixth grade. I started the sixth grade and I didn't go on, because my parents put me to work.

I believe that it was to survive. There was a lot of poverty, you see? There was lots of poverty. Money was scarce; there was none. I believe I worked for whatever they paid me, for sure, which helped buy food. That's the reason I didn't get an education, almost none at all.

What little English I learned, I learned it going to Colorado to work with the Anglos and all of those people over there. That's the way I learned, little by little.

Filiberto Esquibel

Una mestra que no quería a la raza

Más antes no había la ley. Era diferente. No había tal cosa como ora. Ora le da su nalgaa a un muchacho, es *child abuse*. Yo me acuerdo d'en papá cuando me metió en el libro primero. Toca la mala suerte que tuvimos una mestra que no quería a la raza, y le dijo el viejito,

—Si hace mal, dale con una jara.

Pus me agarró mala pica porque íbanos vestíos al estilo rancho. No había tal negocio ora de vanidá d'esto de "Tiene rico. Ése se le echa de ver en la ropa. Aquel viene más mal vistío que lotro." Pues nojotros estáanos criaos en el rancho. Íbanos vestíos poco rancho. No se daa uno cuenta pero estaa vistío poco fiero, y me agarró mala idea la mestra. Si ajerraba en una cosa el día que se levantaa del mal lao de la camalta, me daba con la rula, de fila. En la mano. ¡Y recio! No había quién la reportara porque ese permiso le dio mi padre.

Me acuerdo aquí en Las Vegas había munchos malcriaos. Vinían del rancho. Munchos malcriaos. Estaan criaos poco sueltos y, ende medianos, tomaan mula. Teníanos una mestra aquí poco rigurosa, la Miss Tammy, y teníanos al McFarland. Si hacían mal, la Miss Tammy les daba un revés y con el se quedaba uno. Ésa era una mujer grande. Muy respetiva y, ¡mala! Y muy derecha. Si era bastante más grande el crimen, iba con McFarland. Si era un crimen que podía curalo él ahi con un pedazo de tripa, te ponía las manos arriba de una mesita que tenía. Le daba a uno, dos, tres, golpes con la tripa. A veces que si estaa uno mediano suficiente que lo podía manijar, le daba por el lao de atrás. Y sabes tú que le agarraban miedo.

Ya si era una cosa poco mala, como ora si llevaan alguna navaja o cortaan a alguien o le daan un peñascazo, ya van con los chotas. Más antes eran poco más derechos los chotas. Había algunos, si hacías mal, te llevaan a tu tata. "Güeno, te lo vamos a soltar." Pero cuando se iba el chota, le sonaan a uno bastante. Ése era el modo de castigar más antes. El *Social Welfare* no se metía. Si tenía uno güen ceso no golvías hacer mal. Ora no. Ora le dan su nalgaa a un muchacho pa enderezalo, tanto le agarran mala pica entre la mestra y los otros escueleros, como si se da cuenta el *Social Welfare, Human Services,* diremos, ya es *child abuse.* ¿Y cómo endereza uno una persona asina? No envestigan a ver qué tal grave era lo que lo hizo. Diuna vez tienes poco mal reputación entre los vecinos, o, si eres pobre, te dan diferente. Tavía hay diferencia. Si tienes política, si eres de la política, tienes dinero, te tratan con poco más cariño. Si eres pobre o si miran a uno tirao, pues, te crucifican. Tavía hay diferencia en todo eso. Yo creo que nunca se va acabar.

¿De moo que cómo puee ser *child abuse* par uno dale una nalgaa a un chamaco? No se hace naa. Pero si va uno agarralo de las greñas, o quebrale las costías, ya es más negro. Ése es *child abuse* pa mí. Y eso está malo. Porque yo a mis hijos nunca, nunca usé la mano ni pa dales una nalgaa. A niuno. Y salieron derechos.

Más antes toos casi la lleváanos muy bonito entre toa la plebe. Toos eran vecinos o después se conocían y jugáanos juntos. No había problemas casi nunca en l'escuela. No había que, "Ése le van a pegar un balazo," o ganges. No había tal cosa. Se peliaba uno individualmente. Se peliaban por una pelota; se daba uno sus raiguños. Pero es la diferencia que noto yo ora. Ora está más moderno todo. Ora tiene uno munchas ventajas que no tenía más antes. Más antes estudiabas y lo que aprendías en el libro y es too. Ora hay *computers*, hay *television*. Hay modos de despertar la plebe diferente. Yo voy a eso, que se eduque más pronto una persona.

A Teacher Who Didn't Like Our People

Long ago there was no such law. It was different. There was no such thing as now. Nowadays if you spank a child, it's child abuse. I remember my father put me in the first grade. As luck would have it, we had a teacher who didn't like our people, and my old man said to her, "If he misbehaves, swat him with a twig."

Well, she took a dislike to me because we dressed like farmers. There was no such thing as being vain or "He's rich. You can tell just by the clothing." Or "That guy's dressed worse than that other one." Well, we were raised on the ranch. We were dressed ranch style. You didn't notice it, but we were dressed a bit ugly, and the teacher began to dislike me. If I got something wrong in class and she had gotten up on the wrong side of the bed, she hit me with the sharp edge of the ruler. On the hand. And hard! There wasn't anyone who could report her because my father had given her permission to spank me.

I remember that here in Las Vegas there were many misbehaved children. They came from the ranches. A lot of ill-mannered kids. They were raised a bit loose and from a young age, they started drinking moonshine. We had a teacher who was a bit strict, Miss Tammy, and we also had Mr. McFarland. If they misbehaved, Miss Tammy would slap them and it was her gift. She was a very large woman. Very respectful, but mean! And very straight. If the infraction was of a more serious nature, you had to go with McFarland. If he could cure the so-called crime with a piece of rubber hose, he'd make you put your hands on top of a small table. He would swat you one, two, three times with the hose. At times if you were small enough so that he could handle you, he'd hit you on your butt. And do you know that kids feared him!

If it was something pretty bad, for example if someone carried a knife to school or cut or hit someone with a rock, off you went with the deputy sheriffs. Long ago the deputy sheriffs were a lot more honest. There were some who, if you did something wrong, they would take you to your dad. "Okay, we're going to leave him in your hands." So, when the sheriff left, you got it pretty good. That's the way you were disciplined back then. Social Welfare didn't meddle. If you had any sense at all, you didn't repeat what you did before. Not so now. Nowadays if you spank a child, not only does resentment develop between teacher and students, but if Social Welfare or Human Services gets wind of it, let us say, it's child abuse. And how can you straighten out a person that way? No one bothers to find out how serious the matter is. Right away you develop a bad reputation among the neighbors, or, if you're poor, they treat you differently. There's still a difference in the way you're treated. If you have political influence or money, they treat you a little bit more gingerly. If you're poor or if they look upon you a bit tattered, well, they crucify you. There's still discrimination in all of that. I don't believe that it's ever going to end.

So how can it be child abuse because you spank a child? It's no big deal. But if you're going to grab him by the hair, or crack his ribs, that's a little more ugly. For me that's child abuse. And that's wrong. As for my kids, I never, ever raised my hand to spank them. Not one of them. And they all turned out all right.

Long ago just about everybody got along beautifully among the young kids. We were all neighbors or we got to know each other later on and we played together. There were hardly any problems at school. There was no such thing as, "They're going to shoot him," or gangs. There was no such thing. You fought one on one. Kids got into a fight over a ball. You ended up getting scratched up. But that's the difference that I notice nowadays. Everything is much more modern now. Nowadays you have many more opportunities than you had in the past. Back then you studied and what you learned from books, that was it. Now there's computers, there's television. There's different ways of encouraging kids. I'm all for that—the quicker a person can get educated, the better.

Filimón Montoya

No quería ir más a l'escuela

Yo me recuerdo de l'escuela bien, porque era travieso yo, y me casti-gaba el maestro. ¡Oh! Las travesuras que yo hacía era hacer bolas de papel y tiralas de un lao del cuarto al otro. ¡Mojadas! Y si me pescaba el maestro, pobrecito. Me ponía las manos moradas con una regla d'esas de palo.

Bueno, cuando yo empecé l'escuela, ya no me recuerdo cómo estuvo. Yo creo que no quería quedarme en l'escuela cuando me lle-varon por primera vez. No quería estarme yo en l'escuela. Yo quería irme pa la casa. Pero, güeno, al fin me acostumbré. Empezó a enseñarnos el maestro.

El maestro que me recuerdo yo que comencé l'escuela era un tal Nepomuceno Vigil. Y nos enseñaba en un—¿cómo le llaman?—un *chart?* Y tenía 'l alfabeto. Eso es lo que nos enseñaba—los números y 'l alfabeto, y ahi estaba. Nos enseñaba en inglés. *This is one, number one, number two, number three, number four, and so on,* hasta diez. Loo el alfabeto: *A, B, C, D, E, F, G,* hasta que aprendía toas ésas, pa pode-las reconocer cuando las vieras pintaas, cuando las vieras escritas. Y los números igualmente. Luego ya le cambiaban a uno, y le ponían a uno diferentes números: número uno, número cinco, número siete. Le preguntaban a uno, "¿Qué número es éste?" Si usté se recordaba cuando aprendió, *number one.* "*It's one, number five, it's seven.*" Loo las letras tamién. *An A, an H, or, no,* hasta *G* nomás. *An A, a C, an E and an A.* Loo dijían, "*This letter? An A, okay. This letter?*" *A, B, whatever it was, a D, E, an A.* Cuando ya aprendía uno eso, le daban el restante del alfabeto y más numeración.

Luego ya cuando aprendía too 'l alfabeto, antonces le ponían pal-abras ya escritas, como palabras de dos letras. Y ahi ibas siguiendo tres letras, cuatro letras. Ponían una *A* y una *M, E, M,* y aá mismo tamién le daban a uno el sonido de la *A,* cuando era *A.* "Poner una *H, A, M,*" le dijían a uno. "*Read the word,*" lea la palabra. Dijía uno, "*ham, ham,*" o "*I, F, if,*" y por ahi. Y loo los números, ponían 2, 3, 4, y loo las añaduras tamién. Ya era más avanzado, poco más avanzado.

Cuando yo ya estaa como en el quinto grado, toavía era muy

travieso. Me juntaba con otro muchacho travieso. Pus, empezáanos a reírnos a disturbir a la clas. Entonces tenía otro maestro que se llamaba Maximiliano Luna. Cuando ya se cansaba él de corregirnos y dijirnos que nos calláranos o nos estuviéranos quietos, nos levantaa del banco, nos ponía un palo, un palo en el suelo, y nos hincaba. Dijía, *"You kneel here on this piece of wood or the handle of the broom."* Y ésa sí era una penitencia grande, ¿ve? Pus asina nos castigaba.

¿Sabe usté que nunca le dijíanos a nuestros padres qué hacíamos, qué hacíamos en l'escuela, por qué nos castigaban, ni cómo nos castigaban? No íbanos "con chistes" a la casa, que dicen hoy en día que van con chistes. No, porque le dijían a uno, "Lo merecías. No te, ¿cómo? *You didn't behave yourself* en l'escuela cuando soponías y merecías ese castigo. Y si el maestro no te lo da, yo sí te lo voy a dar." Ya no podía ir uno con cuentos.

Yo verdaderamente nomás hasta el diécimo [libro]. Luego ya se me metió en la cabeza que no quería ir más a l'escuela y me fui a vagamundiar.

I Didn't Want to Go to School Anymore

I remember school well, because I was a real cutup, and the teacher would punish me. Oh! One of the pranks that I used to pull was to make spit wads and shoot them across the room. Wet ones! And if the teacher caught me, that was the end of me. He would spank me with one of those wooden rulers till my hands turned purple.

Okay, when I started school, I don't recall exactly what happened. I guess I didn't want to stay in school when they took me for the first time. I didn't want to remain at school; I wanted to go home. But then I finally got used to it. The teacher started teaching us.

The teacher I remember starting school with was a certain Nepomuceno Vigil, and he used to teach us by using—how do you say it?—a chart. And on it was the alphabet. That's what he taught us— the numbers and the alphabet, and there it was. He would teach us in English. "This is one, number one, number two, number three, number four," and so on, up to ten. Then came the alphabet: *A, B, C, D, E, F, G,* until you were able to learn all of those, so that you would be able to recognize them when you saw them again, when you saw them written down. The same thing was true of the numbers. Then they would rotate things around, by giving you different numbers:

number one, number five, number seven. They would ask you, "What number is this?" If you remembered what you learned, number one. "It's number five, it's number seven." Then the same thing was true of the letters. "An *A*, an *H*," or, no, only up to the letter *G*. "An *A*, a *C*, an *E* and an *A*." Then they'd say, "This letter? An *A*, okay. This letter?" *A, B,* whatever it was; a *D, E,* an *A.* By the time you learned all of that, they gave you the rest of the alphabet and numbers.

And then by the time you learned the alphabet, then they gave you written words, like two-letter words. Then you continued: three letters, four letters, and so on. You would hear an *A* and an *M, E, M,* and you'd hear the sound of the letter *A,* whenever it was an *A.* "Put down *H, A, M,*" they'd tell you. "Read the word." You would then respond: "Ham, ham, or *I, F, if,*" and you took it from there. And then the numbers, they would write 2, 3, 4, plus problems in addition. That was more advanced, a bit more advanced.

When I was in about the fifth grade, I was still a little devil. I used to hang around with another prankish kid. Well, we used to start laughing and disturbing the class. By that time I had another teacher whose name was Maximiliano Luna. When he got tired of disciplining us and telling us to keep quiet, he would pick us up from our desks by the collar and he'd put a piece of wood, firewood, on the floor, and he'd have us kneel. He would say to us, "You kneel here on this piece of wood or the handle of the broom." That was a very severe punishment, you see. That's the way he would punish us.

Do you know that we never told our parents what it was we did, what we did at school, why it was they punished us, or how they punished us? We didn't go home with tales, as they say nowadays. Not at all, because you would be told, "You deserved it. You didn't behave yourself at school when you were supposed to and for that reason you deserve what you got. And if the teacher didn't give you a swat, I'm going to do you the favor." You wouldn't dare go home tattling.

I only went to school until I reached the tenth grade. Then it got into my head that I didn't want to go to school anymore and so I quit so I could bum around.

Andrés Archuleta

¡Por güeno me castigaban!

Yo jui a l'escuela ahi en Trujillo. Casi no me acuerdo a qué libro lle-gara. Too era la misma cosa que ora. Poco diferente el manejo, nomás. El primer mestro que yo tuve, enseñaba nomás en español, porque no sabía el inglés. ¿Cómo lo iba aprender tamién yo? Pus no sabía el mestro, menos yo, ¿eh? Narciso Anaya, se llamaba. No me acuerdo en qué año oiga. Pueda que yo tuviera cinco años.

No quisiera decile, pero a cabo es verdá, porque como le dije al principio, era algo perverso yo. Me la pasaba en un rincón con una piedra en la mano, en cada mano. [Risas] Ahi está, ¿eh? No pesadotas no, no a lastimalo a uno, pero ahi tenía que estarme. ¡Por güeno me castigaban! yo creo. [Risas] Porque asina semos todos, ¿qué no? Usté no va dijir que es malo, ¿eh? Ahi está. ¿Por qué creye usté?

Tenían rulas. Taa las usan, pero ya ora no las usan como las usaan antes. Y con esa rula le daban aquí en la mano. En la palma de la mano. No arriba. ¿Sabe lo que es una rula? Una tablita de madera.

No me acuerdo yo que usaran la tripa ahi en el lugar mío. Posible que más antes sí. O en otros lugares. Ahi, como le digo, le ponían a uno en un rincón hasta en la tarde. No se estaba uno muncho. [Risas] Y cortaban.

I Was Punished for Being Good!

I went to school there in Trujillo. I barely recall what grade I went to [before I quit]. Everything was the same as now. Only the way in which schools were run was different. The first teacher I ever had taught only in Spanish because he didn't know English. How was I going to learn it? If the teacher didn't know it, how was I to learn, huh? His name was Narciso Anaya. I don't remember the year. I must have been about five years old.

I would prefer not to tell you, but it's true anyway, because, as I told you in the beginning, I was a bit rambunctious. I used to spend a lot of time in a corner with a rock in each hand. [Laughter] There you are, see? The rocks were not heavy ones, so as not to hurt you, but I had to stand there. I was punished because of being good, I guess! [Laughter] Because that's the way we all are, right? You're not going to say that you're mean, huh? There you are. Why do you think that's so?

Teachers had rulers. They still use them, but nowadays they don't use them the way they used to. And with that ruler is the way they spanked your hand. In the palm of your hand. Not on the top of your hand. Do you know what a ruler is? It's a little wooden board.

I don't remember teachers using a hose there where I lived. Perhaps a long time ago. Or in other places. There where I went to school, as I say, you'd be put in a corner till the afternoon. You couldn't stand it for very long. [Laughter] And teachers cut down discipline problems.

Guadalupe Luján

Agarramos la poquita educación

En los tiempos que nojotros agarramos la poquita educación que agarramos jue durante la depresión. Yo jui el que agarré más en ese tiempo, yo y mis hermanos. Y me eduqué en l'escuela de la Imaculada Concepción, escuela católica aquí en Las Vegas. Tres pesos, tres pesos al mes teníanos que pagar de *tuition*.

Déjeme platicale otra cosa que se me había pasao. Cuando yo estuve en l'escuela de las hermanas, el padre Reverón [Jean Pierre Adrien Rabeyrolle, 1873–1950], hace munchos años, onde está el Allsups, ahi estaba la iglesia. Le daba a uno reporte y si vía que no estaba bien el *report card,* si no sacáanos el grado que soponíanos de haber sacao, diuna vez le avisaba a los padres de uno. Y el padre lo corrigía a uno en la casa. Es una diferencia que ora no pueden porque le ponen pleito diuna vez. Diuna vez le ponen pleito. Y eso es malo. Les dan más libertá a los niñõs.

What Little Education We Got

What little education we got was during the depression. I was one who got more education back then, along with my brothers. I was educated in the Immaculate Conception School, a Catholic school here in Las Vegas. We had to pay three dollars, three dollars a month in tuition is what we had to pay.

Let me tell you something else that I had forgotten. When I attended the nuns' school, Father Reverón [Jean Pierre Adrien Rabeyrolle, 1873–1950], that's been many years now, there where Allsup's is, that's where the church was. He used to give you your report card, and if you didn't get the grades you were supposed to, right away he would notify your parents. And your father would then straighten you out at home. That's something that can't be done nowadays, because right away they'll file a lawsuit against you. A complaint is filed against you right away. And that's bad. Kids are given more freedom.

3

Curanderismo
Folk Healing

Introduction

Curanderismo, the art of folk healing among Hispanics, has existed in northern New Mexico since the sixteenth century. Like other facets of Hispanic folklore, *curanderismo*'s roots can be traced to fifteenth-century Spain following Christopher Columbus' voyages to the New World. Moorish and Spanish herbal medicinal practices little by little reached Mexico and ultimately northern New Mexico. In Mexico, some ritualistic practices and beliefs that existed among indigenous groups combined with those brought by Spanish explorers. A mixture of Mexican and Spanish folk medicines eventually came into contact with those used by Native Americans of New Mexico.

Under the broad umbrella of *curanderismo*, which derives from *curar*, to heal or to get well (*sanar*, to get well or to give birth, at times has been used interchangeably with *curar* in many New Mexican communities), one can include the following folk healers or practitioners who were common in New Mexico until a few years ago: the *curandera* (home remedies and herbs specialist), the *médica* (one who combines various folk practices), the *partera* (midwife), the *arbolario(a)* or *herbolario(a)* (herb healer once thought of as a witch), and the *sobador* (chiropractor or bonesetter, today known as a masseur/masseuse or massage therapist). Each had a distinctly different calling.

All but the last two traditionally have been females. Women therefore have dominated the field of folk healing, even though one hears of the occasional *partero* (in fact, there was a *partero* in my own community of Ojo del Padre) or a *sobadora*. A principal reason for their dominance was that women felt more at ease in discussing intimate and sensitive subjects with a *curandera* or a *partera* than with their male counterpart. Yet, topics such as menstruation were deemed taboo even among some women.

While each folk healer specialized in specific medicines and ailments, it was not uncommon for a *curandera* or a *médica* to know something about the other professions. Accordingly, a so-called specialist often qualified as a general practitioner. A *curandera,* without a doubt the most popular of all folk healers, is a prime example.

My maternal grandmother was a *curandera* and she, like most *curanderas,* was quite adept at diagnosing and treating a variety of common ailments. The treatment oftentimes involved, as I recollect, no more than blowing cigarette smoke in the ear to treat an earache or applying the soft ashes of a cottonwood tree for a toothache. In many cases, the remedy (*remedio*) consisted of drinking an herbal concoction.

As a five-year old, I sometimes had to fetch from my grandmother's "medicine cabinet" (*alucena*) or *dispensa* (pantry) the proper herb to treat an ailment. Since the dry herbs or roots were not labeled, I learned to tell the difference between them from their fragrance, the shape of the leaves, or their color. For example, she could have asked me to fetch *manzanilla* (chamomile tea), used to calm the nerves; the root *oshá,* ground and boiled and drunk as a tea to break a fever; or *yerba buena* (mint tea), the Hispanic Alka-Seltzer and prescribed for stomachaches or indigestion. A common cure for indigestion, as we learn from Cruzita Vigil, was an egg. In "The Egg Is for Indigestion" she explains how she was able to cure two of her grandchildren using an egg. My maternal grandmother claimed that indigestion was caused by eating the inside of fresh-baked bread and by drinking water.

Her knowledge of herbs, like that of most *curanderas,* was quite remarkable. I can recall countless times accompanying her and my step-grandfather, himself a *sobador,* to the countryside to look for *remedios del llano* (country remedies). She could tell you what any plant was and its medicinal power—and she did so with self-assurance.

Of course, a *curandera* did not rely solely on her knowledge of herbs, referred to as *plantas, matas,* or *hierbas (yerbas),* or her innate ability to diagnose an illness as well as prescribe the proper treatment. She, like most folk healers, believed that whatever illness descended on an individual was due to God's will (*la voluntad de Dios*). Therefore, religion played an important role in curing a patient. The reciting of the rosary, the lighting of votive candles to a favorite saint, or a religious pilgrimage, preferably made by the patient, was of paramount importance in getting well.

If the victim was a baby suffering from the evil eye (*el mal ojo*), then the mother as well as the individual responsible for inflicting the evil eye, which stemmed presumably from excessive admiration of the child, were encouraged to say their prayers as part of the ritual for lifting or getting rid of the evil eye. Even plants or flowers were affected by the evil eye, as we learn from Katarina Montoya in "The Evil Eye Is One Thing I Do Believe In."

One way of curing the evil eye, unless the person responsible for inflicting it could be found, was to summon a Juan or a Juana. Either one had the power to cure a child with the evil eye, but the child had to be treated before the next Friday of the week in which the evil eye was inflicted or he or she could die. A Juan or a Juana would simply take a drink of water, spit a mouthful on the child's face, and make the sign of the cross.

Some of the stories found in this chapter deal with the evil eye. Each story varies in tone—from the serious to the humorous. At least one person, Cesaria Montoya, despite inflicting the evil eye on a nephew and then curing him, was somewhat ambivalent if not skeptical about it. At the same time, individuals such as Filiberto Esquibel, whose eldest son contracted the evil eye, were unambiguous about the phenomenon having existed at one time. The evil eye, to be sure, is still one of the most talked about topics among the old folks.

Illnesses affecting old and young alike ran from *mal ojo, empacho(e)* (indigestion), *caída de la mollera* (fallen fontanel), colds or an earaches, to *susto* or *rebato* (fright). Often my grandmother could tell if a person was suffering from a *rebato,* caused when something unexpected happened to them (e.g., the death of a loved one), which is a bit different from a *susto.* The latter at times was looked upon as emanating from magical powers or caused by someone with evil intentions. In these types of situations an *arbolaria(o),* or maybe even a *médico(a),* not a *curandera,* was considered the logical person to treat the ailment.

Curanderas, because of their role in the community, always commanded utmost respect from both adults and the young. A *curandera's* reputation was well earned because in most cases, she was said to possess a certain *don,* that is, a gift from God. Moreover, she rarely charged for her services, although it was not uncommon for her to accept food or small amounts of money as payment for services rendered. Hence, a *curandera,* unlike a *sobador* or the other folk healers mentioned earlier, enjoyed and wielded considerable power and prestige.

Perhaps the least common folk healer, because of being more of a specialist, was the *sobador,* the equivalent in some respects of our modern-day chiropractor, massage therapist, and orthopedist all wrapped up in one. The most frequent complaints from men who visited my step-grandfather (hardly any women visited him, as I recall), a *sobador,* related to a sprained ankle (*un pie torcido*), *un brazo desconcerta(d)o,* a dislocated arm or shoulder, or a *dolor de cintura,* lower-back pain. He would suggest wearing a *faja de cintura,* resembling a corset made of leather and worn around the waist for this last. Massages for backaches and muscle spasms were common as well. In the main, *sobadores* were rare in most Hispanic communities (a *sobadora,* the female counterpart, was even rarer) and not very much in demand. People sometimes had to travel long distances to see one.

Another less-common practitioner was the *arbolario(a),* an herb specialist. Eventually, the *arbolario,* usually a male, branched out and began treating people who were presumably bewitched (*embruja[d]os* or *enyerba[d]os),* something a *curandera* did not ordinarily treat. As a consequence, an *arbolario* was often thought to possess witchlike tendencies. Part of the reason was because of the incredible stories people would hear regarding the *arbolario,* how, for example, a bewitched person would vomit balls of hair after treatment. This was proof that the patient had been not only bewitched, but also cured of the malady. Whenever the spell was lifted and the victim got well, the *arbolario*'s credibility increased.

A *médico(a)*, in many instances, resembled an *arbolario(a)*. Their similarities or differences in terms of expertise, above and beyond being herbalists, depended in great measure on their reputation. In the eyes of some people, they were either good *médicos(as)* or evil ones. Opinion was predicated on whether a *médico(a)* was thought to practice white (good) or black (evil) magic.

A more benevolent folk healer, and a mainstay herself, was the *partera,* the midwife. Her duties were fairly clear-cut: to deliver babies. My grandmother always said that the trademark of a good midwife was large hands (*manos grandes*) in order to deliver a baby with ease. A midwife, who in most cases had inherited the profession from her mother or grandmother as part of a family tradition, was also well trained and well versed in prenatal and postpartum care. In addition, she knew which foods were healthful and safe for a woman after childbirth for a designated period of time, usually forty days. A *partera* in small communities, like a *curandera,* did not charge for her services. She relied on donations, either money or foodstuffs.

One of the most famous midwives in northern New Mexico is Jesusita Aragón from Las Vegas, a midwife for over eighty years. Her narrative, "I'm Going to Be a Midwife," is an excellent overview of what made up a midwife's responsibilities from the time a woman became pregnant until she gave birth. We also learn of the thousands of babies that she has delivered, some of whom have been born grossly deformed or with animal-like features. Many old folks believed—as I was taught as a child—that these facial traits stemmed from incest or the devil's macabre intrusion. Others assumed a punishment from God for violating the laws of nature. Whatever the reasons, Jesusita Aragón shares both the joy and the pain she has experienced in the miracle of life.

Folk healing among northern New Mexico's Hispanics, to be sure, is a dying art, although young people's utilization of, and belief in, herbal remedies has increased during the past several years. Midwifery has also gained in popularity and is now accepted as a bona fide practice by the medical profession. But, to draw the conclusion that folk healing is bouncing back in New Mexico and thus likely to enjoy the kind of popularity it once enjoyed in Hispanic communities would be stretching the point.

Jesusita Aragón

Yo voy a ser partera

De mi agüelita aprendí. Ella era partera. Lola se llamaba. ¿Sabe qué? Desde chiquita yo, cuando mi agüelita iba asistir a mi tía Petra,

—Vente pacá, —me dijía, y a mí me interesó, porque yo quería ser nodriza, pero no pude.

Dije, "Si no soy nodriza, yo voy a ser partera."

—Vente pacá m'hija. Ahi párate. Cuídame. No todos los días me van a tener a mí, —y es verdá.

A la edá de trece años asistí la primer mujer. No estaba mi agüelita en la casa, y asistí a mi tía. Muy contenta mi agüelita. Yo estaba con las borregas, porque siempre andaba ajuera de la casa. Mi agüelita no estaba. Se jue asistir otra mujer lejos del rancho. De modo que no había niun hombre allí que juera a buscar una partera. Todos estaban trabajando ajuera, ¿ve? Ya sabe cómo se van en el rancho. Mandaron a una de mis hermanas que juera por mí, allá dionde andaba yo con las borregas. Llegó ella.

—Allá te llaman —me dijo—. Mi tía Petra está sanando.

Dije, "Pus allí está mi mamá Ramoncita, mi madrasta, y mi tía Sofía." Agarré la yegua que ella [mi hermana] llevaba, y monté y me vine. Llegué y asistí a mi tía. Muy contenta. Toavía mi agüelita *más* contenta. Era niño. Sesenta y tres años tiene. Eso tiene mi primer bebito.

Güeno, pa asistilas a las mamases, pus yo les dijía que vinieran cada mes pa examinalas y todo, pero algunas vivían muy lejos. Vinían una o dos veces, hasta el día que se me enfermaban, porque vinían de Alburquerque, y vinían de Taos. Siempre me jue muy bien. Siempre, gracias a Dios.

En Trujillo iban por mí en carro de caballos y no me gustaba. A caballo era más fácil. Ya sabía andar bien a caballo. Iba yo caindo agua, caindo granizo, caindo nieve, pero ahi voy asisitir a la mujer ondequiera que me llamaban. En veces a pie.

Preparaba de todo antes de sanar la enferma. Garras, porque antes con garritas. Hacíanos sabanitas de papeles, de *newspaper,* le ponía uno la garra arriba. Antes estaba uno bien impuesta a lo pobre. Ora qué. Ora hay todo propio.

Ya pa sanar yo permitía al esposo ver si quería la enferma, y alguna mujer que ella quería, pero a munchas no les gustaba. Ni al esposo.

—¡Vete! ¡Vete! ¡Salte pallá! ¡Espérame en el carro! O en otro lugar.

A mi agüelita no le gustaba eso. Cuando entraba el hombre en veces allí, le dijía,

—¡Salte! Éste es negocio de mujeres.

Ora no. Tamaños asina chiquititos los traen pa que ellos miren. No me gusta a mí, ¿pero qué puedo hacer? Como dijía mi agüelita,

—Su tiempo se les llega pa que aprendan.

Ya una muchacha de catorce años, sí. Le queda bien que mire todo eso. Pero chiquititos asina, no. Pero sabe usté que las americanas tienen esa idea. Tiene que estar 'l esposo, y una, dos o tres amigas. También las muchitas chiquitas de tres o cuatro años pa que miren.

Cuando ya nace el niño, se le corta el ombligo. Le pone uno una pasa o pedazo de higo pa que se cierre bien. Ora qué. ¡Ora salen del hospital con el ombligo bien largo parriba! Aquí en la casa, no, tengo mis tijeras. Tavía tengo las tijeras que me dieron en la clínica. Con esas tijeritas chiquitas corto. Pa los ojos en aquellos años no se les ponía nada, pero después en la clínica nos dieron gotas de nitriato de plata.

Después de nacer un niño, tres días las tenía yo así cuidándolas a las mujeres en la cama. Y comidas en su cama, y todo, cuidándolas. Eso hacía yo. Ora no. Ya ora tienen su niño y como a las dos o tres horas se preparan y van pa su casa. Ya ora es diferente. Hasta de todo comen.

Yo no. Atole. En primer lugar atole de maiz azul. Atole con brel. Hacía tortillitas y las tostaba bien tostaditas. Atole y pan tostao. Y luego cuando les daba carne a las mujeres, les daba carne de gallina, pal mediodía. Ya en la noche, no. Puro atole en la noche otra vez. Ésa era la dieta que daba. Cuando comían carne de borrega, tenía que ser de borrega que no tuviera borreguito o borrego. No comían carne de marrano ni de vaca. No las dejaban. Es que era muy pesada dijía mi agüelita.

Después de nacer el niño, cuarenta días era la dieta. Y se levantaban a los tres, cuatro días las mujeres poquito. Y en un ratito iban a la cama otra vez. Mi agüelita les daba diez días en la cama. Cuando están sanando voltean muncho 'l estógamo. Pero después les doy té de manzanilla, o té de poleo pa que se limpie el cuerpo. Eso les doy.

Lo más importante era la dieta del hombre. Ésa era la dieta más dura que tenían. Cuarenta días. La dieta del hombre era importante pa que sanara bien la matriz. Ora a los tres, cuatro días ya puede estar con su esposa. Ése es el costumbre de ora. Por eso hay tanta fumerada, porque no guardan su dieta. Su matriz nunca sana, nunca. Mi agüelita sí los hacía esperar. Cuarenta días tenían que esperar.

¿Sabe qué? Más antes cuando yo empecé de partera cobraba diez pesos. Y luego veinte y cinco, y después cincuenta. Después me dijieron en la clínica que querían que llevara los trescientos. Güeno, yo no. Les dije que no.

—Yo voy a llevar cien, —les dije—. Cien. Eso voy a llevar yo.

Después volvieron a llamar que querían que llevara seiscientos. Hoy cobro doscientos, porque todos semos pobres, por eso. Todos semos pobres.

Tengo ochenta y un año [desde 1921] de partera. Eso tengo. Mire. Yo tengo 45,927 bebitos de a uno. Veinte y siete pares de cuates, y dos que tuvieron tres cada uno. Eso tengo.

Yo lo hago de todo corazón. No importa quién sea, la raza que sea, porque ya tengo de todas razas bebitos. De todas. Porque por ondequiera tengo bebitos. Por todo el mundo. Por todo, todo el mundo. Y no tengo licencia pero les digo a todos,

—Esa herencia me dio Dios, y naide me la quita. Naide. Más que me la quieran quitar, no pueden. Esa herencia, no. Es mi negocio, hasta que muera.

I'm Going to Be a Midwife

I learned from my grandma. She was a midwife. Lola was her name. And do you know what? Ever since I was a little girl, whenever my grandma went to assist my Aunt Petra, she'd say, "Come here," and that interested me, because I wanted to be a nurse, but I couldn't. I said to myself, "If I can't be a nurse, I'll become a midwife."

"Come here, little one. Stand there. Watch me. You're not going to have me around forever." And it's true.

I was thirteen years old when I helped deliver the first baby. My grandma wasn't home, so I assisted my aunt. My grandma was very proud of me. I was herding sheep at the time, because I was always away from the house. My grandma wasn't home. She went to take care of another woman far from the ranch. It so happened that there wasn't a single man around who could go after a midwife. They were all away working, you see. You know how they leave the ranch. One of my sisters was sent to go after me where I was taking care of the sheep. She got to where I was.

"They want you over there," she said to me. "My aunt Petra is having a baby."

I said to myself, "Well, my mom, Romancita, my stepmother, and my aunt Sofía are there." I grabbed hold of my sister's mare, hopped on, and took off. I got there and I helped my aunt have the baby. She was very happy. My grandma was even happier. It was a boy. He's sixty-three years old now. That's how old the first baby is that I delivered.

Now, when it came to taking care of the mothers, I used to tell them to come see me every month so I could examine them and everything, but some of them lived very far away. They'd come once or twice, until the day that is was time to have the baby, because they came from as far away as Albuquerque, or they came from Taos. Things always turned out well for me. Always, thank God.

In Trujillo they used to go after me on a horse-drawn wagon, but I didn't like it. It was a lot easier on horseback. I was already very good at riding on horseback. I'd go whether it was raining, hailing, snowing, or what have you, but there I'd go help deliver a baby wherever they wanted me. At times I went on foot.

I used to get all kinds of things ready before the mother had her baby. Rags, tiny rags, because that's what we used back then. We would make small bed sheets from paper, from newspaper. We'd put the rags on top of it. Back then we were used to doing things the poor man's way. Now, forget it. Now you have everything ready-made.

When it came time to have the baby, I allowed the husband to watch if the wife wanted, plus a lady friend, but many women didn't like the idea. They didn't even allow the husband. "Go! Go! Scoot! Wait for me in the car!" Or some other place. My grandma didn't like the idea of men watching. Sometimes when the man came in, she'd say to him, "Scoot! This is women's work."

Not so nowadays. They even bring tiny kids so they can watch. I don't like it, but what can I do? As my grandma used to say, "When it comes to learning, everybody's turn comes."

If a girl is fourteen years old, why, of course, it's okay for her to watch all of that. But when they're small children, no. But do you know that the Anglo women are like that? The husband has to be present, along with one, two, or three female friends. Even little girls three or four years old are allowed to come in to watch.

After the child is born, you cut the umbilical cord. You put a raisin or a piece of fig so the cord can heal. Not so in this day and age. Nowadays babies leave the hospital with their umbilical cord sticking straight up! That doesn't happen here at home. I have my scissors. I still have my pair of scissors that they gave me at the clinic. Those are the tiny scissors that I use to do the cutting. Back then you didn't put anything in the baby's eyes, but later on they gave us silver nitrate at the hospital.

After a child was born, I used to keep women in bed for three days while I took care of them. And I'd feed them in bed while I took care of them. That's what I used to do. Not so now. Now they have their baby and about two or three hours later they get ready and take off for home. It's different now. They even eat all kinds of stuff.

Not me. Blue corn gruel. At first, blue corn gruel, with homemade flat pan bread. I'd make tortillas and I'd brown them really well. Blue corn gruel with toast also. And then when I fed the women I gave them chicken at noon. Not at night. I only gave them blue corn gruel at night. That was the diet I had them on. Whenever they ate mutton, it had to be from a sheep that didn't have a lamb, or the meat could be lamb. Pork or beef was not good. Women weren't allowed to eat either one. According to my grandma, it was very heavy.

After the child was born, there was a forty-day diet. Women would get up for a little while after three or four days. No sooner said than done and they were right back in bed. My grandmother let them stay in bed for ten days. When women are pregnant they suffer a lot from nausea. Afterward, however, I give them chamomile tea, or brookmint [pennyroyal] tea so as to cleanse the body. That's what I give them to drink.

The most important thing was the man's regimen. That was the hardest regimen that the man and the woman had. Forty days. The man's abstinence was important so the uterus would heal. Nowadays after three or four days the man can be with his wife. That's customary now. That's why there's so much of a fuss, because they don't abstain. The woman's uterus never heals, never. My grandma made sure the men waited. They had to wait forty days.

And do you know something? A long time ago when I started off as a midwife I used to charge ten dollars. Then I charged twenty-five, and later fifty. Later on they told me at the clinic that they wanted me to charge three hundred dollars. Well, not me. I told them no. "I'm going to charge one hundred," I said to them. "One hundred. That's what I'm going to charge." Later on they called asking me to charge six hundred. Today I charge two hundred dollars, because we're all poor, that's why. We're all poor people.

I have been practicing for over eighty-one years as a midwife [since 1921]. That's how long it's been. Listen. I have delivered 45,927 single babies. Twenty-seven sets of twins, and two sets of triplets. That's what I have.

I do it from the heart. It doesn't matter to me who it is, what race the person is, because I have babies of all races. Of all races. I have babies all over. Throughout the world. Throughout the entire world. And I'm not licensed. As I tell everyone, "God gave me this gift, and nobody can take it away from me. Nobody. Even if they want to take it away from me, they can't. That gift they can't. It's my calling, until the day I die."

Esa mujer nunca se olvidó de mí

Una vez hasta una alemana nació aquí en casa. Esta mujer y este hombre andaban en vacación aquí, y se enfermó ella de chiquito. No se jue hasta que no sanó. Ella preguntó por una partera. Diuna vez le dijieron de mí, y vino aquí hablar conmigo. La asistí. Hablaba español y hablaba el inglés la alemana. No supe de ella más de cuando cumplió un año la bebita. Estaba en San Francisco ella, en California. Me escribió y me dice,

—Jesusita, ya hoy me voy. Mi hijita cumplió un año. Ya me voy, —tiene quince años ora la hijita.

Una mujer de New York también vino a visitarme, a los veinte años que cumplió su hija. Esa mujer *nunca* se olvidó de mí. No jallaba quién la asistiera porque no tenía dinero, y vino a mi casa. Alguien le dijo de mí, y vino aquí. Yo estaba asistiendo a otra mujer. Y me dice,

—¿Eres Jesusita? ¿Podrás asistirme?

—Sí. Entra.

Americana ella. Y le dije que se acostara en mi cama en lo que me desocupaba yo. Cuando yo me desocupé allá con la otra mujer, ya estaba naciendo el niño de ella. Arreglé todo mi negocio.

—Ora sí. A ver cómo está —y la asistí.

Veinte años después vino pacá a verme.

—Nunca me preguntates nada. Tú no me preguntates si traiba dinero o no. Ora vine a verte porque nunca te me olvidates. Mi esposo me abandonó desde que tuve a mi hijita. Ni conoce a su hija. Como ora te traigo un presente. Ora sí tengo con qué.

Traiba cincuenta pesos ella en su bolsa. Me los dio. Me trujo un cheque. Me trujo un chequecito. Lloró tanto cuando me vido, y yo a ella. De gusto lloramos.

That Woman Never Forgot about Me

One time even a German baby was born here in my house. This woman and this man were here on vacation, and she went into labor. She didn't leave until she had her baby. She asked about a midwife. Right away they told her about me, and she came here to talk to me. I took care of her. She spoke Spanish and English, the German woman did. I didn't hear from her until a year later, when the baby girl was one year old. The mother was in San Francisco, California. She wrote to me and said, "Jesusita, I'm leaving today. My daughter just celebrated her first birthday. I'm leaving [for Germany]." The daughter's fifteen now.

A lady from New York also came to see me when her daughter was twenty years old. That woman *never* forgot about me. At that time she couldn't find anyone to take care of her because she didn't have any money, so she came to my house. Somebody told her about me, and she came here. I was already tending another woman. And she says to me,

"Are you Jesusita? Will you be able to take care of me?

"Yes. Come in."

She was American. And I told her to lie down in my bed while I finished with the other lady. When I was through with the other lady, this other lady's baby was already about to be born. I took care of all of the necessary arrangements.

"Now we're ready. Let's see how you're doing," and I tended to her.

Twenty years later she came by to see me.

"You never asked me anything. You never asked me if I had money or not. Now I've come to see you because you were never out of my mind. My husband left me after I had my daughter. He's never even seen his daughter. Now I bring you a present. Now I can afford it."

She had fifty dollars with her in her purse. She gave them to me. She brought me a check. She brought a nice little check. She cried so much when she saw me, and I, her. We both cried from sheer joy.

A mí me tocó otro desforme

Lo que me acuerdo nomás que nació un niño con las tripas de juera, y llamé al dotor porque los dotores me vinían ayudar cuando yo los necesitaba. Cuando yo llamaba, vinía uno que lotro. Vino un dotor y la nodriza y imediatamente lo volaron pal Alburquerque.

—¡Que tal si hubieras visto el que me tocó a mí! Con el hígado de juera también, —dijo—. Se me hace que ése no vive Jesusita. Éste sí vive.

Y luego lo llevaron, diuna vez, imediatamente en la noche. Otro día llevaron a la mujer pa que juera a estarse con su hijito allá. Y vivió. A los diez años me lo trujo la mujer pa que lo viera. Eso me tocó a mí.

Mi agüelita me platicaba que a ella le tocó aquí un caso, con el corazoncito ajuera. No vivió. Y asina. A mí me tocó otro desforme. Muy triste. ¡Porecitas las mamases! Esta criaturita tenía la faición como una rana. No vivió más que un ratitito.

Pero yo cuando me pasa algo, diuna vez reporto al dotor y él lo ve, y vienen y lo miran y too. La consuelan a la mamá y se ayudan.

Oh, tengo una que no tiene bracitos, ni piernitas. Está viva. Muy brillante niña. Habla las dos idiomas [inglés y español]. Muy inteligente. A gatiar en ruedas. En ruedas. Ya está grande; tiene como diez años. Pero muy bien la trata su gente toda. Que es que comenzaron sus hermanitos ahora a peliar con ella, y los agarró el agüelito y les dijo que no hicieran eso con su hermanita. ¡Porecita! Es muy duro cuando mira uno eso. Muy triste. Pasan algunas cosas.

I Myself Had to Deliver a Deformed Child

The one thing I recall is this child who was born with his intestines sticking out, so I called the doctor because they used to come help me whenever I needed them. Whenever I called, one doctor or the other came. A doctor and a nurse came and they immediately flew the child to Albuquerque. "If you'd seen the one I got! He also had his liver sticking out," he said to me. "I don't believe that that one is going to make it, Jesusita. But this one will survive."

They took him right away, immediately that night. Next day they took the mother so she could stay with her little boy over in Albuquerque. When he was ten years old, the mother brought him here so that I could see him. That's what happened to me.

My grandma used to tell me that she had a strange case, a child with its heart outside its chest. It didn't survive. And cases like that one. I myself had to deliver a deformed child. It's very sad. Poor mothers! This poor little child had the face of a frog. It only lived a little bit.

But whenever something like that happens to me, I right away report it to a doctor and he comes and sees for himself and everything. The doctors console the mother and help each other.

Oh, by the way, I delivered one who has no arms or legs. She's still alive. She a very intelligent girl. She speaks both languages,

Spanish and English. Very smart. She gets around on wheels. On wheels. She's already grown; she's about ten years old. But all of her relatives treat her very nice. I understand that her little brothers started to pick on her, and the grandfather sat them down and told them not to do that with their little sister. Poor thing! It's very hard on a person to see that sort of thing. Very sad. Things like that do happen.

Cruzita Vigil

Yo sané con médicas nomás

Yo sané con médicas nomás. Yo nunca sané con dotores. Con mis agüelas. Mi agüela era médica. Loo mi mamá después fue médica también. De moo que yo nunca jui a un dotor a sanar. Yo sanaba en el rancho. La partera vinía cada luna. Cada luna nueva. A conforme se iba acercando el tiempo de tener el *baby*, ¿ve? Vinía a ver cómo iba caminando la criatura, y el día que ya se llegaba el tiempo, pus ya no era más de llamala. Ea vinía y proponía too lo listo, lo que iba arreglar, hasta que nacía el chamaco, lo bañaba y loo se iba. Y le pagaban; lo que sí que le pagaban. Llevaa veinte pesos por curar a uno.

Ea lo que aprevinía eran los pañales. Aprevinía las frezadas. Aprevinía lo que iba a usar: medecinas pa la mujer; pal *baby* cuando nacía. Eso. Las tuallas onde iba a bañalo. Loo arreglaba a la mujer; la dejaba después que tenía el *baby,* bien limpia. La ponía en su cama limpia y too y loo se iba la médica. Es lo que hacía nomás.

Loo cada dos días le vinía a dar güelta a ver cómo estaa caminando la mujer. Es lo que hacía. Pus las que les gustaba estar en la cama, se estaban hasta los ocho días. Pero yo no. Yo no me estaa más de dos días en la cama. Dos días. En dos días me levantaa ya después de tener el niño. Iba aá, me dicía la médica,

—¿Ya andas andando? ¡Qué bribona!

—Oh, —le dicía yo—, esa cama no sirve más de pa estar uno acostaa y me levanté.

—Pus siempre no vayas a hacer esto y lotro.

No, nomás se iba y hacía lo que me daba gana. [Risas]

—No vayas a barrer, no vayas a lavar los trastes, no vayas hacer . . .

Nomás se iba ea, limpiaba yo mi casa toa.

Eran cuarenta días, hasta que no tuvieras cuarenta días sanaa uno no salías de casa. Isque hasta antonces no se cerraban los poros diuno, onde nacía el *baby*. Isque hasta las venas y too eso no se cierran hasta los cuarenta días.

Ahi estaa uno en una cama, en la dieta. Conque hasta el pan lo tostaban bien, bien pa que lo comiéranos. Si no, no no[s] lo daban. Carne, carne de borrego había de ser, y no de otra clas. Pus quién sabe por qué. Porque eso es lo primero que alistaban, un borrego, pa cuando ya nacía.

Only Midwives Delivered My Babies

Only midwives delivered my babies. I was never assisted by doctors. With my grandmas. My grandma was a midwife. Then later on my mom was a midwife, so that I never went to a doctor to have a baby. I would have my babies at the ranch. The midwife would come visit me with every new moon. With every new moon, just as time for having the baby was approaching, you see? She'd come to see how the baby was coming along, and when the day to have the baby came, it was only a matter of calling her. She'd come and get everything ready, until the child was born, and then she'd bathe it and then take off. And they paid her, that's for sure. She charged twenty dollars for delivering a baby.

What she got ready were diapers. She would prepare the blankets. She'd prepare what she was going to use: medicine for the mother and child when it was born. That stuff. The towels for when they [the ladies helping] bathed it. Then they took care of the mother; they left the baby real clean for her. She was put back into a clean bed and everything and then the midwife took off. That's all that was done.

Then every two days she would come to pay the mother a visit to see how she was doing. That's what she would do. Those who liked to stay in bed did so for eight days. But not me. I only stayed in bed for two days. Two days. Two days after having a child I would get up.

The midwife would go visit me and she'd say to me, "You're up and walking? You rascal!"

"Oh," I'd say, "that bed's only good for sleeping so I got up."

"Well, just the same. Don't go do this or that."

As soon as she left, I'd do as I pleased. [Laughter] "Don't go around sweeping, don't go wash dishes, don't go do this or . . ."

No sooner did she leave then I'd clean my entire house.

Forty days. You had to stay inside the house for forty days after having a baby before you went out. It took that long before one's pores could close after the baby was born. I understand that the veins and all won't close until forty days are up.

There you'd be in bed during postpartum. Even the bread was really well toasted so that you'd be able to eat it. If it wasn't well toasted, they wouldn't give it to you. As far as meat is concerned, it had to be lamb, nothing else. Well, who knows why. That's one of the first things that was prepared, a lamb, so that by the time the baby was born, that's what you were given to eat—lamb.

Katarina Montoya

En el mal ojo sí creo

En el mal ojo sí creo. Sí. Tenía una flor muy bonita atrás de una cortina que no le entrara el polvo. Estaba bien, bien bonita, coloraa, como coloraa y verde en la orilla. Coyos se llaman ora. Y llegó mi sobrino, estaa mediano mi sobrino, puea que como cinco años, y abrió la cortina y empezó a que le gustaba tanto esa flor. Ahi se estuvo, y la voltiaba y le dijía a su mamá,

—Ven mira esta flor que bonita, mamá.

Loo le dijo mi hermana que la dejara sola. No le hizo mal. No le hizo nada que yo viera, porque yo estaa ahi.

Otro día amaneció la flor bien seca. La planta amaneció muerta otro día. Y estaba viendo, que yo siempre cuido mis plantas muy bien y se murió y antonces creí [en el mal ojo].

Y loo a los *babies*, que les hacen ojo. Antonces dije, "Pus puea ser cierto tamién." Pero quizás a los míos no. ¡Toos estaan muy feos! No les hicieron ojo nadien. [Risas] Dijían,

—Persínenlos. No les vayan hacer ojo, —a mí me dijían si yo estaa viendo un niño que admiraba, que qué bonito y too eso, —persínalo, porque si no tienes que dale agua con la boca, —pero a los míos, ¡nunca!

The Evil Eye Is One Thing I Do Believe In

The evil eye is one thing I do believe in. I had a very beautiful flower behind the curtains so that it wouldn't collect dust. It was really, really pretty, red, like red with green around the edges. It's a coyo, as it's called nowadays. And so my nephew showed up. He was young, perhaps about five years old, and he opened the drapes and started admiring the flower a lot. There he was, and he would turn it around and then he'd say to his mother, "Come here and look at this pretty flower, Mom."

Then his mother told him to leave the flower alone. He didn't harm it in any way. He didn't do anything that I could tell, because I was right there.

Next day in the morning the flower was dry, dry. Next day the plant had died. And I was wondering, because I always take very good care of my plants, but it died. That's when I began to believe in the evil eye.

And then there's babies, who suffer from the evil eye. Then I said to myself, "Perhaps it's true as well." But I guess that's not the case with mine. They're all so ugly! Nobody ever cast the evil eye on them. [Laughter] People would say, "Make the sign of the cross on them. Don't go cast the evil eye on them!"

I used to be told that if I admired a baby a lot, because it was pretty and all of that.

"Make the sign of the cross; otherwise you have to give it water with your mouth." But that never happened to my children. Never!

Cruzita Vigil

A mí me hicieron ojo de quince años

Eso sí es verdá, porque, porque mi esposo les hacía ojos a sus mismos hijos dél. Nomás empezaba uno de mis hijos a llorar, chiquitos, y loo le dicía a él,

—Tú le hicites ojo al niño.

—No, que no, que apenas le hice cariño.

—¡Que le hace! Dale agua, y le hace una cruz aquí [en la frente] con sal.

Se le quitaba lo llorón; sanaba.

D'eso sí es verdá. A mí me hicieron ojo de quince años. En los cachetes. Juimos a una trasquila de borregas. Jue en papá tamién, y jui con una de mis agüelas. Había esta mujer too el tiempo me dicía a mí que qué bonitos cachetes tenía. Y, cuento es que, cuando nos vinimos de aá [de la trasquila], comencé yo con comezón en los cachetes. Me untaba de too lo que me dicían, y entre más y más me iba cundiendo la comezón, más y más [comezón], hasta que un día me dijo mi agüela,

—No sabes. Tú dices que quién sabe si aquea malvada te haría ojo.

—Oh no, ya tan vieja, ¿qué me ha de hacer? Y si me llevan a que me dé agua, yo no voy a beber agua. Que me dé agua con su boca, yo no voy a beber. Si no es necesario.

—Oh, ¿quieres murirte?

—No, pus llévenme.

Y me llevaron. No, no, de güena suerte no me dio agua, pero que agarró agua con sal y agua bendita y me bendició y me untó agua salivia de ea misma y sané. Se me quitaron esos cachetes hinchaos que tenía. Eso sí sé yo que es malo—el ojo. Se han muerto munchos asina. Se le secan los ojos al muchacho que le hacen ojo.

Someone Cast the Evil Eye on Me When I Was Fifteen

That's one thing that's true, because my husband used to cast the evil on his own children. No sooner did one of my children start crying, when they were small, than I would say to him, "You cast the evil eye on the baby."

"Why, no, no, I only caressed him."

"Just the same! Give him salt water and make the sign of the cross right on its forehead." He'd stop his crying; he would get well.

That's one thing that's true. Someone cast the evil eye on me when I was fifteen years old. Right here on my cheeks. We happen to have gone to a sheep shearing. My dad went as well, and I went with one of my grandmas. And there was this woman who always told me what beautiful cheeks I had. And, so the story goes, when we returned from shearing sheep, I started itching on my both of my cheeks. I'd rub on whatever I was told to rub on, and the more I treated the itching, the more it itched, until one day my grandma said to me, "You never know. You say that perhaps that scoundrel of a woman cast an evil eye on you."

"Oh, no way. At my age. How could she cast the evil eye on me? And if they take me for her to give me water, I'm not going. For her to give me water from her mouth, forget it! Why, that's not necessary!"

"Oh, so you want to die?"

"Why, no! Take me."

They took me. Well, no, luckily she didn't give me water from her mouth, but she got salt water and holy water and she blessed me and she rubbed her own saliva on me and I was cured. I got rid of the swollen cheeks that I had. That's one thing I know is bad—the evil eye. Many individuals have died because of it. The eyes of a child with the evil eye can go dry.

José Nataleo Montoya

Mi señora le hizo mal ojo a un sobrino

Mi señora le hizo mal ojo a un sobrino. Él estaa, pus, bebito estaa él. ¡Y murre feo! Pus una tarde estaa ésta [mi esposa] con un dolor de cabeza. Que le dolía la cabeza y el chavalo estaa ahi gomitándose y llorando y de todo. Antonces le dice su mamá de ésta, taa estaa viva ea,

—Oye, Lala —porque le dicen Lala—. Lala, dale agua al Melecio.

—¿Por qué? —le dijo.

—Tú le hicites ojo a ése.

—¡Que le voy hacer ojo a ése tare feo! —le dijo.

Pus vino y le dio agua y ahi estuvo. Se arregló. Pero ora quizás no sucede eso. Pero en esos años sí. Y quizás sí era cierto, porque pasaban cosas asina.

My Wife Cast the Evil Eye on a Nephew

My wife cast the evil eye on a nephew. He was, well, only a baby. And very ugly! Well, one evening she was suffering from a headache. She claimed that she had a headache and the child was vomiting and crying and everything. Then my wife's mother said to her—she was still alive—

"Listen, Lala," because they called her Lala. "Lala, give Melecio some water."

"Why?" she said to her.

"You cast the evil eye on that child."

"How could I have cast the evil eye on such an ugly child?" she responded.

Well, she came and gave him water [from mouth to mouth] and that was it. That took care of it. But I guess that sort of thing doesn't happen anymore. But back then it did. And I guess it was true, because things like that did occur.

Cesaria Montoya

¿Qué ojo le voy hacer ese feo?

Pues no creo en el mal ojo, y a veces que me dan ganas de creelo porque me pasó una vez. Teníamos un sobrinito que criaron mi papá y mi mamá, su nieto. Estaba bebito, chiquito. Pos una vez había gente en la casa; llegó gente. El niño al rato empezó a llorar muncho y a subile muncha calentura, y a mí me comenzó a doler la cabeza. Ya yo comencé a deponer, como a gomitarme, y me dijo mamá,

—Ya tú le hicites ojo al niño.

Me rií y le dije,

—¿Qué ojo le voy hacer ese feo? Todos los días lo miro y está tan feo que, ¿qué ojo le voy hacer?

—Pus no le hace —me dijo—. Dale agua.

Tenía uno que dales agua con la boca [a los niños con mal ojo].

—¡Pobre criatura! —le dije—. ¡Qué le voy a dar agua yo con mi boca!

—Dale agua —me dijo—. ¡Tú le hicites ojo!

Pus lo agarré en brazos, le di agua, y loo me acosté en la cama con él. Nos durmimos los dos. Cuando recordamos estábanos bien. No me dolía la cabeza a mí, ni él estaa llorando. Isque ése era, isque le había hecho ojo. Es lo único que me acuerdo yo de eso, del ojo.

How Could I Have Cast the Evil Eye on That Ugly Thing?

Well, I don't believe in the evil eye, and at times I want to believe in it because of what happened to me one time. We had a little nephew who was raised by my dad and my mom, their grandson. He was a small baby, tiny. Well, one time there were people at the house; people came to visit. A little while later he started to cry a lot with a high fever, and I started to get a headache. I began to get nauseated, as if to vomit, and my mom said to me, "You have cast the evil eye on the baby."

I laughed and said to her, "How could I have cast the evil eye on that ugly thing? Every day I look at him and he's so ugly that how could I have cast the evil eye on him?"

"Well, it doesn't matter," she said to me. "Give him water [from your mouth]." You had to give babies with the evil eye water from your mouth.

"Poor child!" I said to her. "There's no way I'm going to give him water from my mouth!"

"Give him water," she said to me. "You're the one who cast the evil eye on him!"

Well, I grabbed him in my arms, gave him water, and then I lay in bed with him. We both went to sleep. When the both of us woke up, we were okay. I no longer had a headache, nor was he crying. I understand that's what it was. I had inflicted the evil eye on him. That's the only incident I can recall regarding the evil eye.

Filiberto Esquibel

Yo ha visto cómo trabaja el mal ojo

Pues yo ha [he] visto cómo trabaja [el mal ojo]. Sí hay tal cosa, porque yo tenía un hijo. El mayor. Eh, había una vecina y quería muncho a la plebe y jue a velo. Le gustaa muncho la plebe y le hizo un agasajo al muchito, y se le voltiaron los ojos bien parriba. No se le vía el ojo. Bien parriba y sí era un dolor bárbaro. No sabíanos qué hacele. No había estao más de ea allí que le hizo un cariño. Le dio un beso. Y loo en papá, se llamaa Juan Bautista. Nació el día 24 de junio. Güeno, y jue muy religioso el viejito, y dijo,

—Este muchacho, este muchacho le hicieron ojo. ¿Quién le hizo un cariño? A ver.

Lo pescó y lo curó. Le dio agua en la boca. Rezó. Y le lavó la cabeza con lo que traiba él, sal, y lo que trujiera en la boca. Cinco minutos después no tenía nada. Yo ha [he] visto no nomás ése. Ha [he] visto varios.

I've Seen How the Evil Eye Works

Well, I have seen how the evil eye works. There is such a thing, because I had a son, the oldest one. Ah, there was a neighbor and she loved kids a lot and she went to see him. She liked kids very much and she made a warm gesture [usually on one of the cheeks], and his eyes rolled up. You couldn't see either one of his eyes. His eyes rolled up, and there was an awful pain. We didn't know what to do. She was the only person who had been there and caressed him. She had kissed him. And then Dad's name was Juan Bautista. He was born on June 24. Well, then, the old man had always been very religious and he said,

"This boy, this boy has been afflicted with the evil eye. Who caressed him? Come now, let's see."

He caught him and he cured him. He gave him water in his mouth. He prayed. And he washed the boy's head with whatever salt [saliva] he had in his mouth. Five minutes later there was nothing wrong with him. I have seen not only that case, I have seen various others.

Cruzita Vigil

El güevo es par un empache

El güevo es par un empache. Como si usté taa mediano, güeno hay una comida que se les cuaja 'l estómago, y no puee comer y le da calentura y too eso. Gómitos le dan y too eso. Viene usté y quiebra un güevo. Conforme está, se lo echa aquí, en 'l estómago. Porque yo hice ese remedio. En 'l estómago se lo echa aquí. Y ahi trae el güevo roando asina con la yema y la clara. Onde se revienta el güevo, ahi está el empache. Y sana. Hasta pa una calentura. Una calentura fiebre que sea.

Si usté conoce que el niño está con muncha calentura, quiebra usté un güevo, y le hace una cruz con sal y se lo pone en la cabecera onde está el *baby*, onde está el muchito, lo que sea, en la cabecera dél. El güevo amanece cocido otro día, y se le quita la calentura al muchito.

Ya yo lo ha [he] hecho. Porque yo lo hice con el Carl, con el hijo de la Marcela. El Ronald. Ése ya hacía un mes que estaa malo. Lo llevaron al dotor y no descansaba. Yo era la que lo cuidaba, ¿ve? Y él era muy particular. Él era, oh, diatiro. Y un día dije, "No, no han de dejar morir al chamaco ese nomás por . . . Voy y lo curo a escondidas, ¿pus qué?" Vine y lo empeloté y le anduve con el huevo asina [en el estómago] y loo lo reventé y le unté too el güevo en too el cuerpo. Loo lo envolví enpelotito en una sábana y lo acosté. Al rato recordó y me dijo,

—Grama.

—¿Qué? —le digo.

—Yo tengo hambre, y quiero comer.

—Güeno —le digo yo.

Jui y le di de comer. Cuando vine a dale güelta a ver cómo estaba de la calentura, ya no tenía calentura. Dijo su mamá,

—¿Pus qué le pasó a mi hijito? ¿Se le jue la calentura?

—¿Quién sabe? —le dije yo—. Seguro que ya se le cortó la calentura. Yo no quise dicir tavía porque era muy particular.

A los dos días le digo yo,

—¿Sabes quién jue la médica de tu hijo?

—¿Quién?

—Yo lo curé, que si no se te había muerto tu chamaco.

—Pus, ¿cómo lo curó?

Ya le estuve diciendo,

—Oh, pus está güeno que lo curara. Ya ora sí sé que es mérica." [Risas]

Ya le digo. El güevo es muy güeno.

The Egg Is for Indigestion

The egg is used for indigestion. For example, if you're a small kid, well, there may be some food that causes indigestion and you can't eat and you end up with a fever and all that. You're nauseated and all that sort of thing. What you do is crack an egg. Just as it is, cracked, you put it on the child's stomach, because I did that myself. You put it on top of his stomach. Then there you have the egg rolling around with the yolk and the egg white. Wherever the egg yolk breaks, that's where the indigestion is located. And he'll be cured, even from the fever, a high fever. If you realize that a baby has a high fever, you crack an egg, and you make the sign of the cross with salt and you put it at the head of the bed where the baby is, where the little boy is, or whatever it is, right at the head of the bed. The egg will be cooked next morning, but the baby will no longer have a fever.

I have done that myself, because I did it with Carl, Marcela's son. With Ronald, who had already been ill for a whole month. They took him to the doctor and he couldn't get well. I was the one who cured him, you see? And he was very hard to please. He was, oh, just terrible. And one day I said to myself, "No. They must not let that child die just because of . . . I'll go and cure him without anyone seeing me, so what?" I came and undressed him and I rubbed an egg like so, on his stomach, and I cracked it and I rubbed the egg all over his body. Then I wrapped him up, bare naked, in a bed sheet and I put him to bed. A little while later he woke up and he said to me, "Grandma."

"What?" I said to him.

"I'm hungry." He wanted to eat.

"Okay," I said. I went and fed him. When I returned again to see how his fever was, it was gone.

"Well, what happened to my son's fever? Is his fever gone?" said his mom.

"Who knows?" I responded. I didn't want to say anything at that time because she was very difficult to please.

"I don't know," I responded. "Surely his fever has gone down by now."

Two days later, I say to her, "Do you know who your baby's folk healer was?"

"Who?" she said.

"I'm the one who cured him. If not, that child of yours would have been history."

"Well, how did you cure him?"

I proceeded to tell her and she said, "Oh, well, it's a good thing that you got him well. Now I know that you're a folk healer." [Laughter]

I'm telling you. The egg is very good [for indigestion].

4

Brujerías y supersticiones

Witchcraft and Superstitions

Introduction

Hispanos in northern New Mexico have enjoyed a long-standing relationship with supernaturalism due to the fascination, allure, mystery, and mirth surrounding it. There is probably not a single Hispano over sixty years of age in the small communities who has not engaged in a conversation about or heard a story related to witchcraft. To an extent, whether individuals truly believe in superstitions is inconsequential, because even the skeptics, either by choice or by default, knowingly or not, have been drawn into heated discussions as part of community gossip (*mitote*) or amusement.

Years ago families used to gather in the evening to exchange all kinds of stories, about ghosts, witches (*brujas*), and peculiar natural phenomena. This custom—now passé—was practiced especially during the winter while family members roasted and ate pine nuts around the potbelly stove. Witches have been a favorite theme among Hispanos from time immemorial.

Every community at one time or another has no doubt laid claim to an old hag suspected of sorcery. Her clandestine nighttime wanderings, bizarre appearance and behavior, or her idiosyncratic home environment and the company she kept merely intensified interest and piqued people's curiosity. At times, even after a witch died, perhaps in peculiar circumstances, she did not disappear completely. Stories abound about neighbors or passersby seeing sparks or balls of fire emitted from the chimney of a dead witch's empty house, testimony to her powers and a vivid reminder that her wretched spirit was still present. Moreover, a witch who did not forsake her evil ways and repent went to hell, and her soul was made to wander in pain for the rest of time as punishment for her malevolent deeds.

As a child growing up in rural New Mexico, I heard countless stories about witches. These accounts came in different forms, some from my relatives. I recall vividly a cousin who came home one night beside himself and with his face full of scratches. It seems a dog kept nipping at his ankles as he passed by the cemetery, whereupon he kicked it. The dog, black with white spots, then jumped up and scratched his face. Black dogs (not white ones) symbolize the diabolical element in Hispanic folklore of northern New Mexico, but in my cousin's case, the dog was black and white. My paternal grandmother claimed that the dog was a witch (in actuality, a lost soul) from the nearby cemetery destined to torment innocent victims such as my cousin. Her advice to us was, whenever we saw a strange object (*un bulto*) at night or something resembling an evil spirit (*una cosa mala*), to utter the words, "Santísimo sacramento del altar" (Holy Sacrament!). There were times when I saw her make a cross with the thumb and index finger and heard her invoke expressions like, "¡Dios le ponga las cruces!" (May God have mercy on it [the ghost or spirit]!), "¡Ave María Purísima!" (Holy Mary of God!), and "¡Dios nos libre de la cosa mala!" (God spare us from all evil!). These utterances were intended to ward off evil spirits.

Witches also were reputed to disguise themselves as owls (*tecolotes*—we used *lechuza* in the Río Puerco Valley), coyotes, or cats, particularly cats with striking green eyes. In *Recuerdos de los viejitos: Tales of the Río Puerco* and *Abuelitos: Stories of the Río Puerco Valley* I have collected stories involving the transformation of a woman (a witch) into a coyote as well as the belief that women with green eyes were suspected of being witches. My paternal grandmother also recounted stories about colts (*potrillos*) and donkeys (*burritos*) as part of the magical lore of my village of Ojo del Padre.

Of course, one can ill afford to forget the inimitable *coco* or its counterpart, *el agüelo,* both bogeymen that, until more recent times, were household words in virtually every Hispanic home. I well recall how my father and, on occasion, my mother would scare my siblings and me when we were small with *el coco* or *el agüelo;* this is the same figure that plays a somewhat different role in Los Matachines (an old Spanish ritual dance whose music can be traced to sixteenth-century Europe). "Si no se están quietos y se duermen, va venir el coco por ustedes" (If you don't keep quiet and go to sleep, the bogeyman's going to come and get you). Eventually, we figured out that *el coco* was nothing more than a mythical figure and not something we should fear. Until that happened, though, *el coco* was quite effective in getting us to quiet down at bedtime because it scared the dickens out of us.

People who believe in bewitchment (*embrujo*), La Llorona (the Wailing Woman), enchanted places (*lugares encantados*), buried treasures (*entierros*), the evil eye (*el mal ojo*), ghostly apparitions (*bultos*), lights (*luces*), or hallucinations (*visiones*) are the ones who for a long time kept the drama of superstition alive. Supernatural tales are still popular with some old-timers.

The narratives in this chapter reaffirm the popularity supernaturalism enjoyed among most old-timers who were interviewed for this work. Most informants' tales are quite traditional. They range from the Wailing Woman to evil spirits to ghosts to sorcery to the devil to witches to mammals and reptiles to remarkable natural phenomena. Others will take the reader into a mysterious and fascinating universe that seems a bit farfetched yet compelling to the narrators because of their personal experiences.

Jesusita Aragón

La Llorona

Yo de la Llorona no sé. Pueda que sí hubiera. En este callejón aquí a lado, vestida de blanco, se oye llorar muy lejos, es que La Llorona. Ella anda llorando. No le hace mal a naide, pero anda llorando. Dijían mis agüelitos que lloraba por su hijo. Cuando el rey ordenó que degollaran a todos los niños, porque quería ver si degollaban al Niño Dios, La Llorona es que dijo, "De ver a m'hijo degollao, mejor lo hogo." Y l'echó en el río y lo hogó. Eso es lo que ella llora, pero no le hace mal a naide.

Una noche cuando estaba yo en el fresco, porque yo cuidé siete hombres pacientes del estao por trece años aquí en mi casa, y loo cuando yo vi mi negocio en la noche de lavar trastes y todo, me salí pal portal al fresco. Estaba m'hijo sentao aá juera platicando conmigo, cuando oigo llorar y llorar. Y había una pobre que le dijían la Chigüila, por mal nombre. Bebía muncho. Me dijo él,

—Ahi viene la Chigüila, Tita.

—¿De veras? Pobrecita, pobrecita —porque vivía tal y mal.

—No. No es —dijo—. ¡Mira! Es un bulto blanco.

Y se paró él y vido la Güila.

—No Güila —le dije—. Es La Llorona. No te hace nada.

No. No juyó. Hasta quién sabe hasta ónde iría llorando. Y loo se desaparece. Daba como un grito. Como un grito nomás. Era todo.

A mí no me daba miedo porque mi agüelito cuando se oía el grito, dijía,

—Ahi anda La Llorona penando.

The Wailing Woman

I don't know anything about the Wailing Woman. Perhaps there was such a thing. Right here in this alley, dressed in white, you hear a woman cry far off in the distance. She walks about crying. She doesn't harm anyone, but she roams around crying. My grandparents used to say that she cried for her son. When the king ordered all the children to be beheaded, because he wanted to see if they would behead the Baby Jesus, the Wailing Woman is reputed to have said, "Rather than see my son beheaded, I'll drown him." And she tossed him into the river and drowned him. That's why she cries, but she doesn't do anyone any harm.

One night when I was outside getting some fresh air, because for thirteen years I took care of seven male patients belonging to the state here in this house. After I tended to my evening chores, washing dishes and all, I went outside to the porch to get some fresh air. My son was sitting outside and talking with me, when all of a sudden I hear this crying and crying. And there was this poor woman they called Chigüila, an unflattering name. She used to drink a lot. My son said to me, "There comes Chigüila, Tita."

"Really? Poor thing, poor thing," because she lived so down and out.

"No. It's not her," he said. "Look! It's a white ghost."

And he stood up and saw the Güila.

"It's not Güila," I said to him. "It's the Wailing Woman. She's harmless."

No. She didn't flee. Who knows how far she went crying? Then she disappeared. She let out, like, a holler. Like a moaning sound. That's all.

I wasn't afraid, because my grandfather, whenever he heard the cry, he would say, "There goes the Wailing Woman, grieving."

La cosa mala

Sí creyo en la cosa mala. Yo creyo que hay. A muncha gente le ha llegao a pasar munchas cosas con la cosa mala. En un tiempo ahi en misa había un casorio, y le dijo el marido a la mujer,

—Orita vengo por ti y por mi mamá. Voy yo a dar la güelta— y jue y se puso una parranda y no se acordó. A medianoche cayó ya por ellas.

—¿Qué horas son éstas de ir al baile? —le dijo la mamá. Y empezó él a desparatiar y qué sabe qué tanto. La borrachera.

—¡Y que me lleve el diantre! —que pallá y que pacá.

—¡Cállate la boca!—le dijo su mamá—. Te puede llevar.

—Que me lleve.

Y se salió pa juera. Pues de allá entró too desgreñao y too rasguñao, la ropa rota y too.

—¡Qué bárbara! —les dijo—. Por tanto y me lleva el diablo. Ustedes ni saben.

—Pus tú querías —le dijo su mamá. [Risas]

Evil Spirits

I'm one who believes in evil spirits. I believe there is such a thing. Many people have had bad experiences with evil spirits. One time during Mass there was a wedding going on. And the husband said to his wife, "I'll be back in a little while to get you and Mom. I'm going to go look around," and he went and got drunk and forgot all about them. At midnight he showed up to pick them up.

"What time is this to be showing up to go to the dance?" said the mother.

And he started to carry on and who knows what all. Talking nonsense.

"And let the devil take me away!" all this, that, and the other.

"Keep quiet!" said his mother. "It can come and get you."

"Let him take me."

And he went outdoors. No sooner had he gone outside than he came back in all disheveled and scratched up, his clothes all torn and everything.

"Good gracious!" he said to them. "The devil almost took me with him. You don't know how close he came."

"You asked for it," said his mother to him. [Laughter]

Filiberto Esquibel

¿Qué no quieres ir al funeral?

Si tú quieres que yo te diga de que hay cosas que no podemos explicar, te voy a platicar una cosa, una cosa que me pasó a mí. Tenía un carro viejo. Güeno, en esos tiempos no había muncho jale. Tenía un carro Chevy, viejo, le di un *overhaul*. Pues yo no había compuesto un carro que no comenzara. Dende un prencipio hasta el otro. Dende chiquito me crie dándole *overhaul* a gatos, *bulldozers* y maquinarias. Le di un *overhaul*. Era un '36 Chevy. No, no, no, no quería prender. Le chequié too y güeno. Teníanos en ese tiempo un funeral entre unas personas muy cerca. Yo estaba acabando de componer el carro pa prendelo. Luego dijo la mujer,

—¿Qué no quieres ir al funeral?

—Pus yo quisiera componer este carro. Lo necesito pa ir al trabajo. Curre tú.

Pues esta persona [el muerto], cierta persona, se nojó porque no quise ir yo al funeral. El día que lo iban a enterrar [al difunto], se enojó. Se me quedó a ver, a componer el carro. Le chequié el carbulador. Le chequié los puntos. Le chequié too. Too estaa bien. Se soponía comenzar. Gaselín. Too tenía. Le di al *starter* hasta que tomé la batería, y los '36 Chevys se les podía dar cranque. Le di cranque. Nada. Ni, ni lucha hacía, y le dejé el cranque puesto al carro. Ya me dolía 'l espinazo. En ese tiempo llegó tal gente pa la casa. Y llegó mi suegro adelante. Me dijo,

—¿Qué no lo has poído componer? ¿No ha prendío el carro?

—No quiere —le dije—. Le cayó hasta la batería. Ya me cansé de dale cranque. Ya me cansé. Ora lo voy a prender atrás de la troca de mi tío y le voy a pegar una jalaa a éste nomás de puro coraje.

Y en ese tiempo vinía cierta persona de allá del funeral pacá, dolientes del enterrao. Ya se le había bajao el coraje al dijunto, y pasó cerquita una mujer.

—¿Qué pasa —dijo—. ¿Qué no puedes comenzar el carro?

—No —le dije—. No quiere comenzar.

Yo no maliciaba nada.

—¡Válgame Dios! —dijo—. Pus yo no sé cómo no comienza y eres muy güen macánico.

Y le alisó el *fender* asina [con la mano], y entró pa dentro. Siguimos platicando yo y mi suegro. Y le dije,

—Pus ya l'hecho el trae a este carro de toos moos. Ya llevo too el santo día. De toos moos y no quiere.

Le puse la llave otra vez. Nomás en cuanto se movió el ingenio y prendió el carro. Explícame tú eso.

Hubo esta cierta persona [el muerto], y no me quería, ¿ves? Tuvimos una dificultá.

Don't You Want to Go to the Funeral?

If you want me to tell you about things that we can't explain, I'm going to tell you something, something that happened to me. I had an old car. Fine, back then you couldn't find work. I had a Chevy, old, and I gave it an overhaul. I had never fixed a car that wouldn't start. From one car to another. Ever since I was small I grew up overhauling caterpillars, bulldozers, and machinery. I gave the car an overhaul. It was a '36 Chevy. It just didn't want to start. I checked everything, but nothing. There was a funeral going at the home of some people who lived nearby. I was about done with the car and getting ready to start it. Then my wife said to me, "Don't you want to go to the funeral?"

"Well, I would like to fix this car. I need it for work. You go ahead."

Well, this person, this certain person [the deceased] got angry because I refused to go to his funeral. The day that they were going to bury him, he got mad. He stayed behind to watch me fix the car. I checked the carburetor. I checked the points. I checked everything. Everything was fine. It was supposed to start. It had gasoline. It had everything. I hit the starter until I ran the battery down, and you could crank the '36 Chevys. I cranked it. Nothing. It didn't even hum, and so I left the crank in it. My back was already hurting. About that time some people stopped by the house. And my father-in-law was ahead of them. He said to me, "Haven't you been able to fix the car? Hasn't it started?"

"It doesn't want to start," I said to him. "The battery's even gone down. I'm tired of cranking it. I'm tired. Now I'm going to hitch it up to the back of my uncle's truck and I'm going to give a good jerk just from anger."

At that moment there was this person returning from the funeral, one of the mourners. The dead person's anger had subsided, and a woman passed close by.

"What's wrong?" she said. "Can't you start the car?"

"No," I said to her. "It doesn't want to start."

I didn't suspect anything.

"Good gracious!" she said. "I don't understand why it doesn't start and you're such a good mechanic."

And she caressed the fender with her hand, and she went inside the house. My father-in-law and I kept on chatting. And I said to him, "I've tried starting this car in every which way. I've wasted the whole blasted day. I've tried everything and it doesn't want to start."

I put the key in the ignition one more time. No sooner had the engine made noise than the car started. You explain that to me.

There was this certain person [the deceased], and he didn't like me, you see. We had a disagreement.

Mi anillo con unas porquerías

Yo con mi esposa juimos al baile un sábado en la noche. Otro día teníanos que ir pa Alburquerque. En la noche juimos al baile. Y dijo,

—Ponte tu anillo, tu *wedding ring*.

Era media celosa. Güeno, es una cosa muy bonita. Me lo puse y juimos al baile. Cuando volvimos del baile le dije,

—Me lo voy a quitar pa no perdelo, porque mañana tenemos que ir pa Alburquerque.

—Güeno —dijo—. Lo echas en mi cajón.

Ahi tenía mis *cufflinks* y prendedores así de la mujer, y eché mi anillo. Tenía mi nombre por dentro y lo eché en la caja. La tapé. Cerré el cajón. Era como la una de la mañana. Durmimos un rato. Luego recordamos a las muchachas de mañana pa ir pa Alburquerque a comprar *groceries* y a visitar a la tía que crió a mi esposa. Güeno, juimos y volvimos el lunes, en la madrugada. Muy de mañana nos vinimos de Alburquerque. Y tenía la idea mi esposa de que llegáanos a la casa y chequiaba el cajón de correo.

—Mira —dijo cuando íbanos entrando—. ¡Mira! Hay una carta; está una carta estampada, estampada aquí en Las Vegas.

Jue echada aquí en Las Vegas, *okay?* Poco gorda la carta. La abrí y tenía un retrato puerco de tal persona. Estaba el anillo mío de casorio adentro la carta, y lo vide. Atrás tenía mi nombre. "¿Pus qué pasa aquí?" Fui a buscalo aá dentro onde lo guardé. Ese lunes en la mañana estáanos allá en Alburquerque antes que pasara el correo. ¿Cómo puee echar esa carta el domingo, y ir el domingo aquí en Las Vegas? Tú explícame eso.

—Mira —le dije a mi esposa—. Éste es mi anillo. Ahi está la carta pegada. Ahi está la carta con la dirición de aquí. Mira qué día salió. ¿Cómo puee el anillo cruzar el tiempo, a que pudiera haber echo día jueves, viernes o sábado pa que hubiera caido aquí?

No había nada en el correo el domingo cuando nos juimos. Siempre le echaba la llave cuando me iba pa alguna parte, porque la plebe estaba cerquita de l'escuela y me sacaban las cartas. Las tiraban. Muy traviesos.

—¿Tú tienes una explicación cómo pudo ir en el correo mi anillo, caminar patrás en tiempo, y venir a esa carta?

—Que si ónde lo había dejao ese anillo, que si lo había dejao en un hotel. ¿Tú no has andao en un hotel? —me dijo mi esposa.

Yo no salía pa ninguna parte, pero alguien me tenía mal idea. Mi anillo estaba ahi en la carta con unas porquerías. ¿Pero cómo jue a dar ahi en el correo?

My Wedding Ring and Some Filthy Stuff

My wife and I went to a dance on a Saturday night. Next day we had to go to Albuquerque. And she said to me, "Put on your ring, your wedding ring."

She was kind of jealous. Fine, it's a very beautiful thing. I put it on and we went to the dance. When we got back I said to her, "I'm going to take off my ring so I don't lose it, because tomorrow we have to go to Albuquerque."

"Okay," she said. "Put it in my chest of drawers."

That's where I had my cufflinks with my wife's brooches and stuff like that, and so I put my ring in the drawer. It had my name on the inside, and I put it in the box. I closed the lid. I closed the drawer. It was about one o'clock in the morning. We slept for a little while. Then we woke the girls up early in order to go to Albuquerque to buy groceries and to visit the aunt who raised my wife. Very well, we went and came back on Monday, very early. We came back very early from Albuquerque. And my wife had the habit of checking the mailbox when we got home.

"Look," she said when we were going in the house. "Look! There's a letter; there's a letter with a stamp, stamped here in Las Vegas."

It was mailed here in Las Vegas, okay? The letter was a bit bulky. I opened it and it had an obscene picture of a certain person. My wedding ring was inside the envelope, and I looked at it. Inside the ring was my name. "I wonder what we have here?" I went to look for my ring inside the house where I had put it.

That Monday morning we were over in Albuquerque before the mail went out. How can that letter have been mailed on Sunday and delivered on Sunday here in Las Vegas? You explain that to me.

"Look," I said to my wife. "This is my ring. There's the sealed letter. There's the letter with our address. Look at the day it was mailed. How could the ring jump backward in time so that it could have been mailed Thursday, Friday, or Saturday so as to get here?"

There was nothing in the mailbox when we left. I always locked it whenever I went anywhere because the school kids were close by and they would take out the letters. They'd throw them away. They were mischievous.

"Do you have an explanation how my ring was able to go

through the mail, for the clock to go backward, and for my ring to come in that letter?"

"Had I left my ring somewhere? Had I left it in a hotel?" my wife wondered aloud. "Have you been at some hotel?"

I never went anywhere, but somebody had it in for me. My ring was in that letter and some filthy stuff. But how did it get there?

Enterraron el cajón delante de mí

Güeno. Pasó otra cosa. Y a ver cómo me lo explicas. Cuando mi madre se murió, tenía ea un anillo que había comprao. El original se le perdió. Se le cayó en el sinke, y no lo jallamos. No lo pudimos jallar. Loo después compró otro baratito. Cuando mamá se murió, yo vide que cuando cerraron el cajón, que se llevaa su anillo de casorio todo bien arreglao. Llevaa las manos hechas cruz. Ahi iba su anillo. *I made darn sure* que estaba su anillo. La enterraron. Enterraron el cajón delante de mí. Ese cajón no se abrió ajuera de mi vista. No se despareció. La enterramos. Otro día me dijo mi esposa,

—Oyes —dijo—. Pus, ¿qué no está el anillo de tu mamá aquí? ¡Cómo se parece! Tiene su nombre por dentro también.

'L anillo que se soponía llevaa mi madre, estaba en mi cajón. *That I remember. I still got the ring. I can't explain that. Maybe she wanted me to have something. I still have it.*

Puea que nunca lleguemos en la vida de nosotros a explicar qué pasó. Pero pasan las cosas. Las ha [he] visto.

The Casket Was Lowered Right before My Eyes

Okay. Another thing happened. And let's see if you can explain it to me. When my mother died, she had a ring that she had bought. She lost the original one. It fell in the sink, and we didn't find it. We couldn't find it. Then later on she bought another one a bit cheaper. When my mother died, I saw when they closed the casket that she had her wedding ring intact. Her hands were crossed. She had her ring on. I made darn sure that she was wearing her ring. They buried her. The casket was lowered right before my eyes. That casket never left my presence. It was never out of my sight. We buried my mother. Next day my wife said to me, "Listen," she said. "Isn't this your mother's ring? It sure looks like it! It also has her name on the inside."

The ring that my mother supposedly was wearing when she was buried was in my box. That I remember. I still got the ring. I can't explain that. Maybe she wanted me to have something. I still have it.

Perhaps we'll never be able to explain in our lives what happened. But things like that happen. I have seen them.

Carmelita Gómez

Pus ésa era bruja, ¿qué no?

Isque había coco. Había La Llorona. Dicían, "Cállense hijitos, va venir La Llorona. Si no se callan va venir La Llorona." Platicaba mi papá que había una mujer. Tenía munchos muchichitos y eran muy atroces. "Cállense, hijitos. Orita viene La Llorona." Pero ahi en onde yo vivía, en Jorupa, isque había munchas brujas. Pus nojotros las víanos. Iban las brasas. Dicía José Lucero,

—Siéntense aquí pa que vean. De aá de Jorupa salen munchas luces paá pa Antón Chico.

Y era verdá. Iban saltando y saltando y saltando. Pero le voy a platicar. Una vez, taa yo soltera, andábanos en un baile en los Torres. Andaba yo. Mi hermano Liberato estaa soltero. Andaba la María, andaba Franque Tapia y andaba Vitoriano. Cuando salimos del baile, vimos venir una luz asina sobre el monte. Venía corriendo sobre el monte, y les dije,

—Ya se le salieron las borregas [brujas] a Adolfo Martínez—porque parecía que venían de abajo y ahi bajó derecho la brasa.

Nosotros veníanos en veces de aá de los Torres por San José y pasáamos el río y pasó la bruja, la brasa, atrás de nosotros. Loo adelante iba. Esta bruja pescó too ahi en los Torres. Pescó too el cañoncito, y no la vimos más. Pus ésa era bruja, ¿qué no?

Why, She Was a Witch, Wasn't She?

People claim there was a bogeyman. There was supposedly the Wailing Woman. They used to tell us, "Keep quiet, children. The Wailing Woman is going to come and get you. If you don't keep quiet, she's going to come." My father would tell us that there was this woman. She had lots of kids and they were terrible. "Keep quiet, kids! The

Wailing Woman's going to come." But I understand that where I lived, in Jorupa, that there were lots of witches. Why, we even saw them. We'd see the sparks flying. José Lucero used to say, "Come and sit down here so you can see. From Jorupa on down to Antón Chico you can see lots of lights [witches] flying."

And it was true. You could see them bouncing and bouncing and bouncing. But I'm going to tell you something. One time, I was still single, we were at a dance in Los Torres. I was at the dance. My brother Liberato, who was also single, was at the dance as well. There was María, Franque Tapia, and Vitoriano. When we left the dance, we saw a light moving like so [bouncing] on top of the mountain. It was bouncing on top of the mountain, and I said to them, "Adolfo Martínez's sheep [witches] are on the loose," because it seemed like they were headed from down below [where Martínez lived], and that's where the light came down.

From time to time we'd come down from Los Torres through San José, cross the river, and the witch, the light, would pass by behind us. Then there she'd be in front of us. This witch took off in the direction of Los Torres. She headed right up the small canyon, and we never saw her again. Why, she was a witch, don't you think?

Reynaldo Gonzales

Había brujas hechiceras

Quién sabe si será verdá o será mentira, pero a mí me contaban historias. Yo estaa muchacho grande. Grandecito estaa yo. Yo y otro muchacho íbanos a aquea escuela a estarnos en la noche. Tenía una puerta grande. Ahi nos sentábanos cuando estaa bonito el tiempo, a platicar. Táanos sentaos cuando vimos de aá lejos, taa la mesa, vinían dos brasas volando en 'l aire. Bajaban y subían. Bajaron cerca onde estáanos nojotros. Por arriba el techo pasaron. Un zumbío lo mismo que l' aire. Se fueron pa bajo. ¿Quién sabe? Seguro qu'eran brujas! No eran más de brujas. Eso jue too lo que vide de las brujas.

Pero había brujas antes: brujas hechiceras y brujas curanderas. Había arbolarios y había malhechores. Le hacían mal a la gente. Pus sepa Dios, porque su papá de mi cuñao mío, ya murió él tamién. Él se jue pa California y vivió aá y dejó a su papá aquí. De ahi de San Agustín, poco más pa abajo, había otra placita. Le dijían la Contación. Ora le dicen a too el pais, Lourdes. Ahi le hicieron mal a ese hombre. ¡Su misma mujer!

Este hombre jue casao dos veces, su papá de mi cuñao. Se llamaba Niceto Tapia. Pero yo conocí a don Niceto. Yo no he visto otro músico como ése. ¡Cómo tocaba bonito el violín! ¡Qué bárbaro! Pero, ¿pus a cuál músico no le gusta beber? ¿Cuál es el que no le gusta beber? Él le gustaba beber muncho. Y antes se iba la gente a buscar trabajo aá onde jallaban. Comenzaron a entrar con borregas aá a Roswell, a Fort Sumner, y too eso de ahi. Se juntaron un montaja de hombres. Había habido un baile en San Agustín, y estuvo tocando el hombre ese, ése que le hicieron mal. Isque dijo,

—Yo mañana me voy. Me voy con toos estos compañeros a la borrega. Voy a cuidar borregas.

No era ni su primer mujer; era su segunda mujer dél. Isque le dijo,

—No te vas.

—Sí me voy. ¿Quién me manda a mí?

Se jueron un bonche de hombres a caballo, burros, hechos chorro. Roswell está lejos. Cuando llegaron aá en la noche, se pararon a descansar los animales y a descansar eos. Mandó la mujer esta que le digo yo, a su hijo. Isque le dijo,

—¡A qué carajada! Aquí olvidó tu papá un encargadito. ¿Los alcanzarás?

Pus él quería a su papá. El hijo tenía un caballo. Otro día nomás amaneció y agarró su caballo y se jue. Los alcanzó. Estaan almorzando eos cuando llegó aá. Su hijo seguro se jue abrazar a su papá. Pues su hijo isque le dijo,

—Aquí le mandó mamá—era su madrastra del muchacho—esta botea que olvidó. Mandó que se la trujiera. A eso vine, a traila.

Pues que la agarró. Diuna vez bebió él. Pus, como le digo yo, ¿cuál músico no bebe? ¿Cuál músico no bebe?

Pa mediodía se jue haciendo loco el hombre. Como loco, estaa. Enpelotaba solo, y disparatiando solo en onde iba con compañeros. Hasta que lo notaron los demás compañeros. Isque dijieron,

—No. Vale más volvernos a llevar este hombre patrás pa San Agustín.

Se volvieron. Lo trujieron patrás. Ya cuando vino acá, taa como tonto el hombre. Pero yo vide ese hombre. Corrían las babas oiga, hasta aquí asina [al pecho]. Como un perro envenenao. Era un babero. Ahi se estaba el probe. Pus no podía ni comer ni naa, por el babero. Se estuvo asina ese hombre hasta que se murió. No podía comer.

Pero era la mujer dél ésa. Jue la mujer dél que l'hizo mal. Pues yo digo qu'era su mujer. L'hizo mal nomás porque no quería que se juera porque no iban a tener bailes aquí. Era el único músico.

There Were Malevolent Witches

Who knows whether it's true or lies, but they used to tell me stories. I was already a big boy. I was a little grown up. This other boy and I used to go to this school at night to kill some time. It had a huge door. That's where we sat down to chat when the weather was nice. We were sitting down one time when we saw in the distance—there was a mesa—two lights [sparks] flying in the sky headed our way. They'd go up and down. They descended close to where we were. They whizzed by over the roof of the house. The humming was just like when the wind is blowing. They took off down range. Who knows? Surely they were witches. That's what they were, witches! When it comes to witches, that's what I saw.

But long ago there were witches: malevolent witches and folk-healing witches. There were herb specialists and practitioners of black magic. They inflicted evil on people. God only knows why, because there's the father of a brother-in-law of mine. He's already dead. The son took off to California and he lived over there and he left his father here. From San Agustín, farther on down from there, there was another village. They called it Contación. Now people call all that area Lourdes. That's where they inflicted evil on that man. His own wife, of all people!

This man was married twice, my brother-in-law's father. His name was Niceto Tapia. But I knew Don Niceto. I've never known a musician like him. Boy, could he play the violin! Wow! But what musician doesn't like to drink? He liked to drink a lot. And a long time ago men went looking for work wherever they could find it. Sheep started gaining popularity over in Roswell, in Fort Sumner, and all those places around there. A large group of men got together. There was a dance there in San Agustín, and this man had been playing, the one who was bewitched. People claimed that he said, "Tomorrow, I'm out of here. I'm taking off with these sheepherders. I'm going to go be a sheepherder."

And she wasn't even his first wife; she was the man's second wife. His wife said to him, "You're not going."

"Yes I am. Nobody bosses me around!"

A whole bunch of men took off on horseback, on donkeys, all strung out in a row. Roswell is far. When they got to a resting place, they stopped to rest their animals and to rest themselves. This woman I'm talking about [the man's second wife], sent her son. She told him, "Good gracious! Your father forgot this little package. Will you be able to catch up with them?"

Of course, he loved his father very much. He had his own horse. Next morning he woke up, grabbed his horse, and took off. He caught up with them. They were eating breakfast when he got to where they were. The son headed straight to embrace his father. His son took out a package and presumably uttered these words, "Mom" (she was the boy's stepmother) "sent you this bottle that you forgot. She asked me to bring it to you. That's why I came, to bring it to you." Well, he grabbed it. Right away he took a drink. As I told you, there isn't a musician who doesn't take a swig. What musician doesn't drink?

By noon, the man began going nuts. He was like crazy. He stripped himself naked, and was uttering nonsense as he followed the rest of his companions. They finally noticed what he was doing. They turned back. They brought him back to San Agustín. By the time they got here, the man was, like, crazy. And I saw that man. You should have seen him. His drool ran down to his chest. Just like a dog that has been poisoned. It was some drooling. There he was, the poor thing. He couldn't eat or anything due to his drooling. That's the way he was until he died.

But it was that second wife of his. She's the one who inflicted evil on him. I believe it was his wife. She inflicted harm on him because she didn't want him to go sheepherding because they weren't going to be able to have a dance here in San Agustín. He was the only musician.

Cesaria Montoya

Se murió su compadre

Mi papá nos contaba, güeno, no mi papá nomás, mi agüelita tamién, que tenía mi agüelita un tío, y se llevaban muncho uno con el otro. Siempre andaban jugando. Y isque le dicía el viejito,

—¡Mire, comadre! Si usté no aprende a decirme "compadre" y un día yo me muero primero que usté, yo voy a venir y me la voy a sacudir.

No le dicía "compadre"; le dicía "mi tío." Así siguieron. Pus muérece el viejito, y oímos algo en la tardecita. Estaba la viejita sola, mi agüelita, con mi papá y con su hermanita, una tía mía. Estaban chiquitos, andaban jugando arriba la cama, y ea [la abuelita] estaa haciendo cena, cuando isque se levantó mi *daddy* de la cama.

—¡Mamá! ¡Mamá! Ahi entró mi tío.

—¿Qué tío?

Ya no me acuerdo cómo se llamaba el viejito. Eh, mi tío Antonio se llamaba.

—Pus, ¿qué es él?

—Pus yo no sé —le dijo—. Entró por ahi por la puerta y parece que se metió ahi atrás de la máquina.

Tenía una máquina de coser atrás de la puerta mi agüelita.

—Oh —le dijo—. Tú estás loco. Qué estás ahi soñando.

—No, mamá. Sí entró.

Y le dijo mi papá cómo andaba vestido, que traiba un vestido pardo, que no traiba zapatos. Nomás el calcetín. Y traiba una camisa blanca y traiba un puño de la manga desabrochao.

Pos, eh, no pasó más. Se acostaron los niños; se durmieron. Ea se quedó alistando cena pa cuando llegara quizás el viejito. Luego en eso oyó que vinía un muchacho chiflando, de una tiendita, porque antonces había esta tienda, y era el nieto del viejito que se murió que vinía chiflando. Que vinía avisale que se había muerto su compadre. Llegó y no le dicía nada el muchacho; estaa chiflando, sentao en el marco de la puerta. Le dice mi agüelita,

—¿Pus qué andas haciendo a estas horas?

—No —isque le dijo—. Vengo de allá de la tienda y llegué por aquí.

—No, no, no —le dijo—. No me mientas, no me mientas. Dime a qué vienes—, porque ea sabía que el viejito estaa enfermo.

—No. Vine avisale que se murió su compadre.

Pus no pasó más. Envolvió a los muchachitos, los levantó.

—¡Vamos! —le dijo—. Ayúdame con la niña.

"Nos juimos a lotra banda," dicían entonces, onde estaba el viejito, y entraron onde estaa el viejito tendido. Ya lo tenían tendido en una mesa. Nomás entraron que se hincó mi agüela a rezar, isque estaa mi papá jalándola. Y ea, que se callara.

—¡Mira, mira, mira cómo está vestido!

Traiba un pantalón pardo, una camisa blanca con el puño desabrochao, y no traiba zapatos. Pus atendido ya muerto. Ya se levantó mi agüelita y se jue pa la cocina a platicar con la viejita [la esposa del viejito].

—Comadre, pueda que sea verdá.

Cuando estaa acabando de platicar, isque levantaba la mano el viejito como pa onde vivía mi agüelita.

—Pueda que sí juera avisale mi esposo esa noche que había acabao.

Será verdá o no será, no sé. Pero, ¿por qué ahora no pasan cosas así? ¡Superstición! Era se me hace a mí que pura superstición.

Her Compadre Passed Away

My father used to tell us—well, not just my father, my grandma also—that she had an uncle, and they got along really well with each other. They were always kidding around. The little old man used to say to her, "Listen here, comadre! If you don't get used to calling me 'compadre' and one day I die before you do, I'm going to come back and shake you [grab your feet]."

She didn't call him "compadre"; she called him "uncle." Nothing changed. Suddenly the little old man died, and we heard something in the evening. The old lady was alone, my grandma, with my father and his sister, an aunt of mine. They were small; they were playing on the bed, and grandma was fixing supper, when all of a sudden my daddy jumped off the bed.

"Mom! Mom! My uncle just came in."

"What uncle?"

I don't recall what the little old man's name was. Ah, his name was Antonio.

"Is it really him?"

"I don't know," he said to her. "He came through that door and it appears that he hid behind the sewing machine."

My grandma had a sewing machine behind the door.

"Oh," she said to him, to my daddy. "You're crazy. Quit your dreaming."

"No, Mom. He did come in."

And my dad told her how he was dressed, that he was wearing a gray suit, and that he was wearing no shoes. Only socks. And he was wearing a white shirt, and one of his cuffs was unbuttoned.

Well, ah, nothing happened. The kids went to bed; they fell asleep. She [Grandma] stayed up fixing supper for when grandpa came home. Right about that time she heard a boy whistling on the way back from the store, because there was a store at that time, and it was the grandson of the little old man who had died who was whistling. He was coming to tell her that her compadre had died. When the boy got there, he wouldn't say anything; he just kept whistling. He was sitting at the doorstep. My grandma says to him, "What are you doing at this late hour?"

"Why, nothing," he said. "I'm on my way back from the store and thought I'd drop by here."

"No, no, no," she said to him. "Don't lie to me; don't lie to me. Tell me why you came," because she knew that the little old man had been ill.

"You're right. I came to tell you that your compadre died."

That's all she needed to hear. She wrapped up the kids and picked them up.

"Let's go!" she said to him. "Give me a hand with the girl."

There was a saying back then: "We've gone to another strato-sphere," where the old man now found himself, and they went in and found him lying in repose. They already had him laid out on a table. No sooner my grandma knelt down to pray than my father began pulling on her. And she kept asking him to keep quiet.

"Look, look, look how he's dressed!"

He was wearing gray pants, a white shirt with the cuff unbuttoned, and wasn't wearing shoes. She paid her respects to the deceased. Afterwards, my grandma got up and headed for the kitchen to chat with the wife of the deceased.

"Comadre, perhaps it's true."

When grandma was about through talking, I understand that the little old man kept raising his hand as if in the direction of where my grandma lived.

"Perhaps my husband did go visit you that night to tell you that he had died."

Whether it's true or not, I don't know. But, why is it that things like that don't happen anymore? Superstitions! I believe it was nothing more than superstitions.

Se había caido la copa

Tenía la cocina mi mamá, como abajo, y loo subían tres pisitos pa entrar pa la sala. Y un muchacho que criaron mi papá y mi mamá estaa sentao acá arriba del último pisito. Tenían un calentón de leña puesto asina como ora en un rincón, con copas muy bonitas. ¿Te acuerdas que había unos calentones que tenían como unas copas muy bonitas arriba? Bueno, cuando menos acordamos—y yo andaba jugando allí en el suelo en la cocina—oímos el golpe. Pasó en el cuarto. Pus el muchacho de una vez se levantó y voló pallá, y loo mi papá y mi mamá y toos juimos allá. Se había caido la copa esa del fogón y estaa tranpada muy juerte. No se podía cae sola; pus se cayó *anyway. So,* ahi se quedó en el suelo. Conque ahi están eos, "¿Qué pasará, qué pasará, pus qué pasaría?" En eso estaban cuando llegó alguen avisar que se había muerto una prima hermana de mi mamá. Figuran que la prima vino avisar.

Tamién tenía yo una tía mía, la hermana de mi papá, una tía muy querida. Ya no me acuerdo cómo se llamaba mi tía. Ea vivía en Colorao, y isque entró un cernícaro. ¿Sabe lo que es un cernícaro? Es un gavilancito, chiquito. Entró. Isque se le paró a mi tía en la cabeza. No lo espantaron; nomás se salió el gavilancito. Pero pronto llegaron avisales a mi papá y mamá que había muerto la tía allá en Colorao.

Eos dicían que era un aviso que al muerto le daba Dios permiso de que viniera hacerlos saber.

The Cup Had Fallen

My mother had the kitchen, like, sunk down below, and then you climbed three little steps to reach the living room. And a boy that my father and mother raised was sitting up here on the last step. They had a wood stove like in a corner, with very beautiful cups sitting on top. Do you remember those wood stoves that had, like, very beautiful cups on top? Well, all of a sudden, and I was playing on the kitchen floor, we heard the thump. It sounded right there in that room. Well, the boy got up right away and flew to the room, and then my father and mother and everybody went there. That cup from the wood stove had fallen off, and it was pretty well attached to the stove. It couldn't fall off by itself, but it fell off anyway. So, there it was on the floor. And there they were speculating—my father, mother, and everyone, "I wonder what's going on, I wonder what's happening? I wonder what could have happened?" They were in the midst of the discussion when someone came to tell us that a cousin of my mother had passed away. The way they figure it is that the falling of the cups was a warning from the cousin that she was dead.

I also had an aunt, my father's sister, a very dear aunt. I can't recall what her name was. She lived in Colorado, and I understand that a kestrel flew into the house. Do you know what a kestrel is? It's a small, tiny hawk. It came in the house. They say that it stood right on my aunt's head. No one scared it. The little hawk then just flew off by itself. No sooner said than done, someone came to inform my father and mother that my aunt in Colorado had died.

My parents claimed that it was a warning, a premonition, that God gave to the deceased as a way of informing people of his death.

Amaneció muerta la viejita

Mi mamá era partera. Yo no sé qué tantos niños hizo *deliver* mi mamá en su vida. ¡Munchos, munchos de eos! Me acuerdo de oyer decir de curanderas, de brujerías. Decían que a mi agüelita la habían enbrujao una vez. No sé cómo ni naa, pero esta otra viejita era curandera. Jueron a verla que viniera a curarla [a su abuelita]. Isque les dijo,

—¡Pus es mi amiga! Pero yo me voy a morir si la curo. Pero vamos. Yo voy con ustedes, pero vengan a medianoche, que no sepa naiden que me jui con ustedes.

Pus llevaron a la viejita. No sé cómo la curaría [a mi abuelita] o qué haría. Cuento es que otro día en la mañana amaneció muerta la viejita que la curó. Y mi agüelita descansó, nada más que quedó— ¿cómo le dicen?—jorobada. Dicían que brujería.

The Little Old Lady Was Dead in the Morning

My mother was a midwife. I don't know how many babies she delivered in her lifetime. Many, lots of them! I remember hearing about folk healers, about witchcraft. The scuttlebutt was that my grandma had been bewitched. I don't know how or anything, but this other little old lady was a folk healer. They went after her to come and cure my grandmother. The little old lady supposedly said to them, "Why she's my friend! But I'm going to die if I cure her. But let's go anyway. I'll go with you, but come after me at midnight, so that no one knows that I went with you."

Well, they took the little old lady. I don't know how she cured my grandma or what she did. Fact is that next morning the little old lady was dead. And my grandma got well, except that she became— what do you call it—hunchbacked. People say that it was all witchcraft.

Filimón Montoya

No le vido el rostro

Pues una vez estaa mi hijo Rogelio allá onde tenían los viejitos [los abuelos de Rogelio] como una dispensa, y era durante el tiempo de la cosecha, y habían cosechao muncho maíz. Lo metieron, sin deshojalo, ¿ve? Despacharon al muchacho a deshojar el maíz, o iba el muchacho a deshojar el maíz. Ya no estaa muy joven. Era en la nochi, no tan nochi, pero ya escuro. Luego dicían que se le había aparecido alguien allá, que él les había dicho que se le había aparecido un individuo o un bulto. Pero no le vido el rostro porque traiba el rostro tapao. Le metió tanto miedo, que salió huyendo y, al tiempo que abrió la puerta, no la abrió suficiente, y pégase en la cabeza con el filo de la puerta onde iba juyendo. Eso jue lo que les platicó a los viejitos.

Jueron allá fuera a ver qué había, pero no vieron naa. Y tenían un farol d'esos de aceite que usaban en esos tiempos colgao en el techo. El farol estaa ahi; no había muvimiento de ninguna clas, pero el muchacho llegó too golpiao. Eso es lo único que me recuerdo yo.

Oh, sí platicaban de brujas pallá y brujas pacá. Yo no sé, isque se juntaban y salían en un bogue, y loo resultaba el bogue, los caballos amarraos en un árbol, en un pino, y no había gente en el bogue. Pero naiden se acuerda de habelas visto que volaban del bogue y iban a otras partes, a otros lugares. Siempre platicaban que vinían pacá pa Mora. Yo no sé, Mora era su desquite. Siempre estaan con el cuento que en Mora había munchas brujas.

He Didn't See Its Face

Why, I remember one time when my son Rogelio was over where the old folks [Rogelio's grandparents] had like a pantry, and it was during harvest time, and they had harvested lots of corn. They stored the corn without husking it, you see? So they either sent the boy off to husk the corn, or he was going on his own. He was no longer a young boy. It was nighttime, not very late, though, but it was already dark. There was talk that someone had appeared before him, because he had told them that a person or a ghost had suddenly sprung upon him. But he didn't see its face because it was covered. He got so scared that he took off running and, at about the time he opened the door to the house, he failed to open it enough, and, whammo, he hit himself on the sharp edge of the door as he was running. That's what he told the old folks.

They went outside to see what they could find, but they didn't see anything. And they had one of those kerosene lanterns that they used to hang on the ceiling a long time ago. The lantern was right there, with no movement at all, but the young man got home all beat up. That's the one story I can recall.

Why, of course, people talked about witches this, witches that. I don't know, but word has it that they would get together and leave in a horse carriage, and then it would turn out that the carriage and the horses would be found tied to a pine tree, but there were no people in the carriage. But nobody recalls having seen the witches fly off from the buggy, and they'd take off in different directions, to other places. People always said that they would head for Mora. I don't know why, but Mora was a kind of place where they fulfilled their wishes. Stories floated constantly about the fact that there were many witches in Mora.

Mató el tecolote

¡Oh, sí! Déjeme contale este cuento. Estaa una viejita que vivía sola. Ya estaa viejita. A nojotros se nos parecía porque nojotros estáanos muy jóvenes. Era una mujer larga y siempre andaba vestida de negro y usaa vestidos largotes hasta que le arrastraan al suelo. Dicían que'ra bruja, que'ra bruja. Toos le echaban que'ra bruja. Yo no sé si sería bruja o no.

Pero, güeno, una nochi, esto era, o ya muncho después, ¿no? Yo pienso que ya estaba hasta casao yo cuando sucedió esto. Estaa un vecino de nojotros que vivía, oh, poco retirao. Y isque vinía un tecolote toas las noches a cantar o lo que hagan los tecolotes, ahi cerca de su casa en un poste, pero estaa en el camino, y su casa estaa junto el camino. Güeno, una nochi se aburrió de estalo oyindo, y sacó el rifle y lo balió. Mató el tecolote. Pocos días después, o un día o dos después, jallaron a la viejita esta muerta en su casa. Estaa bien desnuda, y tenía un' herida en la cabeza como cuando le dan un tiro. Dijían, yo no la vi, pero dijían y creían qu'era el tecolote.

Pero no sé. No era más de lo que oíamos decir.

He Killed the Owl

Oh, yes! Let me tell you this story. There was this little old lady who lived alone. She was already old. We kids thought she was quite old because we were young. She was a very tall and lanky woman who was always dressed in black and she wore very long dresses that came down to the floor. People claimed she was a witch, a real witch. Everybody accused her of being a witch. I don't know whether she was a witch or not.

But, anyhow, one night, this came much later, you see. I believe I was even married when this happened. There was this neighbor of ours who lived, oh, quite a ways from us. And I understand an owl would show up every night to sing or whatever owls do, there on a post close to his house, but the owl was on the road, and the neighbor's house was right close to the road. In any case, one night he got tired of listening to it hoot, and he took out his rifle and he wounded it. He killed the owl, in fact. A few days later, or a day or two afterwards, they found the little old lady dead in her house. She was totally nude, and she had an injury like when you shoot somebody in the head. People claimed, I didn't see it, but people claimed and believed that it was the owl.

But I just don't know. It was all based on what we heard.

José Nataleo Montoya

La culebra mamona

Una vez, güeno, estáanos medianos. Teníanos como unos ocho años, yo creo, y cuidáanos vacas. Había una vaca que tenía una teta *muy,* muy grande. Muy gresa siempre. Ésa no daba leche. Dijían que ésa la había mamao la culebra mamona. Qu'esa era lo que la había mamao y por eso tenía la chiche asina. Tenía la vaca los cuernos bien doblaos. Pus veníanos nojotros y nos metíanos en el corral. Voltiábanos y la agarrábanos de los cuernos. ¿Qué tal si los [nos] levanta parriba el animal ese o algo? Y no se defendía. Pero que eran unas cosas peligrosas y que hacía uno de chiste.

The Milk Snake

One time, well, we were just kids. We were about eight years old, I believe, and we used to look after the cows. There was a cow that had a *very,* very large teat. It was always very large. That one didn't give any milk. The story people told was that a milk snake had sucked it, and that's the reason that teat was that way. The cow had very twisted horns. Well, we used to go into the corral, we'd turn it around and grab it by the horns. What if it had tossed us up in the air or something like that? And the cow didn't defend itself. But those were dangerous things we did just monkeying around.

Cayó llorando Genoveo

Cuando se muría alguien, tocaba que les avisaban de alguna manera. Yo me acuerdo tavía d'este Genoveo. Cuando murió su mamá, vivíanos arriba la mesa, ahi en San Pablo. Estaba la cocina y loo estaba un zaguán. Loo estaba el cuarto. Pus ahi estáanos durmiendo yo y mi agüelita, y una prima de mi esposa y una hija estaan en el zaguán. Y mi tío Estelito, él había llegao de la sierra, y estaa durmiendo en la cocina. Le pusieron la cama en la cocina. Como ora, por ejemplo, ahi la puerta esa. Asina.

En la mañana se levantó la tía esta Rafelita. Así se llamaba ea. Cuando jue a poner lumbre, vido un charco de sangre en los pies del tío, porque el tío este era compadre de la mamá de Genoveo. Pus ya jue y le dijo a mi agüelita que el hijo seguro que estuvo malo, como siempre estaba enfermo él. Pus ya se levantaron. Hasta lo recordaron a Estelito. Taa estaa durmiendo.

—Oyes. ¿Qué estuvites malo anoche?— le dijieron.

—No— les dijo—. ¿Por qué?

—Mira. Ahi taa hay sangre.

—No —les dijo—. Pus yo no me levanté. Yo ni escupí ni naa.

Al rato cayó llorando este Genoveo que su mamá había muerto. Cuando murió isque había echao un cuajarón de sangre. Eso sí me acuerdo yo velo. Yo estaa como de unos seis años, yo creo, antonces.

Genoveo Showed Up Crying

Whenever somebody died, there was a certain way of letting people know. I still remember about this Genoveo. When his mother died, we were living up on top of the mesa, there in San Pablo. There was the kitchen, then a vestibule, followed by a room. That's where my grandma and I were sleeping and a cousin of my wife and a daughter were in the vestibule. And my uncle Estelito, who had just gotten home from the sierra, he was sleeping in the kitchen. They set up his bed in the kitchen. He was like, from here to that door. Right there.

In the morning this aunt Rafaelita got up. That was her name. When she went to build a fire, she saw a pool of blood at my uncle Estelito's feet, because this uncle was a compadre of Genoveo's mother. Well, she went and told my grandma that her son must have been ill overnight, since he was always getting sick. Then everybody got up. They even woke Estelito up. He was asleep.

"Listen. Were you sick last night?" they asked him.

"No," he responded. "Why?"

"Look here. There's blood there."

"No," he said to them. "Why, I didn't even get up. I didn't spit or anything."

A short time later this Genoveo showed up crying that his mother had died. When she died, I understand that she spat a big glob of blood. That's something I recall seeing. I believe I was about six years old at the time.

Isabel Romero

Ahi se acabó La Llorona.

Y eso de La Llorona, había un lugar que lo conocí. Había un río mediano y había una alameda. Luego, pues, munchas veces ahi en aqueos años, la gente usaba tiros de mulas o tiros de caballos en los carros. No había automoviles, naa como ora. Y había un bosque. Pues, ahi en tal bosque salía La Llorona. Güeno, pues, La Llorona era mujer. Viuda. Vieja ya. Y ésa se enbocaa entre las jaras, y cuando iba pasando alguien que llevaa comida, "¡Ayyyy!" Lloraba. Pus arrancaan a juir; le tiraban la comida. Ahi está La Llorona. Y luego, pues, güeno, pus La Llorona se clavaa.

Luego al fin una vez había un hombre, mi tío Abel. ¡Bárbaro! Era muy atroz él y campó en un lugar ahi. Loo se levantó muy en la madrugada él. Era muy madrugador, muy hombrote. Iba por los caballos allí, cuando salió La Llorona, y él, pus, no tenía miedo. Se jue y se asomó. ¡Palo, palo! Tres azotes. "¡Ay, nito! No me, no me, no me pegues."

Pus era La Llorona, una vieja, camaldolera, como dijían. Pus salía, y le tiraban la comida. Ea se clavaba. Ahi cuando le pegó mi tío,

—¡Ay, nito! No me pegues. Soy Julana.

—Pus pa que no güelvas.

Y le pegó una suriguanga. Le daban con un cabresto o con un

chicote. Le pegaban una azotería o le pegaban una turra. Ahi se acabó La Llorona.

That Was the End of the Wailing Woman.

And regarding the Wailing Woman, there was this place I was familiar with. There was a small river and a poplar grove. Then, many times, back in the olden days, people used teams of mules or horse-drawn wagons. There were no automobiles or anything like now. And there was a forest. Well, there in that forest is where the Wailing Woman came out. Now, the Wailing Woman was a widow. She was already old. She would hide in between the shrubs, and whenever someone went by who was carrying food, she would moan, "Ooooh!" She cried. People would toss the food to her and take off. And, of course, the Wailing Woman got the better end of the deal.

Then finally there was a man, my Uncle Abel. He was terrible! He was very mischievous and he went and camped in a place close by. Then one morning early he got up. He was an early riser, quite a man. He was going after the horses, when the Wailing Woman popped out, and he, of course, was not afraid. He went and took a peek. Wham, wham! Three blows. "Ouch, little brother! Don't, don't, don't hit me."

It was the Wailing Woman, known to people as an old, cunning hag. Whenever she came out, people would toss food at her. She had it made. That time when my uncle struck her, "Oh, little brother! Don't hit me. I'm Julana."

"This is so you don't pull this crap again."

And so he beat the dickens out of her. People used to beat her up with a rope or a whip. They finally gave her either a good beating or a good flogging. That was the end of the Wailing Woman.

Se golvió el coyote diablo

Había un hombre. Era soltero, viejo ya. Carlos López se llamaba. Era coyote él. Era mitá francés. Vivía en un rancho, solo. Su mamá dél estaa con él pero ya muy viejita. Y se iba al baile él. Aá se quedaba la viejita. Lego cuando iba al baile a caballo vido un coyote y le rompió. Ya escureciendo, y le rompió en el caballo con el cabresto. Cruzó el *highway,* y había una piedra muy grande. Cuando cruzó el camino, ahi estaba el coyote arriba la piedra [risas], hecho el diablo.

Pues ya no golvió ir al baile Carlos López. Cuando llegó a la piedra, que brincó a la piedra, vido que era un animal negro. Echaba lumbre por los ojos. Era negro con la cola muy larga. Estaba en piedra y tenía cuernos. Se golvió el coyote diablo.

The Coyote Turned into the Devil

There was this man. He was single, already old. Carlos López was his name. He was a half-breed. He was half-French. He lived alone on a ranch. His mother lived with him, but she was already quite old. He used to go to dances, and his mother would stay home. Then when he was on horseback on his way to the dance he saw a coyote and took off after him. It was already getting dark, and he took off after the coyote on his horse to rope him. He crossed the highway, and there was a huge rock. When he crossed the road, there was the coyote on top of the rock [laughter], turned into the devil.

That was the end of going to dances for Carlos López. When he reached the rock, because he jumped on top of the rock, he saw that it was a black animal. It was spewing fire from its eyes. It was black with a long tail. It was on top of the rock, and it had horns. The coyote turned into the devil.

Echaba lumbre por los ojos

Yo estaa mediano pero oía que había una gente, el hombre y la mujer, que peliaban muncho. Tonteras, celos. Y cerca había una laderita y un banquito. Había munchos peñascos allí, y cuando salió la mujer de su casa vido que era un animal que había salido. Qu'era negro. Y loo que se volvió. Isque ea llamó otra mujer, que juera con ea a ver que había visto una cosa muy fea. Fue a ver [la mujer]. Qu'era negro, prieto, con la cola muy larga, y que echaba lumbre por los ojos. Por la boca. [Risas]

Pos ora vas a ver. Cuando andaa [risas] echando lumbre por los ojos, por la boca, era un animal muy largo, con cola larga, y las pesuñas, eh, como muy patón.

Pos la mujer se desamayó del rebato. Se desmayó. Que dicía el hombre [el esposo],

—¿Pus la Juanita, qué hará, qué hará que no, que no entra?

Pues se desmayó la mujer. [Risas] Se desmayó. La jalló desmayada allá.

—¿Pues, qué te pasa?

Al fin jue, enpezó echale agua en la cabeza, hasta que la recordó.

—Pus, ¿qué estás haciendo aquí?

Ahi le contó ea lo que había visto. Jue tal remedio que no más golvieron a peliar. Era el espíritu malo.

Fire Shot Out of Its Eyes

I was just a kid, but I heard that there was this couple, a man and a woman, who used to fight a lot. Foolishness, jealousy. Close by there was a small slope and an embankment. There were lots of boulders there, and when the wife left her house she saw an animal that came out from behind the embankment. It was black. Then she turned back and asked another woman to go with her to see the ugly thing that she had spotted. The woman went. The thing was black, black, with a long tail, and fire shot out of its eyes. Through its mouth. [Laughter] Now, there's more! As fire was coming out its eyes and through its mouth, [laughter] it was a very long animal, with a long tail, and with hooves, like big feet.

As a result, the wife fainted from fright. She fainted. As gossip would have it, the husband kept repeating, "I wonder what Juanita is doing that she doesn't, that she doesn't come in?" Well, the wife had fainted. [Laughter] She fainted. He found her passed out. "What's wrong with you?"

Finally he went and started pouring water on her head until she came to. "Well, what are you doing here?" That's when she told him what she had seen. The remedy was such that they never fought again. It was an evil spirit.

Capitán de los brujos

Esto jue aá en el Sabinoso. Había un árbol nogal muy coposo, muy grande con sombra pa delante la casa. Y había un hombre que se llamaa Paulín. Él era hechicero. Era la mitá brujo. Güeno, pues que había un hombre Celso Martínez, y estaa casao con una prima hermana mía. Era muy pasiador. Andaa pallá pasiándose, en la tarde ya. Muy tarde. Cuando vinía, vido la tecolotera arriba el árbol, y aquí en el suelo andaan pasiándose allí los tecolotes. Él era muy atroz y siem-

pre traiba pistola. Cuando vido, sacó la pistola y enpezó a tirar balazos. Andaan unos en el suelo y otros arriba. Les tiraba balazos.

Güeno, pues, que otro día,

—Pues, ¿qué pasa Celso? ¿A qué le estaas tirando tanto balazo?

—No, —es que dijo—. Pus, ahi andaa de tecolotera hasta mi tía.
Pues, otro día,

—Isque don Paulín está muy malo.

—¿Cómo?

—Pues ahi le pegó [Celso Martínez] un balazo. [Risas] Isque don
Paulín está muy malo.

Resultó con una pierna quebraa don Paulín. Él era d'esos de la
brujería.

Mamá en ese tiempo estaa muy mala. Muy mala que estaa. Que
sabe qué. Pus cuando baliaron al brujo ese sanó mamá. Sei, sanó.

Too el tiempo se la pasaba llorando. Tan mal y tan mal. Ese hombre Paulín, dijía que él la curaba, pero no le curaba nada. Pus él era el
capitán de los brujos. Pus cuando se murió el hombre ese, mamá
sanó. Mamá sanó.

The Head of the Witches

This took place over in Sabinoso. There was a very bushy walnut tree,
large, with shade in front of the house. And there was a man whose
name was Paulín. He was a sorcerer. He was half witch. Okay, there
was also a man named Celso Martínez, and he was married to a
cousin of mine. He liked to run around a lot. It was evening when he
was making the rounds over in Sabinoso. It was late. On his way
back, he saw the owls' roosting place on top of this tree and on the
ground the small owls moving about. He was a real cutup and he
always carried a pistol. When he saw them, he took out his pistol
and started to fire. Here were the owls scurrying about, some on the
ground, others on top of the tree. He was shooting at them.

Very well, next day, "Well, what happened, Celso? What were you
firing so many shots at?"

"Why, nothing!" he said. "Would you believe that even my aunt
was playing the role of an owl?"

Well, next day, there you are. "The word's going around that
Paulín is very ill."

"How could that be?"

"Celso Martínez went and shot him. [Laughter] Paulín is very ill." As it turned out, Don Paulín had a broken leg [he fell from the tree after being shot]. He was one of those who practiced sorcery.

Mother was very sick at that time. I understand she was very sick. Who knows what was wrong with her? Well, when Paulín was shot, mother got well. Yes, she was cured.

She used to spend most of her time crying. She went from bad to worse. That man Paulín would say that he could cure her, but he never did anything. As it turned out, he was the head of the witches. When that man died, mother got well. Mother was cured once and for all.

Un bulto blanco

Yo me acuerdo una vez que había un lugar que iba pacá pa Las Vegas que le dicen la Laguna de Piedra. Había agua siempre ahi, y munchos pasajeros que vinían pacá paraban en la Laguna de Piedra. Ahi campaban y dormían. Pus había una casa, muy, muy vieja. No tenía techo ni puertas. Estaan las paderes. Algunas personas dicían que ahi en esa casa vieja, que se aparecía un bulto y salían juyendo [la gente]. Cuando había luna es que se aparecía un bulto en la casa.

Una vez iba yo de aquí de Las Vegas paá pa la Laguna de Piedra. Yo oía el cuento de la casa, que se aparecía un bulto, un bulto blanco. Yo iba de a caballo, y sí, se vía moverse allá. "Ora voy y me desengaño," dije yo. "A ver si se aparece un bulto ahi en esa casa. Voy a ver." Y me apié del caballo. Llevaa la pistola en la cabeza de la silla amarraa alderedor. Y yo dije, "No. Vale más subirme en el caballo porque si voy a pie y le tiro al bulto, se espanta el caballo y me deja a pie. No. Vale más subirme." Me subí en el caballo y me jui. Me jui.

Pus era una vaca bole que estaba adentro la casa vieja. Cuando se movía, pues, le pegaba la luna. Pero yo dije,

—No. Le hablo al bulto y si no me responde, le doy un balazo.

De güena suerte que se movió, y vide qu'era una vaca, que si no la mato. [Risas]

El miedo. El miedo hace munchas, munchas cosas.

A White Ghost

I remember once upon a time there was a place on the way to Las Vegas called Laguna de Piedra. There was always water in it, and many travelers who were headed this way to Las Vegas stopped at Laguna de Piedra. That's where they camped and slept. There was a very, very old house. It didn't have a roof or any doors. All that was standing was the walls. Some people used to say that right there in that old house a ghost would appear and people would take off running. Whenever there was a moon is when the ghost appeared in the house.

One time I was on my way from here in Las Vegas to Laguna de Piedra. I had heard stories about the house and a ghost appearing—a white ghost. I was on horseback, and yes, something was moving. "Now I'll go and find out for myself," I said to myself. "Let's see if a ghost appears in that house. I'll go see." And I dismounted. I had a pistol tied to the saddle horn. And I said to myself, "No. I better get on my horse because if I go on foot and I fire at the ghost, it will startle the horse and he'll leave me on foot. No. I'd better ride." I got on the horse and I took off. I took off.

As it turned out, it was a Hereford that was inside the old house. Whenever the cow moved, the moon would shine on it. But I said to myself, "No. I'll talk to the ghost and if it doesn't answer me, I'll shoot it." It's a good thing that it moved, which is when I saw that it was a cow. If not, I would have killed it. [Laughter]

Fright. Fright begets many, many things.

Alfredo Ulibarrí

La Llorona

En ese tiempo ahi hasta de noche en el Cañón, cuando iba de ver a mi esposa, antes de casarnos, porque ea vivía lejos de onde vivía yo, iba a caballo a vela. Y cuando iba, too el Cañón lloraba como lloran las zorras. Lloran como un muchito chiquito, y dijían qu'era La Llorona. Las zorras esas sí lloran como una llorona, ciertamente. Pero te espantas. Siempre te espantas. Se te enchira el cuero. Pus le apretaba al caballo y me iba. En la noche que llegaa aá, había veces que metía el caballo contoy silla al corral, porque me daba miedo— pus solo, solo. ¡Y un zurrón! Pero las zorras lloran como un muchito chiquito. Por eso dicen que son las lloronas. Yo creo qu'eran las zorras, porque yo las llegué a ver.

The Wailing Woman

Back then at night in El Cañón, when I was coming back from seeing my wife, before we got married, because she lived far from where I lived, I'd go see her on horseback. And when I was on my way back, all of El Cañón cried just like foxes. They cry like a small child, and people claimed that it was the Wailing Woman. Those foxes really do cry like a wailing woman, for sure. But you get scared. You always get startled. You get goose bumps. No sooner said than done, I would dig my spurs into my horse and head home. By the time I got home at night, there were times when I would put the horse, saddle and all, in the corral, because I got scared. I was alone, alone. I was scared shitless! But the foxes do cry like a small child. That's why people say that it was the Wailing Women. I believe they were foxes, because I saw them.

Un bulto blanco

Una vez, ya estaa casao y vivía aquí [en Las Vegas], y iba por la mujer mía, porque ea trabajaa aá en l'asilo. Dejé a mi plebe aquí, pus estaan chicos. Yo iba como a las once y media por ea una vez de la noche. Tú sabes aquí onde estaa el *tortilla factory, right there,* ahi mero iba yo en la troca. Loo tú sabes el camino ese abajo del *tortilla factory,* poquito pa unas casas que estaan abajo, abajan pa bajo, ahi iba un bulto blanco, blanco, como una sábana blanca. Yo traiba una *spotlight* en mi troca, y se lo puse asina en la cara, y se subió parriba el bordo otra vez. Onde estaa el *tortilla factory,* estaa una cantinita *right* en el *corner* paá pa una callecita que entra pallá. Ahi se paró atrás de un telefón, y me hacía asina con la mano [Vente, vente], y yo poniéndole el *spotlight* pa ver si podía ver yo qué era.
Ése es el único bulto que me ha salido.

A White Ghost

One time, I was already married and living here in Las Vegas, I was going after my wife, because she worked over at the sanatorium. I left the kids here at home because they were small. I was going after her about eleven thirty at night. You know where the tortilla factory is, right there is where I was driving my truck. Then you know the road down below the tortilla factory, a little ways beyond, there are some houses down the hill. That's where I saw a really white ghost moving, like a white bed sheet. I had a spotlight on my truck, and I shined it right in its face, and it went up the hill one more time where the tortilla factory is located. Where the tortilla factory used to be, there was a bar right at the corner that cuts into another small street farther on up. That's where it stopped, behind a telephone post, and it waved at me to come on, while I kept shining the spotlight on it to see what it was.

That's the only ghost I've ever seen.

Teresina Ulibarrí

Se le quitó lo malo

Una vez platicaba mi mamá quisque eos, papá y mamá, criaron este muchacho. Y le dijíanos nosotros mi tío Miguel. Pero isque era muy atroz. Muy atroz era el hombre. Vinía él pa cas'e mi mamá; él vivía en los Chupaderos. Todas las tardes vinía pacá él. Quizás ya estaa casao. Y él, puro hacer, puro hacer mal. Era muy atroz.

Luego, una vez cuando vinía de aá pacá, isque porque hace güelta el camino asina, cuando vinía de aá pacá—se vinía a pie ayudale a mi papá y a mi tío—vido que delante dél vinía un hombre, pero no lo pudo alcanzar. Ya cuando llegó a cierto lugar, ya no vido el hombre. Cuando iba de aquí pallá, pa su casa—se jue noche—y ende mismo que iba él, isque se oyó como que iba un caballo resollando muy recio, y que galopiando, que ya lo tranpaba, y que ya lo tranpaba y que ya lo tranpaba. Y él que iba a greña a greña.

Cuando en eso que, ende cayó en el Chorro, onde cai agua de onde está un ojito le dijían el Chorro. Mi tío Miguel dice que el hombre ese que vido cayó pa bajo del Voladero y sonó como un balazo recio. En eso abrieron su mujer y su suegro la puerta, a ver qué era el grito y too eso y él cayó desmayao pa entro. No sé si de miedo, de lo qué vería. Pero de ahi pallá era un hombre muy güeno. Se le quitó lo malo.

He Quit Being Mean

One time my mom was saying that they, Dad and Mom, raised this boy. My siblings and I called him Uncle Miguel. But I understand that he was horrible. He was a very terrible man. He used to come to my mother's house; he lived in Los Chupaderos. He came here every evening. I guess he was already married. And all he did was to cause mischief. He was terrible.

Then one time when he was on his way from Los Chupaderos to here, because the road bends a little, he would come on foot to help my father and my uncle—he saw a man ahead of him, but he couldn't catch up with him. By the time he got to this one place, he could no longer see the man. Upon his return home—it was already night—right there where he was walking, he heard a horse that was breathing very hard, and it was galloping. It was about to run over him. I mean about to run over him, really run over him. He was running scared as all get out.

All of a sudden, he fell where there's a waterfall, a spring called El Chorro. My Uncle Miguel says that the man he saw fell down the Voladero [a precipice] and sounded like a loud gunshot. At that very moment his [Miguel's] wife and mother-in-law opened the door to see what the shouting and all the commotion was about, and he fell forward and fainted. I don't know whether it was from being scared after what he saw or not. But from then on he turned into a good man. He quit being mean.

Cruzita Vigil

Eso de diablos y de brujas es la misma

Aquí había cuentos cuando nos mudamos pacá pa Las Vegas. Eso de diablos y de brujas es la misma. Dicía un tío mío que él estaa trabajando con un compañero, y este compañero tenía una novia, poco lejos, ¿ve? Isque iba haber baile y le dijo él,

—Yo no jallo cómo ir al baile —el amigo este, a un tío mío.

—'Tonces —le dijo lotro hombre —yo te llevo al baile.

—¿Pero cómo? Pus si no tenemos naa en qué.

—No. Yo te llevo, si tú te atreves ir. Yo te llevo.

—Güeno, el cuento es ir a ver a mi novia.

Nomás se hizo escuro llegó el amigo y le dijo,

—Güeno, pus, ¿ya estás listo? ¡Súbete en mí! [Risas]

Lo llevó hasta la puerta de la sala. Loo, le dijo el hombre ese,

—Cuando ya te quieras ir, nomás me chiflas.

Tuvo bailando con la novia y todo eso. Cuando ya él quería irse le chifló.

—¡Súbete en mí otra vez!

Lo llevó el hombre ese por onde antes estaban otra vez. [Risas] Dicía mi tío que sí lo llevó a su amigo y lo trujo. Taa curiosa la cosa.

The Devil and Witches Are One and the Same Thing

There were all kinds of stories when we moved here to Las Vegas. The devil and witches are one and the same thing. An uncle of mine used to tell the story when he was working with this fellow, and this fellow had a girlfriend, quite a ways away, you see? I understand there was going to be a dance, and he said to my uncle, "I can't find a way of going to the dance," said this friend to my uncle.

"Then I'll take you," said this other man.

"But how? We don't have anything to go on."

"Never mind. I'll take you if you wish to go. I'll take you."

"Okay, the important thing for me is to go."

As soon as it got dark, this man showed up and he said to my uncle's friend, "Okay, are you ready? Climb on piggyback!" [Laughter] He took him all the way to the doorstep of the dance hall. Then the man said to him, "Whenever you're ready to leave, just whistle at me."

He danced with his girlfriend and had lots of fun. When he was ready, he whistled at the man.

"Once again, climb on me piggyback!"

Then that man took him back the way they came. [Laughter] My uncle used to say that that man indeed took his friend to the dance and brought him back. It was a curious thing.

5

Funciones y costumbres religiosas
Religious Ceremonies and Customs

Introduction

Religious customs and ceremonies have been central to northern New Mexico's Hispano communities since 1598, when Juan de Oñate (founder of New Mexico) first came to what was to be called the Land of Enchantment, la Tierra del Encanto. Since that time, innumerable changes have affected our social institutions, but what remained virtually intact among Hispanos until recently was the strong relationship between the local church and the rural community. The church and the people went together like hand in glove.

Among the most critical factors responsible for this coexistence and the strength of the church was the unshakable faith of both adults and their offspring. As Filimón Montoya says later in this chapter, "Religion was always everywhere. Everything that people did culminated in prayers and the like." Devotion to and support of the tenets of Catholicism as people perceived them stemmed from a spirit that transcended the immediate community. Many inhabitants who invariably supported a church did not reside within the local village, where the majority of the population lived and where religious and secular activities took place. Instead, their ranches and homes were found in outlying areas.

Most rural Hispanic communities did not conform to the highly structured hierarchy of urban churches, where parishioners enjoyed a priest in residence. Rather, a priest was generally assigned by the archdiocese to the mother church, and the mission or sister churches from several villages fell under its religious umbrella. As a result, Mass was celebrated every Sunday at the mother church, but only once a month—weather permitting—at the sister churches (during *visitas*). Important functions such as weddings and baptisms took place almost exclusively at the mother church, unless it and the mission churches were great distances apart, which made traveling difficult for the respective families.

Without question, mayordomos played a major role in garnering support for the church in their respective communities. They were, in effect, the spiritual leaders chosen by church members to serve for a designated period of time. In most cases, the position was filled by a husband-and-wife team that was well respected by peers. Mayordomos were primarily responsible for the upkeep of the church, collecting tithes (*diezmos y primicias*), or providing room and board for the priest when he visited the community. The people stood ready to lend a helping hand with whatever duties and responsibilities fell to the mayordomos.

In some cases, a sacristan or sexton (male or female) served as a round-the-clock church caretaker. He or she was charged by the mayordomos with keeping the keys to the church and was responsible for opening it to parishioners whenever they wanted to pray or perform some other religious function.

The Penitent Brothers (Hermanos Penitentes) were also instrumental in providing religious support in many hamlets throughout northern New Mexico. This was particularly true after Mexico gained its independence from Spain in 1821 and after the Treaty of Guadalupe Hidalgo (signed in 1848), under which Mexico ostensibly abandoned northern New Mexico, something Spain had in effect done a quarter century earlier. Prior to these political events, communities suffered from isolation and the neglect of the Catholic Church.

The Penitents were a lay religious group consisting mostly of Hispanic Catholic men who assembled during Lent to pray, sing hymns, and hold religious processions commemorating the death of Christ.

Some women may have helped during Holy Week (e.g., by preparing meals and feeding husbands at the *morada,* a chapel where the Penitents prayed and held meetings).

In addition, the Penitents became spiritual examples in the community, but rarely imposed their beliefs on others. They also did not intrude in the affairs of priests (e.g., by offering the Holy Sacraments), but they did assist in a variety of religious activities. For example, they participated in religious wakes (*velorios*) for the deceased, recited the rosary, dug graves at the local cemetery (mainly for their brothers), and helped with funerals, all of which occurred whether a priest was available or not. Nowadays, the Penitents are fewer in number, but some confraternities (*cofradías*) are less secretive about and less controversial in their religious practices than they were in the earlier part of the twentieth century.

Throughout the year, community activity—baptisms, weddings, First Holy Communion, death, Lent, Christmas, or religious processions—revolved, and still revolve, around the church. Whether the occasion was joyous, solemn, or mournful, the church was pivotal. No one dramatizes the fundamental importance of these practices better than Arsenio Montoya, Sr., in "Crencias." He sets the tone and indeed encapsulates what once constituted genuine spirituality in a Hispanic community and how people came together to celebrate, pray, or grieve.

Every religious ceremony had its own special meaning. The manner in which each was celebrated varied little from one community to another. This uniformity not only reinforced the traditional way of honoring religious customs and ceremonies, but it also gave credibility to people's belief in them. When a religious occasion concerned children, women—mothers in particular—assumed a leadership role in upholding the principles of religion.

I will never forget Holy Week (Semana Santa) during Lent, when we were not allowed to eat meat on Friday, sing, chew gum, get a haircut, or chop wood. I could never erase the memory of traveling by horse-drawn wagon to Midnight Mass (Misa del Gallo) at my local village and then going home to eat a bowl of hot posole and empanaditas my mother had prepared for Christmas. (We never had a Christmas tree.). I can never forget inventing sins as a small boy just so I could go to confession once a month like everyone else when the priest came to our church to celebrate Mass.

The narratives in this chapter mirror many of the cultural trappings I experienced as a child growing up in the Río Puerco Valley. The *viejitos'* words are also a clear testimony to the abiding faith they possessed and treasured. At the same time, some of them offer sobering thoughts about the attitudes of young Hispanics of today with regard to religion; others express grave concern, to the point of being not just pessimistic but cynical. As Alfredo Ulibarrí says, "The old folks are already tired of telling them [the grandchildren] to go to Mass, and then if they don't go, who's going to force them? That's why I think many people are losing their religion." Others, like Filimón Montoya, are much more reflective and philosophical: "Religion is not disappearing. What is vanishing is faith in religion."

Young Hispanics are leaving the Catholic Church; others are indifferent toward religion; divorce and separation have become commonplace. Our old ones recognize that many young people today view their ancestors' way of practicing religion as outmoded and not in sync with a modern society whose priorities are lodged in a hi-tech world that accentuates material things and tangible rewards devoid of spirituality.

In the main, these different points of view are more symptomatic of the times in which we live. The accounts that follow offer a dichotomy of sorts: on the one hand, the old-timers take us back sixty, seventy, or eighty years, when religion in rural villages of northern New Mexico was paramount and a way of life; on the other hand, they also focus on the present and the problems confronting religion, but they do so in a reflective and pragmatic way.

Arsenio Montoya, Sr.

Crencias

Pa la Semana Santa, pus, si toos usaan leña, tenía uno que partir leña too el lunes, martes, y hasta el miércoles a mediodía. Ya del miércoles pa delante no podía uno. Ya no hacía naa. No lo dejaban ni tirar piedras. Le dijían a uno,

—Si tiras una piedra, le pegas al Señor.

Munchas crencias bien bonitas, ¿ves? Y el jueves y el viernes y el sábado, pus eso era nomás puro rezar. Ayunar. Ayunaba uno, y loo a las once, a las once y media iba a comer uno. Y loo llevar comida pa los parientes asina de una casa a otra y se compartían toos. El domingo iba la gente a misa y se confesaban.

Cuando muría alguien tamién era cuento nomás de rezar porque no había más remedio. En ese tiempo ni cajones había. En papá era el que buscaba tablas onde jallaba y los hacía, porque hacía unos cajones, el viejito mío. Cuando se muría, alguien conocido a él vinían a velo pa que le traiban material y too y él les hacía el cajón. Él se los hacía y bien bonitos. Recién muertos nomás los ponían en una tarima, y les abrochaban las medias con un broche, y les ponían una plancha aquí en el estómago pa que no se hincharan, ¿ves? Taa había de esas planchas que planchaban de fierro, muy pesadas planchas. Dijían que porque se iba hinchando el cuerpo. Si se quedaba con un ojo abierto, le ponían un pene pa que cerrara los ojos, un pene, en l'ojo que estaba abierto, ¿ves? Y puro rezar y cantar alabaos toa la noche. Antonces sí los velaban [a los difuntos] toa la noche entera. Taa ora no. Yo veo velorios que llegan toos enbolaos y caen arriba el cajón. Hacen más busla de la gente [del difunto].

Güeno, había cánticos, pero son pa los días de santos. Ya se me olvidaron toos, como el de San Antonio de Padua. Taa otro que dijía,

A orillas de un ojo de agua,
está un ángel llorando,
de ver que le condenabas,
l'alma que traiba a su cargo.

Tamién había casorios. El casorio comenzaba la fiesta ende el día viernes. De modo que ya viernes, sábado, ya del domingo pa delante, era pa' listarse. En ese tiempo casaban nomás los lunes, pa las seis de la mañana. De ahi pallá se hacía cargo el novio y el papá del novio. Pero lo que era antes de eso, viernes, sábado y domingo, era el cargo por el lao de la novia. Y pasaban bonito porque toos repartían. Mataban un becerro y asina.

El día del casorio cuando salían [los novios] de l'iglesia, hacían una marcha, la "Marcha de los Novios," y de ahi los llevaban. Si no estaba muy lejos, iban a pie hasta la casa de la novia onde iban a entrar. Ya cuando entraba uno, ya estaba too decorao con los nombres [del novio y de la novia], tarimas, y echaban espelma en el suelo pa no resbalarse.

Los bautismos tamién eran cosa bonita, porque pus iba uno y convidaba a los compadres, ya jueran parientes o jueran nomás güenos conocidos que hubieran tenido güenas amistades. Y el bautismo, pus, el padrino y la madrina soponen ser los segundos padres de los hijaos. A mí me bautizaron trece por lao de la familia mía. Loo nojotros bautizamos trece a otros compadres, ¿ves? De modo que siendo trece y trece, tengo veintiséis compadres. ¡Munchos compadres de pila! ¿No? Tocó ocasiones que llegamos de estar como asina en una barra, puros compadres por el lao de que yo les bauticé a eos. Y entraban otros conocidos míos asina y,

—¿Cómo está, Montoya?

—Bien.

—Háblale a mi compadre.

—Aá tengo otro compadre.

—¡No, no, no tanto compadre!

Sí, y sí era verdá, pus tenía trece compadres de pila. Muy bonito asina tanto compadre de pila. ¿Sabes tú que aquel Tranquilino Vigil que tiene casa en la calle seis, tiene restaurante, tenía barbería años pasaos, ése es compadre de pila mío? Mi compadre Gerónimo Garduño, ya es muerto él, tamién jue compadre. ¡Y munchos, munchos otros!

Por supuesto que el padrino y la madrina llevaban al hijao ya cuando lo bendicían, ya cuando lo iban a entregar a los padres y dijían,

> Compadre y comadre,
> aquí está esta flor,
> que de la iglesia salió,
> con los santos sacramentos,
> y l'agua que recibió.

Eso tienes que dijir tú que llevas a los hijaos. Y los papases tienen que dijir,

Recíbote, prenda mía,
que de l'iglesia salites,
con los santos sacramentos,
y l'agua que recibites.

Pero ora, éstos [la plebe] no saben naa, y es muy bonito dijir asina:
"Reciban esta flor que de l'iglesia salió," y loo los padres tienen que
dijir, "Recíbote, prenda mía, que de l'iglesia salites, con los santos
sacramentos y l'agua que recibites." ¡Y ahi está!

Beliefs

For Holy Week, well, if everyone burned wood, then you had to chop
wood all day Monday, Tuesday, and up to Wednesday noon. From
Wednesday noon on you couldn't do it. You just didn't do anything.
They didn't even let you toss rocks. They used to tell us, "If you toss
rocks, you'll hit our Lord Jesus Christ."

A lot of very beautiful beliefs, you see? And Thursday and Friday
and Saturday, they were reserved strictly for praying. Fasting. You
would fast, and then at eleven or eleven thirty you went to eat. And
then you took food to your relatives from one house to another;
everyone would share. On Sunday people attended Mass and went to
confession.

When someone died it was also a matter of just praying, because
there was no other recourse. Back then there weren't any coffins.
Dad was the one who would look for lumber wherever he could find
it, because my little old man used to make them. When an acquain-
tance died they'd come and see him; they'd bring him material and
all and he'd build them the coffin. He would make it, and very beautiful. Right after someone died they would put the body on top of a
wooden bench, and they would tie his socks with a safety pin, and
put a flatiron used for ironing clothes on the stomach so that it
would not swell, see? You could still find flatirons made of iron; they
were very heavy. People claimed that they did this because otherwise
the body would begin swelling. If the deceased person died with an
eye open, people would put a penny on the eyelid so that his eyes
would close. A penny on the eye that was open, you see? And all you
did was pray and sing hymns all night long. Back then people used

to stand vigil throughout the night over the deceased. Not so today. I've attended religious wakes where some individuals get there all drunk and stumble into the coffin. They make fun of the people [the dead person].

Now, there were canticles, but those were for saints' days. I forgot all of them, such as the one about Saint Anthony of Padua. There was another canticle that went like this:

> On the banks of a spring,
> there's an angel crying,
> seeing that you were condemning
> the soul that he was responsible for.

We also had weddings. The wedding celebration started on Friday. In other words, from Friday, Saturday, and Sunday on was time to get ready. Back then you could only get married on Mondays, at six o'clock in the morning. From then on, the groom and his father took charge. But prior to Friday, Saturday, and Sunday, those on the bride's side were in charge. And everything turned out very beautiful because everyone pitched in. They would slaughter a calf and so forth.

The day of the wedding, when the bride and groom left the church, they had a march, the "Newlyweds' March," and there they went. If it wasn't very far, they went on foot to the bride's house, where they entered. By the time you went in, everything was decorated with the names of the bride and groom, wooden benches, and wax was spread on the floor in order not to slide.

Baptisms were also a thing of beauty, because you went and asked the prospective compadres to be godparents, whether they were relatives or good acquaintances with whom you had enjoyed a good friendship. As for baptism, well, the godfather and the godmother are supposed to be the second parents to the godchildren. Thirteen of my kids were baptized on my side of the family. Then we, my wife and I, baptized thirteen others for compadres of ours, see? In other words, thirteen plus thirteen, I have twenty-six compadres. Lots of compadres from baptism! Right? There were times when we were in places like a bar, all compadres because I had baptized their children.

And other friends of mine would come in and say, "How are you doing, Montoya?

"Fine."

"Say hi to my compadre."

"There's another compadre of mine over there."

"No, no, there are too many compadres!"

Yes, and it was true. Why, I had thirteen compadres whose children I had baptized. It's a beautiful thing to have so many of this type of compadres. Do you know that that Tranquilino Vigil, who has a house on Sixth Street, he's got a restaurant, used to have a barbershop years ago, he's a compadre from baptism? My compadre Gerónimo Garduño, who's already dead, he was also a compadre of mine. And many, many others!

Of course, the godfather and the godmother would take the godchild, after it was blessed, to the parents with these words:

> Compadre and comadre,
> here you have this flower,
> which left the church,
> with the blessed sacraments,
> and the water with which it was anointed.

That's what you have to say when you deliver the godchildren. And the parents have to respond,

> I accept you, my jewel,
> which left the church,
> with the blessed sacraments,
> and the water with which you were anointed.

But nowadays, the young kids don't know anything, and it's very beautiful to say, "Accept this flower, which left the church," and then the parents have to say, "I accept you, my jewel, which left the church, with the blessed sacraments, and the water with which you were anointed." And that's that!

Filimón Montoya

Alguien tiraba tiros pa romper el día

Ahi en el Cañón [en Taos] dónde yo vivía, que le dijían el Cañón de Fernández, había un día de fiesta que era el veinte de noviembre. Ya no me acuerdo qué santo celebraban. Creo que es la fiesta de la Imaculada. Ése era el día de fiesta. Güeno, empezaban muy tempranito en la mañana a romper el día. Decían,

—¡Vamos a romper el día!

Alguien salía con un rifle y tiraba tiros pa romper el día. Güeno, y luego vinía la misa. La misa era lo principal, además de la rompida del día. Toa la comunidá iba a misa porque toa la gente era católica. No había otra secta allí. Todos éramos católicos. Todos se juntaban y iban a misa. Vinía el padre de la plaza, de la plaza de Taos, que tenía too el barrio de Taos, Ranchos, Cañón, Ranchitos y Prado. Hasta el pueblo de los indios, les daba servicios.

Tamién durante la misa sacaban una prusición, que sacaban a la imagen del santo que estaan festejando. Muy larga [procesión], como una milla iban. En el camino entonces no había tráfico como hoy en día. Hoy no lo pueden hacer porque el carro, automóviles, no es posible. Iban y voltiaban la güelta y iban cantando y rezando al mismo tiempo, hasta que traiban la imagen patrás pa l'iglesia, y entonces ahi terminaba con la misa.

Luego cuando se acababa la misa, llevaban los mayordomos—eran los que tenían cuidao de l'iglesia—al padre a comer a su casa. Pero no podían acomodar a toa la gente de la comunidá. Algunos eran güenos amigos, güenas amistades, y los llevaban a comer a su casa. Luego toa la gente hacía su comida en su casa, ¿ve? Si tenían familiares que vivían ajuera, vinían a visitar durante ese día. Güeno, ahi pasaban el día visitando con los familiares y con las familias.

En la tarde, cuando ya se hacía tarde, tenían un rosario. Durante el rosario iban y ponían luminarias. Era leña y las hacían como un fuertecito a cierta distancia de los laos del camino. Cuando ya se acababa de rezar el rosario, salía otra prusición en la noche y prendían las luminarias estas. Allí estaan alumbrándose con las luminarias y iban tamién en la misma dirección que jueron en la mañana.

Iban cantando y rezando tamién al mismo tiempo. Eran cánticos en el rosario; usaban cánticos de los miembros de la morada no de l'iglesia. Les dijían alabaos. Los rezos eran el Padre Nuestro, el Ave María y por ahi, ¿eh? Y entremedio de cada rezo, cantaban un alabao. Güeno, se acababa la prusición, metían la estuata pa l'iglesia, apagaban las luces y trancaban.

Somebody Fired Shots to Start the Day

There in Cañón where I lived, called Cañón de Fernández, a feast day was celebrated on November 20. I can't remember the saint. I believe it was the Immaculate Conception. That was a festive day. Okay, people started very early in the morning to start the day. They had an expression, "Let's start the day!"

Someone came out with a rifle and fired shots to start the day. And then came the Mass. The Mass was the principal thing, besides beginning the day. The entire community went to Mass because everyone was Catholic. There was no other religion in the area. We were all Catholics. Everybody got together and went to Mass. The priest came from the plaza, the town of Taos. He was in charge of Taos, Ranchos [de Taos], Cañón, Ranchitos, and Prado. The priest even celebrated Mass at the Indian pueblo.

Also, during Mass there was a religious procession in which they took out the statue of the saint whose day parishioners were celebrating. The procession went a long ways, about a mile. There was no traffic on the road like nowadays. Today you can't do it because of the cars; it's impossible. The procession went and then turned around, people singing and praying as they walked, until they brought the religious image back to the church, and that's when the Mass ended.

After the Mass was over, the mayordomos—the ones who took care of the church—invited the priest to go eat at their house. But the mayordomos couldn't accommodate [feed] everybody in the community. Some villagers had good friends, and they invited them to go eat at their homes. All of the people from the community prepared food, you see? If they had family members who lived far away, they went to visit during the day. That's how they spent the day, visiting with relatives and family members.

In the afternoon, when it got late, they said a rosary. During the rosary people set out *luminarias*. They were made of wood, like tiny forts a short distance from the side of the road. When the rosary was over, another procession took place at night, which is when the *luminarias* were lit. The *luminarias* lit the way and the procession followed the same route as in the morning. People sang and prayed at the same time. There were canticles appropriate for the rosary, not those of the church, but ones pertaining to the *morada* or the Penitents. They were called hymns of praise or of passion. The prayers were the Our Father, the Hail Mary, and so forth. And between each prayer, a hymn was sung. Once the procession was over, people returned the religious statue to the church, turned off the lights, and locked everything up.

*Penitentes' process during
Holy Week, 1904*
Negative 3614. Courtesy of
the Citizens' Committee for
Historic Preservation, Las
Vegas, NM.

Alfredo Ulibarrí

El Tiempo Santo

Pus nojotros cuando estáanos aquí, que yo iba a l'escuela en Las Vegas, nos hacían ir como el Tiempo Santo, como ora mismo [la Cuaresma], nos hacían ir toas las tardes a rezar. ¡Toas las tardes nos hacían! A lo menos en los viernes nos hacían ir a las estaciones. Y loo el tiempo que ya se llegaa el Tiempo Santo [la Semana Santa], como que ya estaa llegándose el tiempo ya muy santo, nos hacían ir y estarnos un día entero en la iglesia aquí en la plaza nueva cuando nojotros estáanos medianos. Pero sí, es too lo que nos hacían hacer. ¡Por tres días! O ir a visitar el Santísimo y estarte un rato. En el día. Antes nos hacían ir a nojotros en el día, porque tenían miedo yo creo los papases. Ora van en la noche.

Pero tenían misiones también. A las misiones nos dejaban ir con la gente grande. Vinía un misionero a dijir, tú sabes, platicar tocante la religión y too.

En la Santa Semana no trabajáanos. No, nada. Ni en el rancho que estuviéranos, no nos dejaan ni partir leña. A mí no me dejaan partir leña. Tenía que partir leña esos días antes [del miércoles hasta el Sábado de Gloria] pa no tener que hacer naa yo. Ora ni el carro dejaan. El papá mío no sacaa el carro pa juera, porque isque dijían que iba a trampar al Santísimo o yo no sé qué, al Señor. Que trampaan al Señor, pus, el Señor no iba estar a 'elante. [Risas] No lo iban a trampar, pero ésas eran las crencias diantes.

Holy Week

Well, when we were here, when I used to go to school here in Las Vegas, they would make us go, like, during Holy Week, like right now [Lent], they made us go pray every afternoon. Every afternoon we had to go pray! And on Fridays they for sure made us do the stations of the cross. And then about the time Holy Week came around, when the holiest time was upon us, they made us go and stay at the church a whole day, here at the new plaza when we were kids. But yes, that's all they made us do. Three whole days! Or you had to go visit the statue of Christ and stay for a while. During the day. Back then we had to go during the day, because the parents, I guess, were afraid. Nowadays kids go at night.

But they also had missions [a parish or domestic mission is a set of instructions and exhortations to raise the level of fervor in a village or town. It resembles a revival in a parish church. Jesuits and Redemptionists were especially known for these revivals.] You were allowed to go to the missions with the grown-ups. A missionary came, you know, to talk about religion and all that.

During Holy Week we didn't work. Nothing at all. Even if you were at the ranch, they didn't even let you chop wood. I wasn't allowed to chop wood. I had to chop wood the days before Wednesday so that I wouldn't have to do anything from Thursday to Saturday. You couldn't even start the car. My father wouldn't even take the car out of the garage, because they claimed that he might run over Christ or I don't know who. People claimed that you could run over Christ. Well, He wasn't going to be in front of you. [Laughter] Nobody was going to trample Him, but those were the beliefs of yesteryear.

Filimón Montoya

La Cuaresma

La Cuaresma empezaba el Miércoles de Ceniza, que son como cuarenta días antes del Día de la Resurección, ¿verdá? Toavía se costumbra en la Iglesia Católica de ir a recibir ceniza. Bueno. Ahi se acababan toos los güenos tiempos. Por toa la Cuaresma no había bailes, no se oía música en las casas. Si tenía uno una grafonola, no podía usala. Si era uno músico, no podía tocar el instrumento durante toa la Cuaresma hasta que no pasaba la Semana Santa. Todos los viernes en la noche hacían a uno rezar las estaciones en la casa. Eso fue durante toa la Cuaresma y luego llegó el Domingo de Ramos. Entonces se iban por la rama, y cada quien llevaa su rama pa que la bendicieran en la iglesia. Y luego ahi siguía la función de la Semana Santa. Güeno, tavía por el lunes, martes y el miércoles hasta mediodía, podían hacer su trabajo. Trabajo allá en la labor o lo que tenían que hacer la gente. Las señoras cociniaban too este tiempo, pero ya del miércoles a mediodía pa delante, ahi se paraba too.

Cuando ya estaa más grande yo, nos hacían arrimar la leña pa junto la cocina. A los grandes nos hacían partir suficiente leña pa no tener que partila, porque dijían que lastimaban al Siñor si partían durante los días santos que era el día jueves, el día viernes o el día miércoles después de mediodía.

Entonces tamién la pasaban rezando nomás y loo iban a visitas a la morada onde estaan los hermanos. Les llamaban los hermanos, los miembros de la cofradía. Iba la gente hacer visitas allá a la morada. Loo salían tamién pal Calvario, que le dijían, a rezar las estaciones toos los días, o durante el jueves y el viernes, por lo menos, que yo me acuerde. Hacían las estaciones allá fuera de la morada al Calvario onde tenían crucifico grandote enterrao, una cruz grandota. Ahi iban rezando y cantando alabaos, pero cantaban tanto los miembros de la cofradía que se le metían a uno en los oídos que tavia despúes los oías. Era, ah, no sé, como le da como un temor con estos alabaos que cantaban. Era como atemorizar, hasta que pasaba el Viernes Santo. Ahi se acababa la Semana Santa.

Y el Sábado de Gloria iba la gente por agua bendita a la iglesia. Luego el domingo era el Domingo de Resureción. Ya era el día que resucitó el Siñor. Iba tamién la gente a la misa del Domingo de Resureción, pero no celebraban como hoy en día, que la plebecita anda ahi con que *Easter* pallá, *Easter* pacá. No era too así; too era pura religión en esos días.

Lent

Lent started on Ash Wednesday, which comes forty days before Resurrection, right? It is still customary in the Catholic Church to go and receive ashes. Okay. That's where all the good times ended. Throughout the entire Lenten period there were no dances, nor was music heard in the home. If you had a phonograph, you couldn't play it. If you were a musician, you weren't allowed to play an instrument until after Holy Week, when Lent was over. They made you pray the stations of the cross every Friday at your home. That was during all of Lent, and then Palm Sunday would come, and then everybody went for their palm, and each person would take the palm to have it blessed in church. Afterward, the Holy Week religious celebrations continued. It was true, you could still work on Monday,

Tuesday, and Wednesday until noon. Whether it was working in the fields or whatever chores people had to do. The women cooked during this entire time, but come Wednesday noon, everything stopped.

When I got older, they made us pile the wood close to the kitchen. The older ones like me, we had to chop enough firewood so we wouldn't have to do it during those holy days, because people believed that you would injure Christ if you chopped wood, especially on Thursday, Friday, and Wednesday from noon on.

What they did then was to spend all of their time praying and later they would go to the *morada* where the brothers were to pay a visit. They were called the brothers, members of the brotherhood. That's where worshippers went to pay their respects. Then they would also go to Mount Calvary every day, as it was called, to say the stations of the cross, or at least on Thursdays and Fridays, as far as I recall. People said the stations of the cross between the *morada* and Mount Calvary, where the brothers had a large, huge cross set in the ground. There they were on their way praying and singing hymns of praise or passion, but the brotherhood members sang so much that the hymns would pierce your ears to the point that you could still hear them much later. It was, ah, I don't know, like you got scared with the hymns that they sang. It was, like, eerie, until Good Friday came and went. That was the end of Holy Week.

By the time Holy Saturday came, people went to the church to get holy water. Then Sunday, it was the Resurrection, the day that Christ Our Lord rose from the dead. People also attended Mass on that day, but it wasn't like nowadays, where the children run around looking for eggs on Easter Sunday. It wasn't like that; it was all religion back in those days.

¡Mis crismes!

Pa Crismes era muy calmado too. Tenían un drama que dijían que eran pastores. Eso es lo que hacían pa la Navidá, pa Crismes. Era un drama, ¿no? Y juntaban varios niños, no niños muy niños, niños que ya pueden comprender, digamos, ya de diez años parriba. Le daban a cada quien un relate, una relación, que tenía que aprendela de memoria. Practicaban unas dos semanas antes de la Navidá, toas las noches. Tenían un maestro de los pastores. Tenían un San Miguel, un Lucifer, un Bartolo, un Gil, y loo los otros pastores tamién, pas-

tores que tenían su nombre. Ya no me recuerdo cómo se llamaban—
Gil y Bato y por ahi.

Eso era la diversión de Crismes, de la Navidá. El día de la nochi, la
Nochibuena, velaban. Había velorio. Hacían su *play,* que le dicen hoy
en día, *play,* el drama, y ahi se estaban toa la nochi. Ahi rezaban
rosario también. Siempre estaba la religión. Too lo que hacía la gente
culminaba en rezos y eso. Y luego el día de la Navidá, que es el día de
Crismes, salían los muchachos que estaan, los pastores. Yo nunca
tomé parte en eos. Salían a pedir crismes. Dijían,

—¡Mis crismes! ¡Mis crismes!

Pero verdaderamente soponían ser en la noche antes [de Navidad]
cuando salían. Tenían que salir a pidir oremos, pero la gente grande,
no, los muchachos menores. Luego como estaa mi esposa hablándole
de los agüelos. Bueno. Estos agüelos salían en la nochi, en la
Nochibuena. Andaban de casa en casa. Y ésos soponían ir a pedir oremos. Oremos era cosa que cociniaba la gente. Es too. Les hacían
sopaipillas o pedazos de pastel, bizcochitos, alguna cosa así para
comer. Eso era los oremos que pidían. Nomás que eos [los abuelos]
iban por las ventanas, y tocaban las ventanas y usaban máscaras. Y
su dicho era,

Oremos, oremos,
angelitos semos,
y del cielo vinemos,
y si no nos dan,
puertas y ventanas
quebraremos.

Ésos estaan poco atrevidos, poco altaneros. Pero sí, les daban, sí se
abría la ventana. Les daban por la ventana y si no les dijían,

—Volteen a la puerta.

Los pastores no salían en la nochi. Eos salían el siguiente día, el
mero día de la Navidá.

Y luego tenían las posadas, que les dijían. Iba el maestro de los
pastores, iba a ciertas natales casas, y les dicían que si podían hacele
el favor de dales posada. No era posada *actually,* verdaderamente,
pero era lo que le llamaban. Güeno, iban y daban parte de su drama
adelante la casa esta y loo los dejaban entrar para adentro. Lo que era

un banquete; éste era un banquete. Les tenían bizcochitos y cosas que cociniaba la gente en esos tiempos: pasteles, *sodas,* ya despúes cuando había *soda,* y cosas dulces, pero casi unas cosas dulces nomás. Ésas eran las posadas.

¿La Misa del Gallo? Nomás en la iglesia mayor, no en las iglesias afuera de la iglesia mayor. Allá nomás hacían la Misa del Gallo. Yo no sé por qué le llamarían la "Misa del Gallo." Toavía le llaman, quizás, porque nacía en la medianochi, pero los gallos no despiertan a medianochi. Bueno, que juera lo qué juera, Misa de Gallo, misa de medianochi, iba muncha gente.

¿Sabe que nojotros íbanos cuando estaa yo muy mediano? Si estaa alguno de mis hermanos en la casa, prendía el carro de los caballos, y nos llevaba a la Misa del Gallo. Nos echaban cuiltas pa que nos cobijáranos. Y en el carro de caballos tenía un cajón, ¿no? Un asiento aquí onde iba el arriero y dos pasajeros y luego otro asiento más atrás. Ahi iban más pasajeros. Y luego la plebe nos echaban en el cajón, sueltos. Nos destendían una cuilta y loo nos cobijaban con otra. Pus íbanos a la Misa del Gallo.

Pero si yo no me recuerdo de ver muncho en la Misa del Gallo porque era un gentío. Taa muy acuñaa la iglesia y pus chamaco, ¿qué va a ver uno? Pero iba la gente grande. Pasaba por adelante el altar, y adorando al Niño Jesús, adoraban al Niño Jesús, y daban su donación. Y les daban la comunión ahi tamién. Ésa era la Misa del Gallo.

Después comía uno lo que hubiera en la casa, porque volvía uno con muncho frío, y tenía que consumir alguna cosa caliente. Me recuerdo que mi mamá tenía un perol grandote, y siempre estaa arriba la estufa toa la noche. Le atisaban a la estufa con leña. Entonces no había gas, no había l'etrecidá. ¡Leña! Pus cuando volvía uno estaa muy calentito en la cocina. Y los grandes hacían su cafecito, y nos daban [a los chamacos] chile con carne y posole y sopaipillas, buñelos, les dijían. Luego se acostaba uno.

Merry Christmas!

Well, everything was very quiet during Christmastime. They had a play that depicted the shepherds. That's what they used to put on during Nativity, for Christmas, when Christ was born. It was a play, right? And they would gather several kids, not very young, who already understood and had a sense of appreciation, let us say, ten years old and older. Each one would be given a story, a part to memorize. They had to practice every night for some two weeks before Christmas. There was a teacher who instructed the shepherds: Saint Michael, Lucifer, Bartholomew, and Virgil, and the rest of the shepherds, who had their own names as well. I can't recall their names—Virgil and Bato and so on and so forth.

That was the entertainment during Christmas, for the Nativity. On Christmas Eve, people would hold a vigil. There was a religious vigil. And they also put on a play, as it is called, a drama. There they were all night long. They also said the rosary. Religion was always everywhere. Everything that people did culminated in prayers and the like. Then on the day of the Nativity, which is Christmas Day, the kids playing the role of the shepherds would come out. I never took part in that. They went out asking for Christmas tidings. They'd say, "Merry Christmas! Merry Christmas!"

In reality, they should have gone out the night before. They had to go and ask for what is called "*oremos*" [lit., let us pray], but not the older people, only the young kids. But then there was the matter of the *agüelos* [characters in Los Matachines] that my wife was talking about. Okay. These so-called *agüelos* would come out at night on Christmas Eve. They went from house to house. They were supposed to be asking for *oremos,* which was nothing more than what people baked. That's all. They would bake things like sopaipillas or pies, *bizcochitos* [cinnamon cookies], or something like that to eat. That's what *oremos* was all about. The only thing is that they [the *agüelos*] went to the windows, knocked on the windows, and wore masks. And their folk expression was,

> Let us pray, let us pray,
> for we are little angels,
> who have come from heaven,
> and if gifts you don't give us,
> we shall break doors and windows.

Those verses are a little bit daring, a little bit arrogant. But yes, people would open the windows and give them gifts, through the window; if not, they'd say to them, "Go around to the door." And then

the shepherds, they didn't go out at night. They went out on the following day, right on Christmas Day.

Then there was what is called *"posadas,"* inns [*dar posadas* = to
give shelter]. The teacher for the shepherds would go to certain
nativity houses, and they would ask for overnight shelter or hospital-
ity. It wasn't actually an inn, not really, but that's what it was called.
Very well, the shepherds would put on part of their play in front of
the house and then they were permitted to go inside. The whole
affair turned into a banquet; it was a banquet. The hosts had *bizco-*
chitos and things that people baked back in those days ready for
them: pies, and soft drinks, later on when there was soft drinks. And
sweet things, but only a few sweet things, that's all. That's what the
posadas were all about.

Now, as for midnight Mass? It was held only in the main church,
not in the chapels [the mission churches] away from the main
church. That's the only place where midnight Mass was celebrated. I
don't know why it was called "Misa del Gallo." It's still called that,
perhaps because it started at midnight, but the roosters don't wake
up at midnight. Be that as it may, Misa del Gallo, midnight Mass, or
whatever, a lot of people attended.

Do you know that we used to go when I was very small? If one of
my brothers was at home, he would hitch up the horses, and he'd
take us to midnight Mass. They would load up quilts so we'd wrap
ourselves up. And the horse-drawn wagon had a wooden box, you
see. There was a seat where the driver and two passengers sat and
then another seat right behind. That was for more passengers. As for
the children, we'd be loaded up in the open box of the wagon. They
would spread a blanket and then they'd cover us up with another
one. That's how we went to midnight Mass.

But I don't recall having seen a whole lot at midnight Mass
because there were hordes of people. The church was packed like sar-
dines and, being a small kid, what can you see? But the older people
would go and file by the altar, worshipping the Baby Jesus, praying
to the Baby Jesus, and giving their donations. That's where they
received communion also. That's what the Misa del Gallo was all
about.

Afterwards you went home and ate whatever there was to eat,

because when you got home you were very cold, and you had to consume something hot. Why, I remember that my mom had a huge kettle of food, and it was on top of the wood stove all night long. And they kept poking, feeding the wood stove. Back then there was no gas, no electricity, only wood! Well, by the time you got home the kitchen was nice and warm. The older folks would make their coffee, and the kids were fed chile and meat and posole [a dish consisting of hominy, chile, pork, etc.] and sopaipillas, called *buñelos.* Then you went to bed.

Los velorios de los finaos

Cuando se moría alguien, diuna vez se juntaba la comunidá y, si no tenían la gente del finao manera de conseguir el material pa hacele el cajón, donaban. La gente hacían donaciones. Estaa un hombre ahi en Cañón de Fernández que era experto en hacer los cajones. Él los hacía. No les cobraa naa. Compraba la madera en el *lumberyard,* que le llamamos nojotros hoy en día, y hacía el cajón y loo lo aforraban con material. Casi toos los cajones los aforraban con material negro para los adultos. Para niños usaban blanco, material blanco.

Luego en la nochi pa los velorios se juntaba la gente, y los miembros de la Cofradía de Nuestro Señor Jesucristo iban a cantar. Tamién toa la nochi cantaban. A la medianochi dijían,

—¡Ora es tiempo de rezar el rosario!

Rezaban el rosario y loo los llamaban a cenar. Hacían muncho que comer, como chile con carne. Dijían,

—¡Vamos al chilito!

Lo mismo que pa la Navidá, pero no me recuerdo si cocerían posole, pero frijoles, sí, cocían muncho. Perolotes de frijoles y sopaipillas, buñuelos y chile. El chile no faltaba, el chile con carne. Cenaban y entonces ya se silenciaba poco hasta en la mañana, porque generalmente nomás una nochi velaban a los dijuntos. No podían tenelos muncho más como entonces no los enbalsamaban como hoy en día.

Luego en la mañana se iban toos los que participaron en el velorio. Iban abrir la sepoltura, con pico y pala. Ya pa cuando era tiempo de si le iban a dar misa al finao o finada, le daban su misa y loo lo llevaban en prusición, hasta el camposanto, cemiterio, el pantión

[monumento funerario destinado a enterramiento de varias per-
sonas]. Tiene munchos nombres. Y lo sepultaban. O alguien le echaba la elogía, que le llamaban. Los dolientes iban y ahi se estaban
hasta que enterraban al dijunto, que ya lo tapaban con tierra. Hoy en
día no los dejan quedarse. Hoy en día los despachan antes de sepul-
tar al finao.

Así eran los velorios y las funciones de los finaos.

Religious Wakes for the Deceased

Whenever someone died, the community got together right away
and, if the family of the deceased did not have a way of obtaining
the materials for the coffin, they donated them. The people would
make donations. There was a man there in Cañón de Fernández who
was an expert in making coffins. He's the one who made them. He
didn't charge anything. He used to buy the lumber at the lumberyard, as we call it today, and he'd make the coffin, and then people
lined it with cloth. Almost all of the coffins for the adults were lined
with black cloth. Those for the children were lined with white cloth.

And then at night for the religious wakes people would get
together, and the members of the Brotherhood of Our Lord Jesus
Christ would go sing. They sang all night long. At midnight they
would say, "It's now time to say the rosary!"

They would pray the rosary and then people were invited to eat. A
lot of food was prepared, such as meat and chile. People hollered,
"Let's go eat a little bit of chile!"

It was the same thing for Christmas, but I don't recall if they prepared posole, but lots of pinto beans were cooked, that's for sure.
Huge kettles of beans and sopaipillas or *buñuelos* [a kind of fritter],
and chile. There was always plenty of chile, especially chile and
meat. People ate and then things quieted down somewhat until
morning, because generally the deceased was watched over [you paid
your respects] for one night only. They couldn't keep a body much
more then, the way they do nowadays, because there was no such
thing as embalming.

Then when morning came, all those who had been present at the
religious wake left. They went to dig the grave with pick and shovel.
When it was time for Mass in honor of the deceased, if Mass indeed

was to be celebrated [provided a priest was available], it was done, or the body was taken in a procession all the way to the cemetery, pantheon [family plot], whatever. It has many names. There they buried the deceased. Or someone would deliver the eulogy, as it is called. The mourners would go and remain until the deceased was buried and covered with dirt. Nowadays you're not allowed to stay. Today they send you off before the deceased is buried.

That's how religious wakes and functions for the deceased were celebrated.

Arsenio Montoya, Sr.

Sacaban a los santos por las cosechas

Yo no sé si sería castigo o qué, pero hacían [la gente] promesas que en veces eran poco duras, como si alguien estaba enfermo, lo ponían [al santo] como en una cómoda o eso. No ponía muncha atención yo quizás, pero sí se me hace que había tal cosa asina, como que lo iban a voltiar pa la pader. Y loo resultaba que se les—¿cómo te quiero dijir?—alquerían lo que pidían y loo lo sacaban [de la cómoda] y le prendían velitas y le rezaban su novena o lo que juera. Munchas oraciones de rezar y novenas.

Tamién sacaban a los santos por las cosechas pa que cayera agua. Eso lo llegué a ver yo. Nojotros viníanos por los baños [en Montezuma], en tiempos secos que ni una gota de agua iba cae. Íbanos con los santos, pasiándolos cantando too el camino, haciendo oraciones. No acabábanos de llegar de allá pacá sin que no nos pescaba l'agua en el camino.

Ésas son cosas curiosas cuando parecía que ni una gota iba cae. No, ya cuando acordaba uno, subían las nubes y llegábanos caindo agua a la casa. Se me hace que, yo no sé, son las creencias de cada quien.

En papá cuando sembraba, que vinían feas nubes, hacía su oración. Si andaba escardando, o andábanos escardando, nos dijía que pusiéranos los cabadores hechos cruz y nos íbanos a casa. Loo había veces que tocaa que caiban unos granizales que barría por toos los laos y parecía que la labor de él la habían cortao del cerco pallá asina. Vinían los Vigiles y dijían,

—¡Qué bonita labor tiene, don Isidro!

—Sí —les dijía.

Yo creo que sí era la güena fe que tenía en papá.

People Paraded the *Santos* through the Fields

I don't know whether it was punishment or what, but people made vows that at times were a little difficult to fulfill, like if someone was ill, they'd stick the *santo* in a dresser or something like that. I guess the *santo* didn't pay much attention, but I do believe there was such a ritual, such as having him face the wall. And then it would turn out that—how should I put it?—I guess people would get what they petitioned for and then they would take the *santo* out of the dresser and light little votive candles and say a novena or whatever in appreciation for his deed.

People also paraded the *santos* through the fields so that it would rain. That's something that I got to see. We used to come to the hot baths in Montezuma when it was dry and not a drop of rain. We'd take the *santos*, parading them all along the road, singing and praying. We were hardly able to go to the end of our journey and back without having the rain catch us on the road.

Those are curious things, especially when it appeared that not even a drop of rain would fall. Before you realized it, the clouds were beginning to appear so that by the time we got home it was raining. It seems to me, I don't know, that it has to do with everyone's beliefs.

My father, whenever he planted and he saw dark, ugly clouds coming, he said his prayers. If he was hoeing, or we were hoeing, he'd tell us to put the hoes in the form of a cross, and we'd head home. There were times when we had some terrible hailstorms that swept the fields from one end to the other, but it seemed as though his cornfields had been spared from the fence onward. The Vigils would come and say, "My, what wonderful cornfields you have, Don Isidro!"

"Yes," he'd respond.

I believe that it's the good faith that my father possessed.

Alfredo Ulibarrí

Está perdiendo la religión muncha gente

Pus, la figuro yo que porque no los enseña el mismo papá a los hijos, a que sigan la religión, no van a misa. Están perdiendo too eso. La gente grande sí va a misa, y los hijos no van a misa porque ya andan aá juera o por ahi en la plaza pasiándose, y no quieren ser católicos como munchos. No los enseñan ende chiquitos, *you know.* Los dejan ahi solos, solos, y no les dicen, "Vayan a misa." Ya los viejos están cansaos de dijiles que vayan a misa, y loo si no van, ¿quién los va obligar? Por eso yo creo que está perdiendo la religión muncha gente.

Yo me acuerdo cuando pasiaban los santos de ahi de Jorupa a la Lagunita. O llevaan la santa de la Lagunita paá pa Jorupa, y le rezaban un velorio a case mi mamá y loo otro día la traiban patrás. Tamién de la santa de—¿cómo quiero dijir?—la de Bernal. Tamién la llegaron a llevar aá, porque aá en Jorupa había una cruz, que esa cruz pertenecía a la iglesia de allá. Pero la iglesia, ya cuando yo tuve uso de razón, ya no había iglesia ni placita. No había más que un tío mío que vivía ahi—mi tío Gregorio. Él vivía nomás en su casa, y nojotros vivíanos pa este otro lao. Pero tenían una cruz, y loo mi papá era el dueño de esa cruz cuando tiraron la iglesia.

Se jue quedando la cruz y él se quedó con ella. Loo se la pasaron a mi mamá. Ésa la pasiaban parriba y pa bajo. Loo al fin la dejaron en la Lagunita y de ahi se la robaron junto con la Nuestra Señora del Rosario. Ahi sí se acabó todo. De ahi pallá no siguieron pasando santos. Oh, despúes pasiaba su mamá de ea [mi esposa] los santos, pero en la placita nomás, entiendo yo.

Tamién sacaban los santos a pasiar pa ver si caiba agua. Una vez le dieron a mi mamá una cruz. No me acuerdo cómo se llamaban los gabachos, por no dijir una mentira, no me acuerdo, pero le dieron una cruz negra. Nomás el puro crucifico. La casa de nojotros estaa como pacá, y loo aá delante estaa una lomita. Y dijieron un día, "Vamos a pasiar los santos y a llevar esta crucita y la vamos a poner arriba la lomita." ¡Y no me has de creer tú a mí! Nadien me va a creer, pero los que saben que andaban con nojotros esa vez, sí pueden saber, o pueden platicar. Jueron y llevaron la crucita.

A mí me dejaron en la casa, porque no podíanos atrancar porque perdieron la llave, o no sé qué pasó. Tenía una tranquita de aqueas de palo al lao a entro la puerta. Y dijieron,

—Tú te quedas aquí en lo que nojotros vamos allá a pasiar los santos y a poner la cruz allá arriba de la lomita, y aquí te quedas, y aquí te quedas.

Yo dije,

—No, yo no me voy a quedar solo.

Pus salí por la ventana del cuarto y jui hasta aá. No, puea que caminara como la mitá, como de aquí a la orilla del bloque ese, de la South Pacific, y ahi estaa la lomita.

Pu' sí, llegaron aá a la lomita pero dejaron cae la crucita y no la pusieron porque vinía una nube muy, muy truenando y caindo granizo y too. Cuando ya les pescó el granizo poco grande, salieron juyendo unos pal rumbo del corral y otros pa en casa. Quise quebrar la puerta, pero no la pude quebrar. Al fin me arrimé pa la ventana y la abrí. Antonces siguí metiendo a las muchachas que andaban por ahi pa entro, las que pudieron, y otras que garraron paá pal rumbo de la caballeriza.

Pero por el granizo ese, no pudieron poner la cruz hasta como los tres, cuatro días. A colgala. Que tavía hasta la fecha pienso que está la crucita caida ahi en la lomita. Pero no era más que una crucita de palo. No tenía santito en ea.

Pus a esa cruz l'iban a castigar [risas], y los castigó a todos ea. Mi mamá mía llegó a sacar a esa santa cruz y ponela aá en un palo que tenía poco en l'esquina del cerquito. Onde se daba chile, ahi la ponía en veces atrincaa a la talla, ves, pa ver si caiba agua. ¡Y caiba agua! Yo no sé si serían los tiempos o qué, pero rezaban muncho, porque el santo que rezaban, que mi mamá creía muncho, era San Lorenzo. A ese San Lorenzo tenía como un retrato. A ése le rezaba too el tiempo—pal día de San Lorenzo. Y lo sacaan a pasiar ese día antes y loo hacían velorio y convidaban gente de la misma placita y esos lugares que querían ir al velorio a la noche a rezale a ese santo.

Many People Are Losing Their Religion

Well, the way I figure it, if the father himself doesn't teach his children, so that they practice their religion, they won't go to Mass either. They're losing all of that. The older people do go to Mass, but the children don't go because they're running around or out and about the plaza and don't wish to be Catholics like many others. They aren't taught from the time they're small, you know. They let them do as they please, and they're not told, "Go to Mass." The old folks are already tired of telling them to go to Mass, and then if they don't go, who's going to force them? That's why I think many people are losing their religion.

I can recall when the people paraded the *santos* from Jorupa to La Lagunita. Or they took the patron saint from La Lagunita to Jorupa, and a religious vigil would be held at my mom's house, and then next day the saint would be brought back. The same thing was true of the patron saint from—how should I say?—the one from Bernal. People also took her over to Jorupa, because there was a cross there that belonged to the church in Jorupa. But the church, by the time I was old enough to make sense out of anything, there was no longer a church in the village. There was only one person living there—my uncle Gregorio. He lived alone in his house, and we lived on this other side. But they had a cross there, and my father was the owner of that cross when the church was demolished.

The cross found a home and he kept it. Then it was passed on to my mother. People used to parade that cross up and down the villages. Finally it was left in La Lagunita, where it was stolen along with Our Lady of the Rosary. That was the end of all that. From then on they quit taking *santos* out in processions. Oh, afterwards, my wife's mother paraded *santos,* but only in the village, as I understand it.

People also took out the *santos* to see if it would rain. One time, I don't remember these Anglos' names who gave my mother a cross. I don't recall, so as not to tell a lie, but they gave her a black cross. The crucifix, that's all. Our house was, like, to one side, and in front there was a small hill. And one day the people said, "Let's parade the *santos* and let's take this small cross and put it at the top of the hill." And you won't believe me! Nobody's going to believe me, but those who were with us at the time, they can vouch for me, or tell the story. They went and took the small cross.

They left me at home, because they couldn't lock the door, since the key had gotten lost or I don't know what happened. The door had, like, a little wooden lock or peg on the inside. And they said, "You stay here while we go parade the *santos* and take this cross over there to the top of the hill, and you stay here, right here."

And I said to myself, "No, I'm not going to stay alone." Well, I snuck out the window and I went all the way over there. Why no, maybe I went about halfway, like from here to the end of that block on South Pacific, and there was the small hill.

And sure enough, they got to the small hill, but they dropped the tiny cross and didn't put it up because there was a cloud coming and it was really thundering and hailing and everything. When the large hail finally caught them, they took off running toward the corral and others headed home. I tried to break the door down but I couldn't. Finally, I got close to the window and I opened it. Then I continued bringing the girls in who were still outside, those who managed to come in, and the others headed for the barn.

Because of the hailstorm, people weren't able to put up the cross until three or four days later. That is, to hang it up. And to this day I believe that little cross is still on the ground on top of that little hill. But it was only a tiny cross made of wood. It didn't have a small *santo* on it.

Well, it was that cross that the people were going to punish, and it punished all of them instead. My mom got to take out that holy cross and put it on a post stuck in a corner of this small fence. Where chile was harvested, that's where she leaned it up against the railroad tie, you understand, to see if it would rain. And did it rain! I don't know whether it was the times or what, but people prayed a lot, because the *santo* that people prayed to, that my mother believed in a lot, was Saint Lawrence. She had, like, a picture of Saint Lawrence. She prayed to him all the time—for Saint Lawrence's Day. And people would take him out on a procession and then they would have a religious vigil and invite people from the village and those places around it. This was done for people who wanted to go to the religious vigil at night to pray to that particular *santo*.

Guadalupe Luján

Ya la plebe no quieren ir al catecismo

Aquí, en este lugar mismo de nojotros [Las Vegas], nos han quitao los padres que de veras son de corazón. Ora nos traen uno ahi que no le entendemos lo que dice. Yo he sido católico toda mi vida, y nos habían de darnos lo que necesitamos. Lo que tenemos güeno no[s] lo quitan y se lo llevan par otro lao.

Ya la plebe no quieren ir al catecismo, y los que están poco más grande, tamién que tiene poco sentido, se desaniman. No quieren ir a la iglesia. Pus aquí rezamos en la casa mejor porque no le entendemos al padre. Ora mismo tenemos aquí un italiano, pero voy a misa porque es mi deber. Por mientras Dios me dé licencia, yo voy a ir a misa. No me voy a cambiar porque yo pertenezco aquí. Y hamos tenido muy güenos padres.

Ora este negocio que traen ahi de los padres [pedófilos], es pura especulación de dinero. Les levantan crímenes a munchos de eos. Por unos pagan todos. El justo paga por el pecador. Ésas son cosas que se habían de enderezar. Y el arzobispo [Robert Sánchez, el décimo arzobispo de Santa Fe, entre 1974 y 1993; renunció su puesto tras declaraciones de indecencia sexual], pus ya hizo su equívoco. Dios que lo perdone. Ésa es su responsabilidá dél. No hay que juzgar uno por lo que le dicen a uno, porque no sabe uno que equívoco puee tener uno en esta vida.

Yo creo en una cosa. Mire. Eos [los padres] vienen a representar aquí, los que de corazón vienen, vienen a representar aquí al Divino que es Jesucristo. Hay munchas cosas de éstas que por eso le digo yo que los padres no están corriendo bien. Ya hace años que está asina. Teníanos un padre aá tiempo pasao muy güeno aquí, no[s] lo quitaron. Se lo llevaron yo no sé par ónde. Isque por allá cerca de México está.

Sí le da a uno temor porque semos pecadores, pero tenemos que vivir esta vida. El evangelio es lo que tenemos que abrazar. Y un padre que se basa sobre el evangelio, lo respeta uno. Ése está bien. En munchas ocasiones, casi más ciento por ciento, los que están bien educaos pa ser sacerdotes, se basan sobre el evangelio. No salen con otras cosas ahi.

Ora otra cosa que miro yo es muncha la ambición pal dinero. Nojotros levantamos un lugar nuevo a estos padres, los que vinían pobremente. Nomás empezó la gente a trabajar, hicimos un lugar hermosísimo pa los padres, onde estudiar y *whatever they like to study*, y rezar lo que tengan que rezar. Pero ahora últimamente no, ya la gente no está satisfecha.

Pa las procesions había un *parade*. ¿Cómo le dicemos? Un desfile dende la iglesia y todo alredor del parque. Primero era la misa, y luego se comenzaba la fiesta. Pero muy bonito. Decoraban. Ponían santos. Ponían flores. Ponían de todo. Y ponían como unas capillitas. Ahi se paraba uno y rezaba. Se hincaba y rezaba. Loo siguía lotra, lotra hasta que daban la güelta alredor del parque. Ya todo eso se acabó.

Una vez me acuerdo yo que escondieron un santo porque estaba muy enfermo, no sé quién. Lo escondieron en una petaquilla aá muy lejos y sanó, pero Dios es el que lo sanaba. Cuando se le llega a uno la raya, no hay quien se escape. Ahi vamos, güenos y malos. Todos. Por eso digo yo que no hay que hablar ajuera de orden, porque no sabe uno qué le va tocar. Todos semos pecadores. Pero tiene uno que cuidarse tamién su reputación, porque yo dende que quedé viudo ya no quise ponelos yo mal aquí a mis hijos.

Ya no hay respeto casi como quien dice. Es tanta la perdición que hay y es causa, más que digan que no, de los TVs. Tavía cuando no entraba televisión, había muncho respeto. Pero muncha plebe mira ahi que matan y loo que roban, ya es mal ejemplo pa la juventú.

Yo le debo too al Divino Creador y a mis padres. Porque de ahi pallá, naiden.

Young Kids No Longer Like Catechism

Here, in this very place of ours [Las Vegas], they have taken away the priests who really cared. Then they [the Church] turn around and send us one we can't understand what he's saying. I have been a Catholic all of my life, and the church should give us what we need. Whenever we get a good priest, they take him away from us and put him somewhere else.

As for the young kids, they no longer like catechism, and those who are a little bit older, who also have a bit more sense, get discouraged. They don't want to go to church. As a result, we're better off here at home praying because we don't understand what the priest's saying. Right now we have an Italian, but I attend Mass because it is my responsibility. As long as God allows me to be on this earth, I'm going to go to Mass. I'm not going to change churches because I belong here. And we have had some very good priests.

As for this business of pedophile priests, it all has to do with money. Many of them are accused of crimes. A few end up paying for the misdeeds of others. The upright priest ends up paying for the sinner. Those are the kinds of things that deserve to be straightened out. As for the archbishop [Robert Sánchez, tenth archbishop of Santa Fe, 1974–1993; resigned amid allegations of sexual impropriety], well, he made a mistake. May God forgive him. That's God's responsibility. One must not be judgmental because of what you're told, because you never know what mistake you're likely to make in this life.

I believe in one thing. Look. The priests come here to perform a duty, those who come wholeheartedly. They come here to represent the Divine One who is Jesus Christ. There's a lot of things going on, and that's why I say that priests aren't doing their duty. They've been like that for years. A while back we had a very good priest here, and they took him away. They took him I don't where. I understand he's somewhere over close to Mexico.

Why, of course, you get scared because we are all sinners, but we have to live our lives. What we have to embrace is the Gospel. And if a priest goes by the Gospel, you respect him. He's accepted. In many cases, almost one hundred percent of the time, those who are well educated to be priests are guided by the Gospel. They don't come out with some other thing.

Now, there's something else I see—the thirst for money. We built a new place for these priests, the ones who came here very poor. As soon as people got together and began working, we built a very beautiful place for the priests where they could study or whatever they liked, and to pray whenever they wished. But lately things have changed; people aren't interested anymore.

For the religious processions there used to be, like, a parade. What do you call it? A parade from the church and all around the park.

First came the Mass, and then the fiesta got going. But it was very beautiful. They would put up decorations. Statues of saints. Flowers. They'd put up all kinds of things. And they used to put up, like, little chapels. That's where you stopped and prayed. You knelt and prayed. Then you went on to the next one, and the next one, until you went around the park. All that sort of thing is history.

I remember one time that people hid a *santo* because someone, I don't who, was very ill. They hid the *santo* in a footlocker somewhere far away and the sick person got well, but it's God who cured him. When your day comes, there's no escaping. There we go, the good as well as the bad. Everyone. That is why I say that it doesn't pay to speak out of school, because you never know what's going to come your way. We're all sinners. But you also have to watch your reputation, because ever since I became a widower, I didn't want to put my children in a bad light.

There's hardly any respect left. So much has gone awry, and it is as a result of television, even though some people may say not. Before television, there was still a lot of respect. But a lot of kids watch killings and robberies on television, and that's setting a bad example for the youth.

I owe everything to the Divine Creator, to my parents. Because from there on I don't owe anybody a thing.

Filimón Montoya

Lo que se está acabando es la creencia en la religión

Pus no. La religión no se está acabando. Lo que se está acabando es la creencia en la religión. Eso es lo que se está acabando. Y tal vez sean las iglesias, porque la gente se está aumentando o huyendo de las iglesias. Diremos de religión, que se comenzó en la iglesia. Hay religiones, diferentes religiones que hoy en día no tienen iglesias. Ahi ondequiera hacen servicios, en el campo. Pero sí digo yo que la creencia es la que se está acabando. Ya la gente no quiere creer lo que nuestros antepasados nos enseñaban—ya la mayor parte de los jóvenes, o los más jóvenes hoy en día, diremos. Tavía los jóvenes de

cuarenta años para arriba, tavía tienen respeto a la religión. Pero ya
los jóvenes, pior los *teenagers*, menos.

Antes sacaban los santos. Tenían tal santo que le dijían San Isidro,
San Isidro Labrador. San Isidro era el patrón de los labradores de la
tierra. Y si había una resequedá fuerte o un destrozo como cuando
caía granizo y destruía las labores, sacaban a San Isidro y lo pasiaban
por las labores, por el medio de la labor. No importaba que piso-
tiaran. "Para que vea lo que estaa sucediendo," dijían. Y luego sacaban tamién a l'estuata de María Santísima. Tamién sacaban Nuestra
Señora de los Dolores, la Imaculada, Nuestra Señora de Guadalupe, y
por ahi.

Y quizás tenían tanta fe que se les cumplían sus deseos. Pero la fe
yo creo era muy grande en esos días. Asina viene siendo ora que la
pérdida de la religión es que ya no hay fe. De respeto no hay fe.
Bueno, no habiendo respeto, ¿qué fe puede haber? Porque la misma
cosa que la pérdida del respeto a los mayores y la pérdida del respeto
a las propiedades ajenas, asina están perdiendo el respeto a la
religión. Asina es; asina la miro yo.

Lo que hacía mi mamá cuando había una tormenta muy fea, que
vinía el viento muy fuerte, casi como—¿cómo le dicen hoy en día?—
Los *tornadoes,* más o menos. Pero no eran *tornadoes.* Era *what you say,
what you would call miniature tornadoes.* Taramotes les llamaban. Y
levantaban muncho polvo y se escurecía too, too el valle. Lo que
hacía mi mamá de acuerdo con las costumbres de la Iglesia Católica,
que bendicen rama pal Domingo de Ramos, vinía y tenía siempre su
rama, y agarraba un ramito del brazo de rama que tenía, que estaa
bendicido, y lo echaba en la estufa. Le llamaba a Santa Bárbara o
alguien otro que calmara la tormenta, y se pasaba la tormenta. Ahi
estaa calmao too otra vez. Pero tenía la fe de hacer eso.

What Is Disappearing Is Belief in Religion

Why, no. Religion is not disappearing. What is disappearing is belief
in religion. That's what is coming to an end. And, yes, perhaps it's
because of the churches, because, increasingly, people are leaving the
church. At least leaving religion, which started in the church. There
are religions, different religions, that nowadays don't have a place to
worship. They conduct services in just about any old place, including out in the countryside. But, I reiterate, what is disappearing is

faith in religion. People no longer want to believe what our forefathers taught us—including the majority of young people, that is, today's youth. At least the young folks forty years and older, they still respect religion. But the younger ones, above all the teenagers, much less so.

A long time ago people used to have religious processions in which they paraded statues of the saints. They had a certain saint they called Saint Isidore, Saint Isidore the Farmer. Saint Isidore was looked upon as the patron saint of agricultural workers. And if a bad drought hit, or a disaster came, like from a hailstorm, and destroyed the cornfields, people would take out Saint Isidore and parade him through the cornfields, right smack in the middle of the cornfields. It didn't matter if they trampled all over them. "So that he can see what a mess he made," is what people would say. People also used to have religious processions during which they paraded Our Lady of Sorrows, the Immaculate Conception, Our Lady of Guadalupe, and so on.

And I guess people had so much faith that their wishes were fulfilled, yes indeed. But faith, I believe, was very strong back in those days. What is happening nowadays regarding the loss of religion is that people simply have lost faith. They've lost respect as well as faith. Consequently, there being no respect, how can there be faith? The same thing as a loss of respect toward elders, and the lack of respect for somebody else's property, that's what happening with regard to the loss of respect for religion. That's the way it is; that's the way I see it.

What Mom used to do whenever a very ugly thunderstorm came, when the wind blew really hard, almost like—what do you call it nowadays?—like tornadoes, more or less. But they weren't tornadoes. They were what you would call a miniature tornado. Whirlwinds is what they were called. They would raise a lot of dust and the entire valley would get dark. What Mom used to do, in accordance with Catholic Church tradition—the blessing of palms on Palm Sunday—is that she always had palms at home. She'd go and grab a tiny branch that was blessed and toss it in the wood stove, whereupon she called on Saint Barbara or some other saint to pacify the sandstorm. The sandstorm would pass, and everything would be calm once again. But a lot had to do with her faith in performing the ritual.

Cruzita Vigil

¡Han cambiao tanto los tiempos!

¡Han cambiao tanto los tiempos! De moo que ya está llegando la finación del mundo y too eso. Yo sí lo creo en la finación del mundo porque en la Biblia lo dice. Porque yo lo que hago leer mi Biblia y yo sí lo creo. Entre más y más aá vamos a llegar a cosas que nunca las hanos visto. Ya ora por eso no hay respeto de nada. Si matan una persona, ya lo mismo que matar un animal, porque ya hoy en día no hay lástima de nada. Ya hoy en día too va dediao, dediao. Ya too va del diablo. Ya too lo que está pasando ora está pasando del diablo, no de Dios.

The Times Have Changed!

The times have changed! The truth of the matter is, the end of creation and all that sort of thing is coming. I for one believe that the world is going to end, because the Bible tells us. Because what I do is read the Bible, and I believe in it. The more we stop to think about it, the more we're going to see things we've never seen in the past. That is one of the reasons why there's no respect for anything. If a person is killed, it's the same thing as slaughtering an animal, because nowadays there's no compassion for anything. Nowadays, everything is related to the devilish kinds of things. Everything stems from the devil. Everything that's happening nowadays is because of the devil, not God.

6

La política de siempre
Politics as Usual

Introduction

In looking across New Mexico's history, from the colonial period to the twenty-first century, politics has invariably played a major role. In more modern times, the political scene has been of great interest even to the average citizen, particularly in the northern part of the state. Certain counties, among them Río Arriba, Mora, and San Miguel, have attracted their share of attention—both favorable and unfavorable—since the early part of the twentieth century.

When I returned to New Mexico in 1986 after a long absence, I heard an anecdote concerning politics in my native state. The episode goes as follows: If you want to earn a B.A. in politics, you go to Boston; if you wish to pursue an M.A., you go to Texas; but if you opt for a Ph.D., you come to New Mexico. Furthermore, not long ago a newspaper in Albuquerque carried a wire story citing our state as one of the most politically corrupt in the nation. Whether this is true is not for me to judge.

Within a few months of making Las Vegas, New Mexico, my residence, I was reminded by a number of people, including colleagues at New Mexico Highlands University, of the politics endemic not just to San Miguel County, but also to Las Vegas in particular. Undaunted, I was proud to inform people that my maternal great-grandmother hailed from Mora, New Mexico, north of Las Vegas.

Politics in Mora County, I was told, has enjoyed no more or less of a good reputation than in San Miguel County.

Little by little I began to appreciate the warnings concerning local political tendencies—not from those born here but from outsiders. Some non-natives viewed politics as something "cultural," a euphemism attributed in part to the *patrón,* or patronage, system associated with Hispanics, both Democrats and Republicans.

As I was growing up in rural New Mexico, I learned by observing my immediate and extended families that the wives had to toe the political line and vote according to the husband's party affiliation. As offspring came of voting age, they, too, were expected to follow suit. Eventually, children (such as my father) broke ranks with tradition (most farmer-ranchers like my paternal grandfather evidently belonged to the Republican Party) and switched parties—from Republican to Democrat.

From time to time I heard the following expression from grown-up men during elections: "Ése no quiere más de estar mamando de la chiche." Loosely translated, albeit the literal interpretation is much more earthy, it means, "All that guy wants to do is to feed at the public trough." In some circles the words are not restricted only to politicians; rather, they refer to underlings or cronies and to all those who in some way reap the benefits of supporting the winning candidate on election day. The payoff comes, for example, in securing jobs for supporters in state, county, or city government.

On a larger scale, those payoffs nowadays are categorized as pork-barrel politics. It is a national phenomenon (some call it a cancer) that transcends political ideology and is pervasive from Washington, D.C., to state capitals, where politicians wield a certain influence. Pork-barrel handouts, often disguised as capital outlay in New Mexico, range in the tens of millions of dollars. Politicians with seniority flex their political muscle to get more money for their districts. These monies may include millions of dollars for public buildings or hundreds for speed bumps in a neighborhood.

Pet projects come to the forefront at the end of a legislative session, which is when pork-barrel largess is doled out to remind voters that their governor, senator, or representative is hard at work on their behalf (capital outlay monies are usually divided equally between the governor, the House, and the Senate). Critics claim that such projects are nothing more than quid pro quo political favors to ingratiate public officials to voters, especially at election time.

Nevertheless, in the eyes of the layperson, politics is a game politicos play. While politics may well be the art of compromise, the average citizen—if the countless oral interviews I have conducted with Hispanic old-timers since the late 1970s are any indication— has a different perception of politics as well as an unflattering assessment of politicians. Perhaps a good analogy is the pendulum on a grandfather clock: it swings back and forth without holding a firm position. Ordinary people look on politicians as being fickle for political expediency's sake.

Virtually none of the *ancianos* featured in this chapter (eight men and one woman) are very sympathetic when speaking about politics or politicians. Arguably, it is not fair to paint everyone with the same brush, because there are, after all, honorable and decent elected officials at the national, state, and local levels. On the other hand, private citizens believe that politicos are probably their own worst enemies. My informants talk about payoffs, bribery, dead voters, broken campaign promises, vote buying, a lack of respect for the public, and almost total disregard for the voters once someone is elected. None of this endears politicians to the average citizen.

Cesaria Montoya and Alfredo Ulibarrí set the tone for this chapter in "Politics Has Always Been the Same" and "Politicians Haven't Changed," respectively. Alfredo Trujillo unloads a scathing attack on politicians, especially the Republicans, in "There Was No Honesty in Politics."

Some of the interviewees' depictions of politicians are blunt and to the point. Filiberto Esquibel, who was politically inclined but became disillusioned with politics, calls politicians "a bunch of liars," although he does have some kind words for one or two of them. While equally harsh in his treatment of politicos, Andrés Archuleta describes them in a more humorous vein. He says, "Politicians are like pigs. All day long they hit each other with their snouts but at night they sleep together." (Politics makes for strange bedfellows!) Filimón Montoya is no kinder when he talks about "rancid politicians."

As for the political scene in Las Vegas of years gone by, Guadalupe Luján, a native, enlightens us about what politics was like in the early twentieth century, when he was a young Democrat in

Republican-dominated territory. "Politics," he says, "was very corrupt here in Las Vegas. . . . It was like the Wild, Wild West." He
talks about politicians killing and shooting each other right in his
own neighborhood.

If one examines closely each of the stories in this chapter, perhaps
the unflattering portrayal of politics and most politicians is not so
farfetched. Let us consider for a moment some of the rhetoric that
state and local politicians used between 1994 and 2002—which has
appeared in newspapers—to lambaste their opponents during elections: fraud, lies, misstatements, dirty tricks, smear tactics, attacks,
mudslinging, dirty politics, half-truths, and so on. A state party
chairman even described a member of his own party as having a rot-
ted brain.

Maybe people's attitudes about politics and politicians, as Cesaria
Montoya and her contemporaries tell us, have changed very little
over the course of time. What appears to have intensified, in addition to negative rhetoric and personal accusations, is a lack of deco-
rum among elected officials. Within recent memory, some politicians in New Mexico have been accused of, and in some cases
indicted for, drunken driving, sexual misconduct, battery, bribery,
mismanagement of funds, filing false per diem and mileage reim-
bursement claims, and malfeasance. Who knows but what there may
be some truth to Andrés Archuleta's assertion that "politics isn't
sweet even when it's sugarcoated." His account, coupled with those
of his contemporaries, serves as personal testimony to the Machi-
avellian approach politicians take to justify their actions.

Cesaria Montoya

La política siempre ha sido igual

Todo lo que me acuerdo es que no me gustaban las—¿cómo les
dicían?—cometivas. Que iban los políticos, oradores que les dicían. A
mí no me gustaban sus oraciones, o cómo se llamen [risas], porque se
me hacía que no íbanos a bailar. Ahi estaban hable y hable y hable.
Eso es lo que me acuerdo que a mí no me gustaba. El baile que había
después, eos llevaban vino.

La política siempre ha sido igual. Siempre ha sido igual. [Risas] ¡Puras mentiras! Agarraban el aposento y ahi se acabó lo güeno. No se volvían acordar de uno. Uno de los candidatos, aquí [en Las Vegas]—que taa ni lo conocía bien—jue y me dijo que si le iba ayudar. Güeno, sí lo conocía, *you know,* pero no, no muy bien. Y le dije,

—Te voy ayudar, pero si ganas, ¿qué va pasar? Si cuando entres, si tú ganas, ¿me vas a conocer despúes tú a mí?

—Pus ya la conozco.

—Sí— le dije—, pero yo te apuesto que nomás ganas ya no te vuelves acordar quién soy. Si me topas en la calle, a qué no me vas a saludar.

—Le prometo— dijo—, que si no le hablo, la dejo que me dé mis patadas.

—Tú lo has dicho— le dije. [Risas]

No. Ni me acuerdo qué pasó. Oh, sí, sí ganó. Pero cuando lo vide le dije,

—¿Te doy tus patadas ora o te las doy después?

—No—dijo—. No me puedes dar patadas porque gané y voy hacer lo que prometí.

Y sí, jue güen político. [Risas] Oh, la mayor parte no son más de que quieren la chanza. Ya agarrándola, ahi se acabó.

Politics Has Always Been the Same

What I recall very well is that I didn't like—what do you call them?—political rallies. That's when the politicians, orators as they were called, showed up. I didn't like speeches or whatever you call them [laughter], because it seemed to me as though we were never going to get to dance. There they were talking and talking and talking. That's what I recall that didn't please me. The dance that came after the rally included wine that they brought.

Politics has always been the same. It's always been the same. [Laughter] Nothing but lies! Once politicians won the race, that was the end of their dignity. They forgot about you completely. One of the candidates here in Las Vegas—whom I didn't know very well—went and asked me if I was going to help him out. Well, I did know him, you know, but not very, very well. And I said to him, "I'm going to help you out, but what's going to happen afterwards? When you get into office, if you win, are you going to know who I am later on?"

"Well, I already know you."

"Yes," I said to him, "but I bet you anything that once you win you won't even know who I am. If you bump into me in the street, I bet you won't greet me."

"I promise," he said, "that if I don't say hello to you, I'll let you kick me in the butt."

"You said it, not me," I responded. [Laughter]

Why, no. I don't even remember what happened. Oh, yeah, he won. But when I saw him I said to him, "Do you want me to kick you in the butt now or later?"

"No," he remarked. "You can't kick me because I won and I'm going to carry out my promises."

And yes, he turned out to be a good politician. [Laughter] But yes, the majority of them, all they want is a chance to get voted into office. Once they're in, that's the end of their promises and everything.

Alfredo Ulibarrí

No han cambiao los políticos

Nomás cuando había las cometivas esas de los políticos, antonces íbanos a los bailes de ahi de Jorupa. Iba yo tamién a los bailes allá a La Lagunita. Ésos eran los únicos bailes que iba. O al Chapel. Too eso de ahi andaba.

Güeno, los políticos que andaban corriendo eran como Ceferino Quintana y asina de los puros políticos que yo conocí. Al dijunto Lorenzo Delga[d]o. Ésos sí los conocí yo cuando iban a las políticas y eso. Es too lo que yo sé de eos. Taa estaa muy mediano yo, pero yo llegaba ir en ese tiempo cuando eos andaan corriendo política.

Comenzaan [en los bailes] como hablar de lo que estaan corriendo, a esto o lotro. Loo después tocaan una pieza y la bailaan y loo comenzaa hablar otra vez el político. Iban varios políticos. Cada político hablaba pa qué andaa corriendo, y loo bailaban otra vez, una pieza *in between*. Ya después acabaan de hablar y seguían con su fiestecita, 'andoles trago o esto y lotro a la gente allí. Loo seguía el baile hasta las doce o la una de la noche.

Los políticos eran a lo mismo los de ora. Porque ora [risas], es la misma cosa de antes. No han cambiao los políticos. Por mi parte no han cambiao. Ora son más enbusteros. [Risas] Güeno, antes eran más decentes, *you know*. A lo menos hablaban y si te prometían alguna cosa, te la cumplían si eras del lao de eos. Te la cumplían; te ayudaban. Y ora más que les hables tú o éste o lotro ahi te traen en güeltas y no te hacen nada. Pero antes, sí te ayudaban.

Antes cuando el tiempo de las eleciones un hermano mío sacaba el carro de mi papá y iba a correr paá pa diferentes ranchos porque antonces los del Pino vinían a votar a La Lagunita. Los de Solano y too eso los traiba él de aá de Solano a votar ahi. O algunos de ahi de Chapel que no tenían con qué, porque del Ojito pa bajo corrían pal rumbo de La Lagunita a votar, y los de Chapel ya corrían pacá pal rumbo de Bernal o pal Tecolote.

Me acuerdo de una mujer candidata. La—¿cómo se llamaa aquea?—Higgins, Ann Higgins, y la mujer del Franque. Ann se llamaba también ésa. Había algunas [mujeres].

Politicians Haven't Changed

Whenever there were those political rallies, then we'd go to the dances there in Jorupa. I also went to the dances in La Lagunita. Those were the only places I went to, or in Chapel. I went to all of those places around there.

Well, the politicians who were running for office were like Ceferino Quintana and so forth, of the real politicians that I knew. The late Lorenzo Delgado. Those are the ones I knew myself whenever they held their political get-togethers and that sort of thing. That's all I know. I was still young, but I got to go to them back then when they were running for office.

At the dances they kicked things off by talking about their platform, or this or that. Then came a dance, which politicians danced to, and then a politician resumed his speech. Several politicians used to attend. Each politician spoke about what office he was running for, and then they danced again, a dance in between speeches. Later on, when the speeches were over, their little celebration went on, as they gave a drink or this or that to the people present. The dance then went on until midnight or one o'clock in the morning.

Politicians back then were the same as the politicians of today.

Because nowadays [laughter], it's the same thing as before. Politicians haven't changed. For my part they haven't changed. Nowadays, they're even more of a liar. [Laughter] Well, long ago they were more decent, you know. At least if they promised you something, they fulfilled their promise, provided you were on their side. They kept their promises; they helped you out. And now, even though you may talk to them about this or that, they do nothing but give you the runaround. But long ago they did help you out.

A long time ago, during elections, a brother of mine would take out my father's car and he made the rounds to different ranches, because at that time people from El Pino came to vote in La Lagunita. He used to bring people from Solano and places around there to vote there in La Lagunita. Or he brought people from Chapel if they didn't have a way, because from El Ojito on down they went to La Lagunita to vote, but people from Chapel voted in Bernal or in Tecolote.

I can recall a woman candidate. What was her name? Higgins, Ann Higgins, and Frank's wife. Ann was also her name. Yes, there were female candidates.

José Nataleo Montoya

Embusteros como orita eran los políticos

Pus embusteros como orita eran los políticos. [Risas] Toos iban ahi a San Pablo. Hacían bailes. En esos tiempos hacían cometivas. Oradores les dijían en ese tiempo. Pus llegaban y ponían eos su música. Ahi vinía el Luis Encinias. Me acuerdo qu'era uno de eos de los muy mentaos en ese tiempo. Y deje ver quién otro. Meregildo Romero. Varios asina, pero hablaban muncho. Todos hacían unas historias tremendas. Pus a mí se me hacía que se estaan muncho, porque hablaban muncho y logo tocaban una pieza y loo vinía lotro y asina.

Luego salía el director de l'escuela. Tamién hablaba su parte él y los comisionaos de los del precinto y por ahi. El cuento es que todos hablaban y algunos hablaban bien, pero otros, no. Otros se salían del ajuero del olla. Hablaban de cosas que no habían de hablar, como que su familia era muy güena y por ahi. De cosas asina. "Y que éste es mi primo, anda corriendo, y que muy güena gente," y echándole al otro lao tamién. Como si eran los republicanos, le echaban a los demócratas, y los demócratas a los republicanos. "Si los sacamos de ahi, pus vamos a quedar mejor. Y el día que vayan, si yo soy electo, el día que vayan paá pa mi ofecina, yo estoy listo." No, pus, si le tocó que ganó éste, iban y no lo jallaban. Sí. [Risas]

De modo que, sí, siempre andaan echando mentiras. ¡Pus no podían cumplir con todos! Que tavía este Ernesto Ribal, ¿no lo ha oido mentar, comisionao? Era de allá de San Gerónimo. ¡Qué comisionao era! Ahi cuando andaba corriendo me dijo,

—Oye, Joe. Ayúdame.

—¿Pus qué andas haciendo corriendo? —le digo yo.

—Usté sabe. Ando corriendo pa comisionao.

—Güeno —le digo—. Y si ganas, ¿cuándo nos vas hacer el puente?

—Después que gane —dijo.

Le respondí,

—Pus estaa un señor que andaa corriendo política ahi, pa tal puesto, y que si él ganaba les iba hacer un puente en el pueblo ese que onde estaba. Tocó la casualidá que no había ni río. [Risas] Asina estás tú—a los de hoy.

Oh sí, es muncha diferencia hoy porque antonces tenían los políticos la oportunidá de hablar todo lo que quisieran eos, y salían en cometiva, ¿ve? A todos los pueblos andaban asina. Ahi llevaan su galón o unos galones de vino y embolaban a toos los mayores, porque a la plebe cuasi no les daban puerta con el trago. Pero munchos sí se emborrachaban de los de ahi que les gustaba el licor.

Pus ya las cometivas salieron a la orilla. Ésas ya ni se oyen mentar. Pus una cometiva es onde se juntaban los candidatos, los candidatos de un partido. En igual de andar como ahora que andan por una casa, queriendo agarrar votos, hacían la cometiva esta pa que se juntara toa la gente. Era onde explicaban eos [los políticos] el detalle pa qué andaban corriendo.

Politicians Back Then Were Liars, Just Like Today

Politicians back then were liars, just like today. [Laughter] They used to go to San Pablo. They had dances. Back then they had what were called political rallies. Politicians were called orators back then. They'd get there and they started the music. There came Luis Encinias. I recall that he was one of the better-known names in those days. And let me see who else. Meregildo Romero. There were several like him, but they talked a lot. They all came up with some humdingers. I thought they spoke too much and then in between dances, there came another politician and so on.

Then it was the school principal's turn. He also had his say, as did the commissioners from the various precincts, and so forth. Fact is that they all spoke and some were quite articulate, but others were not. Others missed the point entirely. They spoke of things that were irrelevant, such as that their families were good citizens and so on. Things like that. "And this is my cousin who's running for office, and he's a very good person," and at the same time criticizing the opponent. For example, if they were Republicans, they spoke badly of the Democrats, and the Democrats did the same thing to the Republicans. "If we vote them out of office, we're going to be better off. And if I'm elected, the day you go to my office, I'm ready to help you." Why, no, if by chance this guy won, people went over there and they couldn't find him. [Laughter]

Fact is, of course, that they were always telling lies. Why, they couldn't please everyone! Like this Ernesto Ribal, have you heard of him, a commissioner? He was from over there in San Gerónimo. What a commissioner! One time when he was running for office he said to me, "Listen, Joe. Help me."

"What's up? Are you running for office?" I said to him.

"You know. I'm running for commissioner."

"Okay," I responded. "And if you win when are you going build us our bridge?"

"After I win," he remarked.

I said to him, "It so happened that there was this gentleman who came around politicking for a certain position and promised that if he won he was going to build a bridge for the people in the village where he was campaigning. And there it was. There wasn't even a river. [Laughter] That's the way you are, just like everyone else."

Oh, yes. There's no question but what there is a lot of difference today, because in the past politicians had the opportunity of speaking for as long as they wanted, and so they'd show up at these political rallies, you see? That's the way they were in every village. There they went with their gallon or gallons of wine and they'd get all the adult men drunk, because the young men barely got their foot in the door when it came to getting a drink. But many men, those from the community who liked liquor, did get drunk.

As for the political rallies of yesteryear, they've gone by the wayside. You don't even hear them mentioned anymore. A so-called political rally is where the candidates gathered, those from a particular party. Instead of going house to house, as they do now, trying to win votes, they would hold their rallies so people would attend. It was a place where politicians explained in detail why they were running for office.

Alfredo Trujillo

No había honestidá de la política

Oh, los políticos, pos nomás eos querían estar logrando de todo. Porque ya de que un partido estaa arriba, ése nomás lograba. El que estaa abajo, no. No podía levantar. Y luego iban éstos, los que tenían *business* ahi en la política, iban pa los lugares allá a cuidar la gente que votaba.

No había honestidá de la política; no había honestidá. ¡Nada! No, ninguna. ¡Nada, nada! El que fregaba, fregaba, y ése es todo. El que estaba arriba eos querían mandar. Luego nojotros como estáanos jóvenes, pus toa la familia tenía que votar como votaba el papá. ¡Toa la familia! De modo es que ahi estábanos nojotros. Teníanos que votar como él mandaba. Yo jui republicano como veinticinco años. No toqué nada, hasta que me cansé yo d'esa política.

Cuando ya me cambié pacá pa Las Vegas [del rancho], pus iba yo pallá pa que me dieran trabajo tan siquiera en el asilo allá arriba. No había chanza. Estaan los republicanos toos ganaos ahi. Eos nomás mandaban. Nomás eos ocupaban los que les daba gana, ¿ve? El que estaba en el partido que estaa caido, pus ahi estaba. No había chanza. Y yo iba pallá a ver si me daban trabajo. "Que ven lotra semana, que ven lotra y lotra y lotra." Pasaban las semanas. Ahi me traiban, hasta

que me cansé yo y le dije a uno que estaba allí encargao d'este negocio de agarrar gente pa trabajar, le dije,

—Güeno, pus yo creo que yo voy a comenzar a trabajar de otro
modo.

Y ¿qué cree que me dijo?

—Ya había de haber comenzao.

—Munchas gracias— le dije—. *Thank you*— y me salí.

Y lego estaba Polonio Durán de *chairman* de los demócratas,
porque como no me querían hacer aprecio los republicanos, yo dije,
"Vale más cambiar porque, pus, éstos [los republicanos] no me dan
nada," y yo lo que quería era trabajar. No quería que me dieran dao
nada. Pero no, no había chanza. Loo vino Polonio Durán pacá pa mi
casa. Él supo que yo estaa nojao con los republicanos. Vino a dar
aquí. Antonces me dijo,

—Oye, Alfredo— me dijo—. ¿Pus qué no me quieres ayudar tú? Si
tú nos ayudas a nojotros, yo te ayudo a ti.

—Que no se diga más. "*O'right, o'right*— le dije.

—Yo te ayudo— me dijo. Y cierto. Como a la semana me mandó
una carta que me reportara aá en el Meadow Home [para los
ancianos]. Antonces ya comencé yo a trabajar.

¡Pero cuarenta años se estuvieron los republicanos ganaos! Y los
demócratas estaban en la caida, pero despúes cuando Polonio subió
el partido demócrata parriba, antonces se voltió toa la gente [en Las
Vegas] demócrata.

Más antes lo compraban a uno, pero a mí no me pudieron comprar, porque no me gustaa a mí eso—vender mi voto. Me llegaan a
ofrecer dinero y me llegaan a dar trago. Y les dije,

—No. Yo soy un hombre ciudadano y yo mi voto yo lo mando.

Porque aquí mismo don Severo [Lucero?] una vez era de los
grandes ahi, que compraa la gente con dinero o algo, y quería a
huevo las cosas. ¿Sabe cómo le digo? Quería que hablara con en
papá, que lo consiguiera porque en papá estaa nojao con eos porque,
pus, seguro que no consiguía naa. Y don Severo un día me llamó
pallá par una junta que tenían eos privada. Estaan varios en la junta
esa. Pero me llamó a mí pallá; me envitó pa dijirme que hablara con
en papá, que yo podía con él, y a ver si lo consiguía yo pa que se con-
tentara con eos de algún modo.

—¿Qué no puees hablar tú con tu papá y dijile que nos ayude?

—No— le dije—. Yo no pueo. Él manda su voto solo y yo mando el mío. No pueo hacer eso. Yo mando mi voto nomás y el dél es el dél.

—No— dijo—. Toma dinero.

—Si no necesito su dinero.

Me daba dinero a mí. Aunque estuviera pobre como estuviera no iba agarrar su dinero. Y no lo agarré.

—Muchísimas gracias— le dije.

Ahi nos peliamos en la maldita junta esa, porque yo me defendía bien.

—Y ustees— le dije yo—, los que estaan en esos negocios de política, son muy gentes ustees cuando viene la política pa que los voten. Y usté, don Severo, me ha encontrao en la plaza munchas veces, y no me habla. ¿Por qué ora? [Risas]

—¡Mientes tú!— me dijo.

—Pus no miento, porque yo lo he topao en la calle ahi, y nunca me habla. ¿Por qué ora?

Nos peliamos en la junta. Yo me defendía muy bien; no me dejaa. Pus no volvió.

No eran muy honestos [los políticos]. Ni son toavía ora mismo. Hay gavillas ahi que son gavillitas eos, y nomás los que eos quieren. Ponen un *mayor,* y el *mayor* no manda nada. El grupito ese que está es el que manda, porque eos quieren estar nomás mamando. No puee entrar otra persona si eos no les dan el trabajo. Meten a los d'eos. A la gente d'eos meten. Asina estaa antes también. Nomás que ora no está tanto asina, pero antes sí. Estaa pior.

There Was No Honesty in Politics

Oh, politicians, why, they wanted everything for themselves. Because once a party was on top, it was the one that profited. Not the party that was down and out. It couldn't pick itself up. And then you had these guys, those who had their fingers in politics, they'd go to the voting places to spy on the people who voted.

There was no honesty in politics; there was no honesty. None at all! No, none whatsoever. None, none! The one who screwed you, screwed you, and that's all there was to it. Those who were on top wanted to run things. Then those of us who were young, why, we all had to vote just like our fathers. The entire family! So, there we were. We had to vote just as he told us to. I was a Republican for about twenty-five years. I didn't get anything out of it, until I got fed up with their politics.

By the time I moved to Las Vegas from the ranch, well, I'd go over there so they would give me work at least at the sanatorium [State Hospital] located up north. No chance. All of the Republicans were in control. They were the political bosses. They hired whomever they felt like, you see? He who belonged to the defeated party, there he was. He didn't have a chance. And I'd go over there to see if they would employ me. "Well, come back next week, and next week, and next." Weeks would go by. They had me going round and round, until I got fed up and I said to one of the political kingpins who was in charge of hiring people, I said to him, "Very well. I guess I'm going to have to start using a different tactic."

What do you think he said to me? "You should have started a long time ago," he said.

"Thank you very much," I said to him. "Thank you," and I left.

And then, as it happened, Polonio Durán was chairman of the Democrats, because it was the Republicans who didn't want to pay any attention to me, and I said to myself, "I better change parties because these guys [the Republicans] won't give me anything," and what I wanted was to work. I didn't want a handout. But no, there was no chance. Then Polonio Durán came over to my house. He knew I was mad at the Republicans. He stopped by. Then he said to me, "Listen, Alfredo. Wouldn't you like to help me out? If you help us, I'll help you."

"Say no more," I said to him. "O'right, o'right."

"I'll help you," he told me, and sure enough. Within a week he sent me a letter to report to Meadow Home [for the aged]. And that's how I started to work.

But the Republicans were in power for forty years! And the Democrats were the underdogs, but later on, when Polonio put the party on its feet, then all of the people in Las Vegas turned Democrat.

Long ago you were bought, but nobody ever bought me, because I didn't like that sort of business—selling my vote. There were times when I was offered money or offered a drink. And I said to them, "No. I'm a private citizen and my vote is mine."

Because right here in Las Vegas, one time there was Don Severo [Lucero ?]. He was one of the bigwigs who used to buy people off with money or something, and he wanted his way by hook or by crook. Do you understand what I mean? He wanted me to talk to my father, for him to come around because Dad was mad at them because, well, he couldn't get anything out of them. And so one day Don Severo asked me to attend a private meeting that they were having. There were several present at the meeting. But he called me over; he invited me to tell me to talk to my father, since I could approach him, to see if I could somehow get him to mend fences with them.

"Can't you talk to your father to ask him to help us?"

"No," I said to him. "I can't. His vote is his and mine is mine. I can't do that. My vote is mine and mine alone and his is his alone."

"Why, no," he said. "Here's some money."

"Why, I don't need your money!"

He wanted to give me some money. Even though I was poor I wasn't about to take his money. And I didn't take it.

"Thank you very much," I added.

And that's where we got into it, in that damn meeting, because I could defend myself pretty well.

"As for all of you," I said to them, "those of you who meddle in politics, you're very much the gentlemen when election time comes around so that people will vote for you. As for you, Don Severo, you've bumped into me out in the plaza many times, and you haven't said boo. Why now?" [Laughter]

"You're a liar!" he said to me.

"I don't lie," I countered, "because I have run into you in the street, and you never talk to me. Why now?"

We got into it in the meeting. I could take care of myself pretty good. I didn't let anybody push me around. That was the end of that.

They [the politicians] weren't very honest. No, nor are they even now. There's these gangs, these little cliques, and only those they favor are part of their group. They put a mayor in and the mayor doesn't have a say. The clique is the one that runs things, because those in the group want to be constantly feeding at the public trough. No one can join their group or get a job unless they let you. They only take care of their own. That's the way it was a long time ago. Not so much so today, but in years past, yes. It was worse.

Filiberto Esquibel

¡Son una bola de embusteros!

No hay diferencia. No hay diferencia. Hay algunos políticos que dicen, "Pues, si yo entro en un puesto de ésos, se va enderezar esa cosa." Algunos hacen lo que prometieron. Muy pocos. ¡Los demás son una bola de embusteros! Sale un embustero y entra lotro que estaa más antes y asina. D'ese moo la miro yo. No hay verdá. Hay muncha leperaa hoy en día entre la política. Y cuando menos acuerda uno, hay algunos que ni a l'escuela jueron. Cuando andan corriendo pa política, tienen unos sartificaos grandes y que sabe qué tanto. Loo los topa uno y no saben nada. O se echan el caldo pallá que pallá.

Yo estoy muy quemao. Yo los políticos, yo no les abro la puerta. Si a mí me gusta un hombre que yo lo conozco, es derecho, anda corriendo, yo hago too lo posible por ayudale. Pal beneficio de toa la gente, no par uno. Ni par un grupo que sea legal. Toa la raza semos iguales. Toos semos ser humanos. A todos nos duele; toos sintemos. Toos tenemos la misma necidá—bebemos y comemos y pisamos la misma tierra.

Y eso se sopone ser una persona que anda corriendo par un puesto como sea, concilario, que son los que jalan más duro, o correr pa *mayor*, correr pa gobernador, pal beneficio del público. Porque pa toos es la misma cosa l'agua—a unos nos hace bien, a otro le echó a perder. Pero hace bien y hace mal. Va uno figurando pa uno o pa lotro [político], porque no toos pueen tenernos contentos. Lo que es bien par uno puee ser mal par otro.

Pus yo no me junto muncho con los políticos. Pero ora la política la entiendo muy bien poco yo. Yo conozco a toa la gente [los políticos] aquí en Las Vegas hoy día. ¡A toos! Diun moo los ha conocido, pero la verdá, ya no es sólida [la política]. Más antes, usté le chakiaa la mano a un hombre, y le daba su palabra. No nesitaa papeles; no nesitaa naa. Valía su palabra.

¡Ora no! "¿Me puees comprar esto o puees comprar lotro?" ¡Mal por abajo! Eso miro yo que no me gusta, y no me gusta monquiar con la política a mí por eso. Por esa razón. Porque hay en veces que éste jala pa lotro. "Es mi cuate; aquél me ayudó. No, no vamos a comprar a naiden." No son individuales ora. Ora son en grupos. Eso no sirve. Un hombre tiene que ser derecho pa los dos laos. No agarrar lao. Y siempre la política se ha podío comprar uno al otro. Se compraan los jueces, se compraan los políticos, y eso no se cambiará. Lo vemos de bien abajo—de un concilario, hasta los grandotes en Washington.

De moo que toa la vida ha 'bido léperos ende que se comenzó, yo creo, el mundo. Hasta el día que se acabe, yo creo va a ver d'eso. Eso no se acabará. Ahi está. Ahi está mal y no tiene uno que vivir por la porquería que hizo el político. "Él que hizo el pozo, no se revolcó en él." Asina está la política.

Yo jui deputado tres veces abajo de tres diferentes sherifas: el sherifa Frank Bergan y loo Pat Romero. Y fueron hombres muy, muy derechos. Eran hombres muy, muy derechos. En ese tiempo había hombres mayores. Tenían diferente valor al respeto.

They're a Bunch of Liars!

There's no difference. There's no difference. There are politicians who say, "Well, if I'm elected to one of those offices, things are going to get straightened out." Some keep their promises. Very few. The rest, they're a bunch of liars! One liar is defeated, and another one who was in office before gets back in, and so it goes. That's the way I see it. There's no honesty. There's too much connivance nowadays in politics. And when you least expect it, you find out that some politicians didn't even go to school. When they're running for office, they claim to have very important certificates [credentials] and who knows what all. Then you run into them and they don't know anything. Or they boast here and there about one thing or another.

I'm an old hat at that sort of thing. When it comes to politicians, I won't open the door. If I like a man I know, and he's straight [honest], who's running, I do everything possible to help him, for the benefit of all of the people, not just for one person. Nor just for one group, even if it's legitimate. All of our people are equal. We're all human beings. We all hurt; we all have feelings. We all have the same needs—we drink and eat and walk the same earth.

And that's what a person running for office supposedly represents, whether he's a city council candidate, who are the ones who do more for you, or a mayoral or gubernatorial candidate, for the benefit of the people. Because the water is the same for all of us—it helps some of us, and others it ruins. It has its good and bad effects. You begin to lean toward one politician or the other, because they can't all keep us happy. What's good for one individual may be bad for another.

Well, I don't mix much with politicians. When it comes to today's politics, I understand it very little. I know all of the present politicians in Las Vegas. Every one! I've known them in one way or another, but the truth is, politics is no longer honorable. Long ago, you were able to shake a man's hand, and he'd give you his word. You didn't need papers; you didn't need anything. His word was worth something.

Not so now! "Can you buy me this or the other?" Bad stuff under the table! That's what I see that I don't like, and that's one reason I don't like to monkey around with politics. That's the reason. There's times when this guy pulls for the other. "He's my buddy. He helped me. Why, no, we aren't going to buy anyone." Nowadays, they're not their own man. Now they belong to this guy's group and so on. That's not good. A man has to be honest with both sides, not take sides. And in politics one party or another has been able to buy this person or that one. Judges used to be bought, politicians could be bought, and that won't change. We see it from top to bottom—from a city council member all the way up to the bigwigs in Washington.

Fact is that there's always been petty thieves, ever since the world began, I suppose. Till the day the world comes to an end, I guess you'll have thievery. That will never stop. There you are. That's what's wrong, and we shouldn't have to suffer because of the crappy mess that the politician makes. "He dug his own hole, but didn't wallow in it." That's the way politics is.

I was deputy sheriff three times under three different sheriffs: Frank Bergan and later Pat Romero. And they were very, very honest men. They were very, very straight. Back then men were older. They had a different sense of value when it came to respect.

Andrés Archuleta

Los políticos son como los marranos

¡Ahi, me dio en la cabeza! No. No hay ninguna diferencia entre los políticos de antes [y los de hoy], ni habrá, porque yo tengo experiencia. Yo jui político, hasta que me desengañé que too era lo mismo. Y me quité, y me ladié, porque too es lo mismo.

Como dijían los viejos de antes, "Los políticos son como los marranos. Todo el día se tronpean y en la noche duermen juntos." ¿Eh? No es mentira. Ése es la política. Yo no jui candidato de ninguna forma, pero peliaba en la política. Trabajaba, como le digo, hasta que me desengañé. Éste jue un condao [San Miguel] por más de yo no sé cuántos años, y estuvo en lo que le nombran republicano. Y yo pelié por ver un cambio, hasta cuando ganó el Roosevelt, que hubo cambio del republicano al demócrata. Hubo cambio nomás de políticos asina, pero cambio de manejo, no. Siguió lo mismo. Y no tiene cambio. La política no tiene cambio. Es como le digo. Son [los políticos] lo mismo que los marranos. ¿Entiende usté, o ha visto una cría de marranos? Es la misma cosa. En el día, todo el día, se tronpean. En la noche duermen juntos.

Toda la vida ha 'bido de toas clases de hombres. Ora mismo hay honestos y hay sinvergüenzas, pero eso lo ha 'bido toa la vida. Usté lo sabe.

Por eso le digo que la política ni de azúcar es duce. [Risas]

Politicians Are Like Pigs

Boy, you really hit me between the eyes! No. There's no difference between the politicians of yesteryear and today's, nor will there be, because I know from experience. I was a politician once, until I found out that everything was the same. And I quit; I stepped aside, because everything's the same.

As the old-folks of years gone by used to say, "Politicians are like pigs. All day long they hit each other with their snouts, but at night they sleep together." Huh? It's not a lie. That's politics for you. I was never a candidate for anything, but I got involved in politics. I used to work at it, as I mentioned, until I became disillusioned. This county of San Miguel, for I don't know how many years, was in the hands of the Republicans. And I fought for a change, until Roosevelt won, which is when there was a change in parties from Republicans to Democrats. There was a change in politicians only, but a change in how business was conducted, no. Things continued the same old way. And it hasn't changed. Politics never changes. Just as I'm telling you. Politicians are the same as pigs. Do you understand what I'm saying? Have you ever seen a litter of pigs? It's the same thing. During the day, all day long, they hit each other with their snouts. But at night they sleep together.

Throughout life there's been men of all types. Right now you'll find honest ones as well as scoundrels, but that's always been true. You know that yourself.

That's why I'm telling you that politics isn't sweet even when it's sugarcoated. [Laughter]

Filimón Montoya

Los políticos rancios

Pus siempre ha 'bido políticos buenos y ha 'bido políticos rancios, que les dijían. Los políticos rancios eran los que no largaban el puesto, que querían estar ahi too el tiempo, too el tiempo, hasta que vinía otra generación y los echaba juera. A ésos les llamaban los políticos rancios.

Güeno, algunos sí eran muy honestos, pero algunos no eran tan honestos. Compraban votos. Verdá que estaa el que tenía dinero podía comprar votos. El que no tenía dinero, pus, tenía que depender en su palabra nomás. Y, como el dinero era muy escaso en esos días, pus, los políticos que ya estaan inpuestos [a correr], y estaan corriendo otra vez, ésos tenían dinero porque estaan ocupados, ¿no? Tenían posiciones onde ganaban salario, y ésos podían comprar votos. A munchos los compraban; muncha gente les vendía su voto.

¡Muncha gente no! Muncha gente era muy orgullosa. Yo me

recuerdo que mi papá era muy orgulloso, y muy fiel en su partido. No lo hacían dirisar, diriar por naa en su partido. Ni comprar su voto, no. Dijía que no. Eso no era ser honesto. Pa elegir un oficial honesto, tenían que ser honestos en la votación. Pero, güeno, siempre que hacían sus treces ahi pallá y pacá, los que les valía, y compraban votos y ganaban. Pus estaan bien puestos, ¿ves?

Pero no se echaban [los candidatos] personalmente. Ésa es una cosa que veo yo hoy en día, que tocan las personas de los candidatos unos a los otros. Entonces se dirigían nomás en el trabajo que hacían, qué era lo que proponían hacer si eran elegidos, qué calidades tenían en trabajos que habían tenido más antes, o tal cosa así. Pero no dijían que él andaa con aquella mujer o aquella mujer andaa con aquel hombre y ora anda queriendo ser oficial, como hoy en día. Eso no se me hace a mí que es correcto usar en la política. Es una cosa muy, muy cochina, muy sucia. O que ese hermano de aquel [candidato] estuvo en la penitensaria. ¿Pus qué culpa tiene que su hermano juera a la penitensaria? O hermano de aquel [otro candidato] que mató a tal y tal. Pus, mientras que él no lo hiciera, él no tenía culpa.

Así la miro yo. Pero muncha gente no la mira así.

Rancid Politicians

Why, there have always been good politicians as well as rancid politicians, as they were called. Rancid politicians were the ones who never turned loose of their office, because they wanted to hang on to it all the time, forever, until another generation came along and kicked them out. That's who was called a rancid politician.

Well, some politicians were really honest, but others, not so. They bought votes. Truth is, the one who had the money could buy the votes, whereas the one who didn't had to rely on his own word. And since money was very scarce back in those days, well, those politicians who were used to running, and who ran over and over again, did so because they were employed and had the money, right? They had positions that paid them a salary, and they could buy votes. Many voters were bought; many people sold their vote.

Not so with other people! Many people were very proud. I remember that my father was very proud, and very faithful to his party. You couldn't get him to stray from his party for anything. Least of all, sell his vote. He refused. That wasn't being honest. For people to elect an honest official, they had to be honest in their voting. But, anyway, they still did their number here and there, those who could get away with it, and so they'd buy votes and win. They were well entrenched, you see.

But candidates didn't attack each other personally. That's one thing I see nowadays, that candidates attack one another's character. In the past, they only referred to the kind of job they were doing, what they proposed to do if elected, what qualifications they possessed for the jobs or positions they had held in the past, or some such thing. But they didn't go on to say, as is the case today, that he [the opponent] was running around with such and such a woman, or that that woman was cavorting with that man and now he was aspiring to be a public servant. That, it seems to me, is not right in politics. That's a very, very nasty and filthy thing to do. Or to say that that guy's brother was in the penitentiary. What fault is it of his [the candidate's] if his brother ended up in prison? Or that the brother of so and so killed such and such a person. As long as he—the candidate—didn't do it, he's not to blame.

That's the way I see it. But a lot of people don't see it that way.

Reynaldo Gonzales

Los políticos eran tan sinvergüenzas

Los políticos eran tan sinvergüenzas, que válgame Dios, porque el político más grande fregaba al más chiquito, y a la demás gente. Les robaba a esta gente pa dale aquea. Los políticos estaan regüeltos con los Hermanos de Nuestro Padre Jesús. Penitentes. Eos estaan en compañía con los políticos, porque comían de la misma . . . le robaan al otro, le robaan al otro, pa vender eos o pa comer o quién sabe qué. Pa comer eos, yo creo.

Yo conocí aquí en Las Vegas varios políticos muy grandes. Estos Romeros. ¿Los oyó mentar usté? Uno se llamaa Secundino, y lotro se llamaba Cleofes. Eran de esos políticos sinvergüenzas. Loo se mixtiaron con los Armijos y los Delga[d]os. Lorenzo Delga[d]o era sobrino de estos Romeros. ¡Salió más sinvergüenza! Yo lo conocí bien, bien. A en papá le hicieron muncho mal [ladrones]. Le robaan muncho. Too el tiempo agarraba en papá ladrones ahi [en el rancho] y los traiba a la corte. ¡No les hacían naa! Pues el juez Armijo, usté lo ha oido mentar, ése era de la misma rueda de los ladrones esos. Y Lorenzo Delga[d]o, pus era de los mismos. Yo llegué a salir con papá de la casa de corte. Le dijía Lorenzo,

—Vete sin pena. Ahi te la pagamos. Nojotros lo arreglamos.

¡Nunca le pagaron nada! ¡Nunca arreglaron nada!

[Los políticos de hoy] no roban tanto a vistas como los de antes. No roban muncho a vistas. Pus, el político grande [más antes] ponía sus jueces, los que él le gustaban. ¡Hasta los muertos hablaban!

Politicians Were So Unscrupulous

God save our souls, but politicians were so unscrupulous, because the more powerful the politician, the more he would screw the little guy, and the rest of the people. He would steal from these people to give to the others. Politicians were mixed up with the Brotherhood of Jesus Christ, the Penitents. The latter were in cahoots with the politicians, because they fed at the same . . . [public trough]. They would all steal from this guy or the other in order to sell what they stole or who knows what. I guess it was to feed one another.

I knew several big-shot politicians here in Las Vegas. The Romeros. Have you ever heard of them? One was Secundino, and the other was Cleofes. They belonged to those shameless politicians. Then they got mixed up with the Armijos and the Delgados. Lorenzo Delgado was a nephew of these Romeros. He turned out to be such a scoundrel! I knew him well, well. They did a lot of nasty things to my father. People stole a lot from him. My father used to catch thieves all the time at his ranch and he'd bring them before the courts. Nothing happened to them! Judge Armijo, you've heard of him, he belonged to the same ring as those thieves. And Lorenzo Delgado was cut from the same cloth. I left the courthouse with my father more than once. Lorenzo would say to him, "Go on. Don't worry. We'll make it up to you. We'll take care of it."

They never paid anything! They never made any amends whatsoever!

Today's politicians aren't as blatant in stealing as those of the past. They don't steal out in the open as much. Well, the bigwig politician long ago would set up his own judges, his favorites. Why, even the dead rose from the grave to vote!

Guadalupe Luján

Jui a dar a la cárcel porque voté demócrata

En 1930 voté la primera vez—y voté demócrata. Eran unos cuantos los demócratas en este condao [San Miguel]. En la noche que juimos a entregar las cajas de boletos, porque votáanos en papeles antonces, boletos de papel, jui a dar a la cárcel. La única vez que yo ha estao en la cárcel en mi vida, porque voté demócrata. Y no había demócrata quién nos sacara. Tenía de güena suerte un tío qu'era republicano, y ése jue y me sacó, que si no, no me hubieran soltao. Hasta garrotazos nos dieron cuando nos metieron a la cárcel.

De ahi pallá me junté con munchos muchachos que estaban desarrollándose en la política. Y les dije,

—Tenemos que hacer alguna cosa pa mejorarnos. Si no, siempre vamos a estar bajo los pies de estos dictadores [los republicanos].

Formamos un grupo que le llamáanos los Jóvenes. [Woodrow] Wilson era el presidente. Antonces comenzaron a subir los sueldos porque ganaban más de tres pesos al día. El presidente comenzó a subir más el sueldo. Agarró mi padre trabajo. Trabajaa por el ferrocarril, y comenzamos a ponernos mejor en pie. Había algunos muchachos muy vivos de naturaleza aquí, y nos desarrollamos y formamos ese grupo de Jóvenes Demócratas. Trabajáanos por el WPA en la administración de [Franklin] Roosevelt. Ahi poníanos dos reales, cincuenta y cinco centavos al mes, pa poder tener un fondo con que operar.

El señor Tom Doren era demócrata antonces. Y ése era el dueño del Fidel, hotel aquí en Las Vegas. Él nos hizo una petición. Juntamos una petición entre los Jóvenes Demócratas. Era pa que firmara el gobernador en Santa Fe pa que nos dieran el permiso de descubrir los libros y hacelos *purge,* del condao de San Miguel. Se tardó un año y medio pa que juera pa la Corte Suprema. Antonces dio una orden ejecutiva el gobernador de que soltaran los libros aquí, y que nojotros íbanos a trabajar en eos. Teníanos que firmar por el libro cuando lo sacáanos y cuando lo volvíanos.

En 1934 ya comenzamos agarrar más juerza. Comenzó agrandecer los Jóvenes Demócratas. Teníanos un muchacho aquí qu'era muy vivo de naturaleza, Luis Encinias. Ya es finado, pero ese hombre nos comenzó a guiar a los que teníanos poquita educación. En 1936 tuvimos que trai la Guardia Nacional aquí en Las Vegas pa que cubrieran las eleciones. Es el primer año que los demócratas ganaron aquí, y el que ganó con más poquito jue el alguacil mayor. Ganó con dos mil votos, porque habíanos sacao mil cien nombres de los libros qu'eran dijuntos de diferentes precintos. Los votaban [los republicanos] alfabéticamente. Hacían como les daba su gana.

El señor Delga[d]o era el teniente de la comisión central. Era el mayor y era el alguacil mayor. Ese año que juimos entregale nojotros los libros allá, el señor Fidel Gonzales antonces había entrao en polecía de estao, y le pidimos que viniera con nosotros pa que no nos jueran a golpiar [los republicanos] cuando juéranos a entregar los libros. No, nomás entregamos los libros. Lorenzo Delga[d]o era un hombre muy vivo. Políticamente nació con ese don. No estaba muy educao pero nació con el don de ser político. Quizás Dios le dio esa sabiduría.

Cuando nojotros trujimos la Guardia Nacional, dijieron,

—¿Quiénes son los oficiales aquí?

Ya les dijimos que estáanos en la minoría porque los comisionaos republicanos nombraban los que iban a sirvir en la eleción. Ahi me pusieron a mí de secretario en 1936. Yo era el secretario, pero eos tenían toa la ventaja del mundo. Cuando le entregaron al dijunto Lorenzo los libros—porque tráibanos una orden de la Corte Suprema—ya habíanos sacao toos los nombres de dijuntos y toos los que votaan. Cuando se los entregamos a él, brincaron dos diuna vez a querernos pegar y entró el State Police con nojotros, y les dijo,

—No me maltraten estos muchachos, porque si ustedes los van a maltratar, yo no los voy a llevar a la cárcel. Los voy a llevar a la penitensaria. Ellos vienen con negocio aquí de la Corte Suprema.

Antonces el dijunto Lorenzo salió y dijo,

—Muchachos, tengan respeto. Ésta es una cosa de ley.

Luego como a los dos, tres meses comenzó él a tomar muy pesao. Y dijo,

—Muchachos, ya me fregaron.

Ya lo habíanos quitao, porque ganaban porque votaban alfabéti-camente, y los dijuntos votaban ondequiera. Unos votaban aquí; otros votaban allá en Pecos. *All over! All over the county!*

Cuando nosotros les ganamos la primer vez, antonces el dijunto Lorenzo Delga[d]o falleció. Había estao muncho en poder. También tuvo la oportunidá de correr pa teniente gobernador cuando los demócratas. Antonces corría el teniente aparte del gobernador. Ya cuando corrió de teniente gobernador, se le cayeron las alas y el Par-tido Demócrata comenzó a desarrollarse. Antonces el Partido Repub-licano se deshizo del todo, y algunos que estaan republicanos se vinieron con los demócratas a ayudar porque querían eos siempre quedar en algo. Reconocieron. Ahi jue onde se ganó la primera ele-ción, en 1936. De ahi pacá siguió demócrata [el condado] todo el tiempo.

Tamién entre los demócratas ha 'bido algunos que son medios . . . Vinían aquí y prometían torres de viento y nunca cumplían con nada. Tuvieron gobernadores ahi qu'eran poco anti-mexicanos. Yo me metí en política por la razón de que mi gente se desarrollara.

Tuve munchas güenas posiciones, pero le ayudaba yo a mi gente too el tiempo, porque yo no nomás tenía que comer. Eos tenían que comer también. Y onde había una oportunidá de conseguirles dinero, que les dieran más *increases* en el pago, iba yo y hablaba por eos y me escuchaban. Ya sabían que yo no estaba nomás interesao en lo mío.

Al fin, con el tiempo, se jue desarrollando la juventú. Ora después no había quién les tapara el sol con la mano. Ya la gente había agar-rao muncha experencia. Y antes no.

Antes no había auditorios que auditara las ofecinas. ¡Oh, robaban! No se sabía ónde iban a dar los votos. Cuando ganó el Partido Demócrata, ya pusieron diferentes regulaciones, onde la persona tenía calificaciones. Si había algún desfalco de alguna manera, diuna vez vinía un auditor y lo chequiaba. Sí ha 'bido algunos desfalcos, que eso es natural, pero antes, no tenían auditor ni naa d'eso.

I Ended Up in Jail Because I Voted Democrat

In 1930 I voted for the first time—and I voted Democrat. There were only a few Democrats in this county [San Miguel]. The night that we went to turn over the boxes containing the ballots, because we used paper ballots, I ended up in jail. It's the only time in my life that I ever went to jail, just because I voted as a Democrat. And there wasn't a Democratic soul who could bail us out. Luckily, I had an uncle who was a Republican, and he went and bailed me out; if not, they wouldn't have set me free. They even beat the tar out of us when we were jailed.

From then on I got together with a bunch of the guys who were learning about politics. And I said to them, "We have to do something to better ourselves. If not, we're always going to be under the control of these dictators [the Republicans]."

We formed a group called the Young Democrats. Woodrow Wilson was president. It was then that salaries started to climb because workers earned more than three dollars a day. The president began increasing the salaries. My father got a job. He worked for the railroad, and we started to get back on our feet. There were some very bright guys around here, and that's when we formed that group called the Young Democrats. We worked for the WPA [Works Progress Administration] in Franklin Roosevelt's administration. That's when we used to put in twenty-five or fifty-five cents a month, so that we could have funds to operate with.

We had a Mr. Tom Doren at the time, who was a Democrat. He was the owner of the Fidel Hotel here in Las Vegas. He drew up a petition for us. We circulated a petition among the youth. It was for the governor in Santa Fe to sign so that we could get permission to examine the books [voting records] and purge them here in San Miguel County. It took a year and a half for it to reach the Supreme Court. It was then that the governor issued an executive order for the books to be released—opened to the public—and that we were going to be examining them. We had to sign for each book when we checked it out and when we returned it.

In 1934 we started to gain more power. The Young Democrats started to grow. We had a young man here who was naturally very intelligent. Luis Encinias was his name. He's already dead, but that man started to guide those of us who had little education. In 1936 we had to bring in the National Guard to oversee the elections. That's the first year that Democrats won here in Las Vegas, and the one who won with the fewest votes was the sheriff. He got 2,000 votes, because we had purged 1,100 registered voters from the books from the different precincts who were already dead. The Republicans used to vote them in alphabetical order. They used to do whatever they felt like.

Mr. Delgado was the head of the central commission. He was the oldest and the sheriff. That year when we went to turn over the books, Mr. Fidel Gonzales had become head of the State Police, and we asked him to come with us so that the Republicans wouldn't beat us up when we turned over the books. No. We handed over the books without incident. Lorenzo Delgado was a very smart man. Politically, he was born with that gift. He wasn't very well educated but he was born with that political gift. I guess God gave him wisdom.

When we brought the National Guard, they asked us, "Who are the officials in charge here?"

We told them that we were in the minority because the Republican commissioners named those who were going to be in charge of the elections. I was one of those put in charge in 1936. I became the secretary, but the Republicans had all of the advantage in the world. When we turned the books over to the late Lorenzo Delgado—because we had an order from the State Supreme Court—we had already purged the names of all those dead people who usually voted. When we turned the books over to him, two men right away jumped us and tried to beat us up, but Fidel Gonzales, head of the State Police, went in with us, and he said to them, "Don't mistreat these young men, because if you do, I'm not going to take you to jail. I'm going to take you to the penitentiary. They're here with orders from the Supreme Court."

Then the late Lorenzo Delgado came out and said [to his cronies], "Boys, have a little respect. This is a legal matter."

Then within about two, three months he started to drink heavily. And he said, "Boys, I've been had."

We had voted him out of office, because the only reason the Republicans won is because those who were dead voted everywhere, in alphabetical order. Some voted here; others voted over in Pecos. All over! All over the county!

When we defeated the Republicans the first time, it was then that the late Lorenzo Delgado passed away. He had been in power a long time. He also had the opportunity of running for lieutenant governor when the Democrats were in control. At that time the lieutenant governor ran separate and apart from the governor. By the time he ran as lieutenant governor, his wings were clipped, and the Democratic Party started gaining power. It was then that the Republican Party came apart at the seams, and some who were Republicans came over to the Democratic Party because they wanted at least to hold onto something. They realized they had had it. That's when the Democrats won the first election, in 1936. From then on the county turned completely Democrat.

Among the Democrats there's also been some who were a bit . . . They'd come here and promise ivory towers, but they never came through with anything. The Democrats had a few governors who were anti-Mexican. I went into politics for the simple reason of having my own people get ahead.

I had many good jobs, but I helped my people all the time, because I wasn't the only one who had to eat. They had to eat as well. And wherever there was an opportunity of getting more money for them, increases for them in their paychecks, I'd go and speak for them and they'd listen to me. People knew that I wasn't just interested in my own well-being.

Finally, in due time, the young people started getting ahead. Later on, there wasn't a soul who could pull the wool over their eyes. People had gotten wise. And before that, not so.

A long time ago there were no auditors who would audit the offices. Boy, did politicians steal! People didn't know where the votes went. When the Democratic Party won, different regulations went into effect, where a person had to be qualified. If some kind of embezzlement took place, right away an auditor would show up and check it out. There have been embezzlements [under the Democrats], which is quite natural, but long ago there weren't any auditors or anything of the kind.

Se echaban bala

Déjeme dicile aquí en Las Vegas onde yo vivía, en la calle Grand, había antonces como el Wild West que estaba aquí. Había unos ciertos individos que no quiero mencionar sus nombres a que no salga, y uno de eos tenía pica cabra de la señor. Y aquí en una esquina de la calle Pacífica, se escondió uno de ellos y lotro iba a la calle Morrison. Tocó una calle más arriba, y aquí éste que le tenía mala pica al otro, agarró el rifle. Voló del caballo aquel otro hombre que iba a caballo. Lo mató. Lo soltaron libre, porque estaba en el partido del que estaba en juerza. Era un *commissioner.* Uno solo manijaba todo.

Pues yo le voy a platicar a usté la verdá. La política era muy corrupta aquí en Las Vegas. A mí me tocó ir a sirvir de secretario de varias eliciones, y se echaban bala. Dos individos se echaron bala, y nosotros tiramos las cajas y nos salimos pa juera. ¡Pero se echaban bala! Era una cosa muy fea.

They Used to Shoot at Each Other

Let me tell you that here in Las Vegas where I lived, on Grand Street, it was like the Wild West what we had here. There were certain individuals whose names I don't want to mention, and one of them really had it in for this other guy. And here at a corner on Pacific Street, one of them hid and the other one was headed up Morrison Street. It was one street above Pacific, and the one who had it in for the other guy grabbed a rifle. He blew that other man off his horse. He killed him. They turned him loose, because he was a member of the party in power. He was a commissioner. One individual alone handled everything.

Well, I'm going to tell you the truth. Politics was very corrupt here in Las Vegas. I got to serve as secretary in several elections, and they used to shoot at each other. Two individuals exchanged gunshots, and we tossed the boxes aside and headed outside. But they used to exchange gunshots! It was a very scary thing.

7

Dichos y adivinanzas
Folk Sayings and Riddles

Dichos

Introduction

Folk sayings (*dichos*) and riddles (*adivinanzas*), coupled with stories, remain an indelible component of my childhood in rural New Mexico. As I was growing up in the Río Puerco Valley southeast of Chaco Canyon, often piqued by the irresistible curiosity of a young boy, I listened attentively to the adults' stories, folk expressions, and riddles. The folk sayings commanded a special importance because they were invoked to instruct and to impart wisdom to us children as part of everyday life.

Dichos are deeply rooted in the Hispanic tradition of northern New Mexico. Some of these cultural and linguistic gems date back to the sixteenth century and were born right here in my native state; many others can be traced back to the Middle Ages, the Renaissance, and the Golden Age periods of Spanish literature. Numerous *dichos* can be found in classical works such as *El libro de buen amor,* by Juan Ruiz, Archpriest of Hita (1283[?]–1350[?]), the anonymous *Lazarillo de Tormes* (1554), and Fernando de Rojas' *La Celestina* (1492). But myriad folk sayings, or proverbs, as some people choose to call them, can be traced to Miguel de Cervantes' *Don Quixote* (part 1, 1605; part 2, 1615) in the utterances of the inimitable Sancho Panza.

Countless times I heard elders in my community, most notably, old men, pepper their conversation with, "Pues había un dicho" (There was a saying), or "Pus había un dicho que decía . . ." (There was a saying that went like this . . .). The latter was followed by a neatly crafted expression within a broader context as the old-timers offered words of advice to the younger folks. To this day in New Mexico we hear, "Del dicho al hecho hay gran trecho" (There's many a slip twixt the cup and the lip), that is, "It is easier said than done." This saying is found, incidentally, in *Don Quixote*.

My parents used folk sayings to teach us about life's trials and tribulations. Some of us still recall their words of counsel—oftentimes exhortations—with delight and profound reflection. My father, who passed away in 2001 at eighty-eight years of age, and whose ancestry in New Mexico dates back at least two hundred years, without fail resorted to the use of folk expressions in Spanish, his native tongue, most strikingly when he discussed topics of grave concern to him (e.g., the lack of respect among our youth toward their elders). A saying that made up part of his repertoire from my earliest recollection was, "No hay mal que por bien no venga" (Every cloud has a silver lining). Nonetheless, his optimism was tempered with sayings such as, "Son días de uno y vísperas de otro" (Life has its pluses and minuses). Yet, after all is said and done, he truly believed that God was the sole determiner of a person's destiny. "Uno propone y Dios dispone" (Man proposes and God disposes) are words that my father took to heart, especially in his golden years.

One of my mother's favorite sayings, particularly when we children complained about her favoring one of us over the other, was, "No todas las uñas de los dedos son iguales" (Not all the fingernails are identical). In other words, "You children are not all the same," hence each one is treated differently. When we got too rambunctious, she would say, "Lo que ustedes hagan con sus padres, sus hijos harán con ustedes" (Whatever you do to your parents, your children will do to you), that is, "What goes around, comes around."

Dichos are culturally charged expressions that were never

explained to us. Somehow we understood what they meant. The first time I heard my paternal grandmother say, "Hijito, raspa la puela, pero no quiebres la muela" (My dear child, scrape the pan, but don't chip a tooth), I sensed the underlying message behind these words: when offered something to eat, don't abuse the privilege; leave some for others.

The contributors of folk sayings in this chapter are presented in alphabetical order. Each saying, followed by both a literal (in parentheses) and a free translation or an equivalent proverb in English, represents a sampling of what the old folks in Las Vegas and its environs used in years past. It should be noted that *dichos* are difficult to produce spontaneously; consequently, most informants shared their folk sayings with me in writing. Nevertheless, even those interviewees who were unable to come up with one or two folk expressions held them in high regard at one time. Nowadays, their attitude is much more cynical, because even in families where Spanish is spoken people tend to view *dichos* as anachronistic and of little relevance in an age of technological frenzy, economic affluence, and cultural indifference or rejection. Regardless of the old-timers' attitudes, however, their sayings, like those of many of their contemporaries in other parts of New Mexico, are inextricably bound to their native language and are often a product of their environment.

Filiberto Esquibel, with his philosophical deftness about life, perhaps best sums up the didactic importance of *dichos* : "Pues sí, hay veces que dichos no se te olvidan tan fácil como un consejo. Si yo te digo un consejo, puea que se te olvide lo que te dije, pero un dicho se te queda enprentao en la cabeza más" (Of course, there are times when you won't forget folk sayings as easily as words of advice. If I give you advice, maybe you'll forget what I told you, but a folk saying remains embedded much more in your head).

It almost goes without saying that the old folks took *dichos* to heart. The following *dicho* aptly underscores the importance of these linguistic jewels: "Los dichos de los viejitos son evangelios chiquitos"; that is, "Much can be learned from the advice [cultural tidbits] of old-timers." [Some translations are adapted from Rubén Cobos, *Refranes: Southwestern Spanish Proverbs* (Santa Fe: Museum of New Mexico Press, 1985) and Wolfgang Mieder, *The Prentice-Hall Encyclopedia of World Proverbs* (New York: MJF Books, 1986).]

Jesusita Aragón

1. Dicen que me han de quitar las veredas por donde ando, las veredas quitarán, pero las querencias cuándo?
(They say that I'll be deprived of the paths on which I travel, and it may well be so, but my favorite places, when?)

People may steer me off course, but I will always reach my destination.

2. Donde pone uno los ojos, el diablo mete su cola.
(Where one puts his eyes, the devil sticks his tail.)

Where evil is at stake, the devil is always one step ahead of you.

3. El que de mañana se levanta, tiene cien años de vida y en su trabajo adelanta.
(He who rises early has one hundred years of life and gets ahead in his work.)

Early to bed and early to rise makes a man healthy, wealthy, and wise.

4. El que solo quiere ser, solo se queda.
(He who wants to be alone, alone will be.)

Misery loves company.

5. El que ha de ser para tamales, del cielo le caen las hojas.
(Cornhusks will drop from the sky on the person destined to be a tamal.)

He who was born to be slow will be slow.

6. El que con niño se acuesta, mojado amanece.
(He who sleeps with a child wakes up wet.)

If you lie with dogs, you'll get up with fleas.

7. El que de noche se pinta, de día parece mal.
(He who paints himself at night looks bad during the day.)

You can't tell a book by its cover.

8. El que al cielo escupe, en la cara le cae.
   (He who spits upward gets the spittle in his face.)

   People that live in glass houses shouldn't throw stones.

9. El que corre y va a su casa, cuenta lo que le pasa.
   (He who runs and goes home can tell what happened.)

   A live coward is better than a dead hero.

10. En la ciudad de los ciegos, el tuerto es rey.
    (In the city of blind men, the one-eyed man is king.)

    In the land of the blind, the one-eyed man is king.

11. El que es de mala suerte, desde la cuna comienza.
    (Bad luck begins while the unlucky are in the cradle.)

    Some people are born under an unlucky star.

12. Los hermanos y los gatos todos son ingratos.
    (Brothers and cats are all ungrateful.)

    Friends and mules fail in hard times.

13. No dejes camino por vereda, ni preguntes lo que no te
    importa, ni te partas con la primer nueva.
    *(Don't abandon the road for a path, or meddle in someone else's
    affairs, or choose the first new path that comes along.)*

    Keep to the straight and narrow path.

14. No te apures en comer, que hambre no te ha de faltar.
    (Don't eat fast, for you will always have an appetite.)

    Slow and steady wins the race.

15. Vale más vecino cerca que hermano lejos.
    *(A neighbor nearby is more helpful when in need than a brother far
    away.)*

    Better a neighbor near than a brother far.

16. Vale más solo que mal acompañado.
    (It's better to be alone than in bad company.)

    A man is known by the company he keeps.

17. Corre buena fama y acuéstate a dormir.
    (Chase a good reputation and go to bed.)

    Acquire fame and go to sleep.

18. Corre mala fama y arranca a huir.
    (Risk a bad reputation and take off running.)

    Play with fire and you'll get burned.

19. El hueso que ha de ser tuyo, aunque otro perro lo lamba.
    (The bone is to be yours, even though another dog may lick it.)

    What rightfully belongs to you will always be yours.

20. El que ha de ser de real y sencillo, aunque ande entre los doblones.
    (He who is destined to be a simple coin will remain so, even though he is surrounded by doubloons.)

    The common person is common even among the elite.

21. Cuando estés en abundancia, acuérdate de las Eucaristías.
    (When you find yourself in plenteousness, remember the Eucharist.)

    When you get to be rich, remember where you came from.

22. ¿Para qué son esos brincos estando el suelo tan parejo?
    (Why jump when the floor is level?)

    Don't make a mountain out of a molehill.

Elba C. de Baca

1. Agua que no has de beber, déjala correr.
   (Water that you're not going to drink, let run).

   Don't be a dog in the manger.

2. Quien mucho duerme, poco aprende.
   (He who sleeps a lot learns little.)

   The early bird gets the worm.

3. Al que quita, le sale una jorobita. Después viene el diablo, y se la corta con su navajita.
   (He who gives and then takes away will develop a tiny hunchback. Later, the devil shows up and cuts it [the hunchback] off with a tiny knife.)

   It's not wise to give someone a gift and then take it back.

4. La codicia rompe el saco.
   (Covetousness rips the bag.)

   All covet, all lose.

5. Cuando se resbala un santo, hasta el infierno no para.
   (When a saint slips, he doesn't stop until he lands in hell.)

   The higher they fly, the harder they fall.

6. La noche es la capa del pecador.
   (Night is the cover of the sinner.)

   Night is the mother of plots.

7. El que solo se ríe, de sus maldades se acuerda.
   (He who laughs alone remembers his misdeeds.)

   When alone, we have our thoughts to watch.

8. Perro que no sale, no encuentra hueso.
   (A dog that doesn't go out won't find a bone.)

   Nothing ventured, nothing gained.

9. No se puede repicar y andar en la procesión.
   (You can't ring the church bell and take part in the procession.)

   You can't have your cake and eat it, too.

10. Cuenta tus duelos y deja los ajenos.
    (Count your hardships and leave those of others alone.)

    Mind no business but your own.

11. No firmes cartas que no leas, ni bebas agua que no veas.
    (Don't sign letters you haven't read or drink water you cannot see.)

    Read carefully; sign cautiously.

12. No hay atajo sin trabajo.
    (There's no shortcut without toil.)

    No pain, no gain.

13. Se le tantió el barco.
    (The boat tilted on him.)

    He was hoist by his own petard.

14. Por el templo del trabajo se entra la fama.
    (Fame passes through the temple of hard work.)

    It takes hard work to attain one's dreams.

15. El amor va a donde quiere, no a donde su dueño lo manda.
    (Love goes where it pleases, not where it is sent.)

    Love is blind.

Filiberto Esquibel

1. El que carrea saco, sabe lo que trae.
   (He who carries his own sack knows what's in it.)

   Only the person suffering knows what it's like.

2. El que no agarra consejo, no llega a viejo.
(He who doesn't follow advice doesn't reach old age.)

Wise men listen to the counsel of others.

3. Tanto vino el viejo malcriao, como el muchacho que crió.
(The ill-bred old man is no better than the boy.)

Like father, like son.

Reynaldo Gonzales

1. Por aquí sale el sol, por aquí se mete; cuando cai agua, hay muncho zoquete.
(The sun rises here, but sets there; when it rains, there's much mud.)

God showers blessings on everyone.

Fred W. Korte

1. El que rieso anda, presto para.
(He who goes fast, stops quickly.)

Haste makes waste.

2. El que adelante no mira, atrás se queda.
(He who doesn't look ahead, lags behind.)

Foresight is better than hindsight.

3. Vale más pájaro en la mano que cien volando.
(A bird in the hand is better than a hundred on the wing.)

A bird in the hand is worth two in the bush.

4. Dios da el frío conforme la capa.
(God doles out the cold according to the cape.)

God tempers the wind to the shorn lamb.

5. Hazte el tonto y comerás con las dos manos.
(Pretend to be a fool and you shall eat with both hands.)

It is a cunning part to play the fool well.

6. Tanto peca el que amarra la pata, como el que mata la vaca.
(He who ties the leg sins as much as the one who kills the cow.)

The accomplice is as bad as the thief.

7. El que tiene boca, a Roma va.
(He who wags his tongue gets to Rome.)

Better to ask the way than to go astray.

8. Con lo que no cuesta, se hace fiesta.
(With something that doesn't cost, one makes merry.)

One celebrates with fewer precautions when using someone else's possessions.

9. Cuando no hay de lomo de todo como.
(Where there's no sirloin, I eat all kinds of stuff.)

Beggars can't be choosers.

10. A tu tierra, grulla, que ésta no es tuya.
(Off to your own home, crane, for this is not your land.)

People are often better off among their own folks than with strangers.

11. El que anda entre la miel, algo se le pega.
(He who plays with syrup, something is bound to stick.)

Play with fire and you'll get burned.

12. Lo que con tu padre hicieres, tu hijo contigo hará.
   (Whatever you do to your father, your son will do to you.)

   What goes around, comes around.

13. Para cada perro hay un garrote.
   (For every dog there is a cudgel.)

   If there's a will, there's a way.

14. Habiendo pan y cueva, más que [aunque] llueva.
   (As long as there's bread and a cave, who cares if it rains.)

   As long as one has food and shelter, the rest is easy.

15. En la ropa del tonto, se enseña el sastre.
   (One can tell the tailor by the clothes the fool wears.)

   A man is known by the company he keeps.

16. Nunca es el león como lo pinta.
   (The lion is never as it's painted.)

   The leopard does not change its spots.

17. Ojos que no ven, corazón que no siente.
   (Eyes that don't see, a heart that doesn't feel.)

   Out of sight, out of mind.

18. Los locos, los niños y los inocentes sí dicen la pura verdad.
   (Madmen, children, and the innocent tell the real truth.)

   Fools and madmen speak the truth.

19. Te casastes, te fregatas.
   (You got married, you've had it.)

   Marry in haste, repent at leisure.

20. Dios da almendras aquel que no tiene muelas.
   (God gives almonds to the person without molars.)

   God brings good fortune to fools.

Guadalupe Luján

1. Haz bien y no acates a quién.
   (Do good things but don't take credit for them.)

   Charity is its own reward.

2. Lo que no te pueas comer tú, dáselo a tu prójimo.
   (Whatever you can't eat, give it to your neighbor.)

   Share and share alike.

3. Cada cabeza es un mundo.
   (Each head is a world.)

   No two people are alike.

4. Los que saben más, entienden menos.
   (Those who know more, understand less.)

   They that think they know everything, know nothing.

5. El justo paga por el pecador.
   (He who is fair pays for the sinner.)

   The innocent person pays for the sins of others.

6. Él se tapa el sol con la mano
   (He blocks out the sun with his hand.)

   He who lies, hides the truth.

7. Cuando se le llega a uno la raya, no hay quién se escape.
   (When you've reached the end of the line, there's no escape.)

   In this world nothing can be said to be certain, except
   death and taxes.

José Nataleo Montoya

1. Lo que puedes hacer hoy, no lo dejes pa mañana.
   (Whatever you can do today, don't leave until tomorrow).

   Don't put off until tomorrow what you can do today.

2. No dejes camino por vereda.
   (Don't give up a road for a path.)

   Keep to the straight and narrow path.

Katarina Montoya

1. Tanto va el cántaro al agua hasta que cai adentro.
   (The pitcher goes to the well once too often until it breaks.)

   The law of averages always catches up with you.

2. No pretendas ser más de lo que eres.
   (Don't pretend to be what you're not.)

   Don't put on false airs.

3. Gane el pinto, gana el pinto, y sale el pinto y quedamos en la misma.
   (The pinto may win, and in fact wins, and you still have the pinto, so you're back where you started.)

   What goes around, comes around.

4. Ustedes hacen su cama, háganla bien, porque pasan más tiempo en su cama.
(You make your bed, but make it nice, because you spend more time in it.)

As you make your bed, so you must lie in it.

You made your own bed, now lie in it.

María Trujillo

1. No falta un roto para un descosido.
(For every ragged person, there's always a tattered one.)

Every Jack has his Jill.

2. Con hambre, no hay mal pan.
(When you're hungry, there's no such thing as bad bread.)

Hunger is the best sauce.

3. A la hija pan y comida; a la nuera pan y afuera.
(For the daughter there's bread and food; for the daughter-in-law, bread and out the door.)

There's nothing like your own children.

4. Si zapato le queda, se lo pondrá.
(If the shoe fits him, he'll wear it.)

If the shoe fits, wear it.

5. Una buena cuenta, buenos amigos.
(A good account means good friends.)

Don't mix business with pleasure.

6. No guardes para mañana lo que puedas hacer hoy.
   (Don't save for tomorrow what you can do today.)

   Don't put off until tomorrow what you can do today.

7. Panza llena, corazón contento.
   (A full belly, a happy heart).

   A full stomach gladdens the heart.

8. A todos los santos se les llega su día.
   (Every saint has its day.)

   Every dog has his day.

9. Barriga de pobre primero revienta que sobre.
   (The poor man's belly bursts first before he has enough.)

   Greed has no boundaries.

10. El que para burro nace, de macho muere.
    (He who is born a jackass dies a mule.)

    Like father, like son.

11. Más vale el viejo conocido, que el nuevo por conocer.
    (The familiar old man is worth more than the new one you've yet to meet.)

    Better the devil you know than the one you don't.

12. Perro que no sale no encuentra hueso.
    (The dog that doesn't go out, doesn't find a bone.)

    Nothing ventured, nothing gained.

13. Le dan cama y pide colchón.
    (They offer him a bed and he asks for the mattress.)

    Give someone an inch and he'll take a mile.

14. Lo mismo es pobre que ser perro, para tratar a uno mal.
(Being poor and a dog is the same thing; either way you're mistreated.)

A poor person is treated like a dog.

15. Al pobre lo echan afuera, y al perro le dicen "¡Sal!"
(The poor man is tossed out, but the dog is told, "Shoo!")

A dog is sometimes treated better than a man in dire straits.

Teresina Ulibarrí

1. Dime con quién andas, y yo te diré quién eres.
(Tell me with whom you run around, and I'll tell you who you are.)

A man is known by the company he keeps.

2. El que con lobos anda, a aullar se enseña.
(He who hangs around with wolves learns to howl.)

Live with a wolf, howl like a wolf.

Adivinanzas

Introduction

Riddles, like folk sayings, have survived for several centuries in New Mexico, and a number of them can also be found in Spain today. From time to time I have shared New Mexican folklore, including riddles, with friends and colleagues in Spain, and invariably they have been amazed at how Hispanic culture was able to reach as remote a part of the New World as New Mexico. Even more surprising to them is the fact that Hispanic culture is still important in New Mexico. A cursory glance at José Luis Gárfer and Concha Fernández' *Adivinancero antológico español* (Madrid: Ediciones del Prado, 1994) puts the reader in touch with a corpus of riddles that clearly connects Spain with New Mexico.

Moreover, by juxtaposing several riddles, this connection becomes even more dramatic. One of the more popular riddles in New Mexico among Hispanic old-timers is identical to the Gárfer and Fernández version:

> En alto vive,
> *She lives up high,*
> en alto mora,
> *she dwells up high,*
> en alto teje,
> *she weaves up high,*
> la tejedora.
> *the so-called weaver.*
> ¿Qué es?
> *What is it?*
> RESPUESTA: LA ARAÑA.
> ANSWER: THE SPIDER.

A lesser known New Mexican riddle, but still exactly like the one found in Gárfer and Fernández, is the following riddle shared with me by Cesaria Montoya:

> Caballito,
> *Little horse,*
> de banda a banda,
> *that rocks from side to side,*
> que no come,
> *that neither eats,*
> ni bebe,
> *nor drinks,*
> ni anda.
> *nor walks.*
> ¿Qué es?
> *What is it?*
> RESPUESTA: EL PUENTE.
> ANSWER: THE BRIDGE.

Some riddles in New Mexico have been modified somewhat, as we see in a riddle offered by Alfredo Trujillo. The variations between the New Mexican version shared with me by Alfredo Trujillo and the one from the Gárfer and Fernández anthology are noteworthy:

NEW MEXICO
El que lo hizo,
He who made it,
no lo quiso,
didn't want it,
y el que lo compró,
and he who bought it,
no lo vio.
didn't get to see it.
¿Qué es?
What is it?

SPAIN
Quien lo hace no lo goza,
He who builds it doesn't enjoy it,
quien lo goza no lo ve,
he who enjoys it doesn't see it,
quien lo ve no lo desea,
he who sees it doesn't wish it,
por más bonito que sea.
however beautiful it may be.
¿Qué es?
What is it?
RESPUESTA: EL ATAÚD/CAJÓN
ANSWER: THE COFFIN.

Notwithstanding the differences between the two riddles, the spirit, intent, and answer remain intact, further evidence of the unbreakable bond between New Mexico and Spain.

Other riddles in New Mexico, because of their strong cultural attributes, obviously have their genesis in New Mexico or perhaps Mexico. To be sure, the answer to many New Mexican riddles—as is also true in Spain—may be an animal, a religion, a person, a vegetable, a letter of the alphabet, a food, or a variety of other possibilities that more than likely are identified with Hispanic culture in general or New Mexico's culture in particular.

Riddles, unlike *dichos,* once upon a time were shared with children and grandchildren more as entertainment than as a didactic tool. My *agüelitos,* or Papá Grande and Mamá Grande, as I called my grandparents, were primarily responsible for sharing these tantalizing "head breakers" with their grandchildren. I can still remember one of the first riddles that my maternal grandmother taught me, when I was about five years old. Its musicality brought instant joy and gratification even though I could not guess the answer:

> Redondito,
> *It's round,*
> redondón.
> *a little bit round.*
> No tiene tapa
> *It doesn't have a lid,*
> ni tapón.
> *or a cork.*
> ¿Qué es?
> *What is it?*
> RESPUESTA: EL ANILLO.
> ANSWER: THE RING.

The combination of the diminutive and augmentative uses of "*redondo,*" coupled with the rhyme scheme, sounded like music to me. Nonetheless, my joy turned to frustration as I tried in vain to unravel the mystery locked in these verses.

My disappointment soon disappeared as my grandmother repeated the riddle in rhythmic and songlike fashion while visually offering me a clue here and there. It did not take me long to realize—with some coaching and prodding, of course—that the secret of unlocking riddles depended on a play on words, hidden meanings, cultural attributes, and a host of other clues.

Above all else, I learned the importance of using my imagination to search for the correct answer. The answer to the ensuing riddle by Teresina Ulibarrí is found in a play on words:

> Ya ves,
> *You see,*
> el que no me lo adivine,
> *he who doesn't guess,*
> bien tonto es.
> *is indeed quite dense.*
> ¿Qué es?
> *What is it?*
> RESPUESTA: LAS LLAVES.
> ANSWER: THE KEYS.

The words *adivine* and *tonto,* meaning "guess" and "stupid," respectively, for obvious reasons did wonders to sharpen my wits. At the same time, coming to the realization that the combination of *"ya"* plus *"ves"* produced a word that sounded like *llaves* (keys), the answer to the riddle, opened up a new and exciting world for me in riddle solving.

The following riddle, unlike this last one, is simple and to the point:

> Yo aquí,
> *I'm here,*
> y
> *and*
> tú allá.
> *you're there.*
> ¿Qué es?
> *What is it?*
> RESPUESTA: LA TOALLA.
> ANSWER: THE TOWEL.

The words *tú* and *allá* combine to produce *"tualla"* in the Spanish dialect of New Mexico, which sounds like *toalla.*

It is clear that the translation, which loses the play on words, is of little help in determining the correct answer to this riddle and others similar to it. English does, however, have its own riddles that use plays on words, for example, "What is black and white and 'read' all over?" A newspaper.

Some riddles in Spanish are also rather straightforward, devoid of rhyme scheme and in the form of a question. An example is the following riddle told me by Jesusita Aragón:

> ¿Qué le dijo el piojo al pelón?
> *What did the louse say to the bald-headed man?*
> RESPUESTA: NO TE AGACHES PORQUE ME CAIGO.
> ANSWER: DON'T BEND OVER OR I'LL FALL OFF.

To be sure, *adivinanzas* (the word comes from the verb *adivinar,* "to guess, to discover intuitively, or to divine") can be difficult, but they also can evoke fun and laughter. My aunt Teodorita García-Ruelas, in an interview, commented on the entertaining aspect of riddles in our village in rural New Mexico when she was a small girl. "In every home at night," she said to me, "people gathered to exchange riddles. They used to pass the time telling riddles, and the one who lost, they made him pray [usually a boy or a girl preparing for First Holy Communion] . . . the Our Father, the Hail Mary."

Incidentally, grownups held their own riddle sessions, and clearly or even implicitly risqué double-entendre riddles were reserved until after children were tucked into bed. Katarina Montoya's only riddle here is a vivid example of the implied erotic element when the intended answer in fact is far from sexual.

The contributors of riddles are also listed in alphabetical order. Each riddle is translated, but its answer comes at the end of the chapter in order to challenge the reader, in particular the Spanish speaker. I reiterate that the translations may be of little value in solving most, if not all, of the riddles.

Jesusita Aragón

1.¿Qué animal anda con las patas en la cabeza?
What animal walks with its feet on its head?

2. Blanca salí de mi casa,
   I left my house white,
   y en el campo mi hice bola.
   and in the countryside turned into a ball.
   Para volver a mi casa,
   In order to come back home,
   me metieron de la cola.
   they brought me in by the tail.
   ¿Qué es?
   What is it?

3. Fui a la huerta,
   I went to the garden,
   y corté una d'ella.
   and I cut one of them.
   Llegué a mi casa,
   I returned home,
   y lloré con ella.
   and I cried with it.
   ¿Qué es?
   What is it?

Elba C. de Baca

1. Mariano está en el llano,
   Mariano is on the plains;
   tiene cruz,
   he has a cross,
   y no es cristiano.
   but is not a Christian.
   ¿Qué es?
   What is it?

2. Una señorita muy aseñorada,
   She's a prim little lady,
   que no sale de casa,
   who never leaves home,

pero siempre está mojada.
but is always wet.
¿Qué es?
What is it?

3. Siempre va y siempre viene,
It goes back and forth,
mas en un lugar se detiene.
yet it never moves.
¿Qué es?
What is it?

4. ¿Qué santo tiene más huesos?
What saint has the most bones?

5. ¿Cuál es la cosa que,
What object,
siendo del tamaño de una vela,
although no bigger than a candle,
puede llenar una habitación?
can fill the whole room?

6. Un zapato acabado de hacer,
A shoe that has just been finished,
¿qué le falta?
What does it lack?

7. ¿Qué es lo que entre más
What is it that the more you
se le quita, más grande es?
take away from it, the bigger it gets?

8. Se pela lo de afuera,
You peel the outer covering,
se cuese lo de adentro.
you cook the inner part.
Se come lo de afuera,
You eat the outer covering,

se queda lo de adentro.
but you still have the inner part.
¿Qué es?
What is it?

9. ¿Por qué compran zapatos las mujeres?
   Why do women buy shoes?

10. Peludito por fuera,
    Furry on the outside,
    peludito por dentro.
    furry on the inside.
    Alza la pata y
    Raise your foot (leg)
    métela adentro.
    and put it in.
    ¿Qué es?
    What is it?

11. ¿Por qué mueve el perro la cola?
    Why does the dog wag its tail?

12. Federico va,
    Fred takes off,
    Federico viene.
    Fred comes back.
    Federico se entretiene.
    Fred enjoys himself.
    ¿Qué es?
    What is it?

13. Una cajita muy chiquitita,
    A tiny little box,
    blanca como el sol.
    as white as can be.
    Todos la saben abrir,
    Everyone knows how to open it,

pero nadie la sabe cerrar.
but no one knows how to close it.
¿Qué es?
What is it?

14. Si los amarro,
    If I tie them,
    se van.
    they go away.
    Si los desato,
    If I untie them,
    se quedan.
    they stay.
    ¿Qué es?
    What is it?

15. ¿Cuántas vueltas da el gato para acostarse?
    How many times does a cat go around in circles
    before going to bed?

16. ¿Qué hace el buey al salir al sol?
    What does the ox do when it goes out in the sun?

17. ¿Qué decía la bruja cuando la estaban quemando?
    What did the witch say as she was being burned at the stake?

Guadalupe Luján

1. Montera sobre montera,
   Bonnet upon bonnet,
   de muy rico paño.
   bonnet of fine cloth.
   El que no adivina ora,
   He who fails to guess now,
   no adivina en too el año.
   will not do so in a year.
   ¿Qué es?
   What is it?

Filimón Montoya

1. Lana sube,
   Wool goes up,
   lana baja.
   wool comes down.
   ¿Qué es?
   What is it?

Katarina Montoya

1. Te la saco y te la meto,
   I take it out and put it in,
   y cosquillitas te hago.
   and I tickle you in the process.
   ¿Qué es?
   What is it?

Alfredo Trujillo

1. Santa soy sin ser nacida.
   I am a saint without being born.
   Santa soy sin ser bautizada.
   I am a saint without being baptized.
   La iglesia me llama santa,
   The church calls me a saint,
   y santa soy santificada.
   and a saint I am who's sanctified.
   ¿Qué es?
   What is it?

2. Blanco salí de mi casa,
   I left my house dressed in white,
   y en el campo enverdecí.
   and in the countryside I turned green.
   Para volver a entrar a mi casa,
   In order to enter my house,
   de colorado me vestí.

I dressed up in red.
¿Qué es?
What is it?

3. De Guadalajara vengo.
   I come from Guadalajara.
   Jara traigo,
   I bring a sandbar willow,
   jara vendo.
   and a sandbar willow I will sell.
   Arriar vendo, cada jara.
   I deal each sandbar willow.
   ¿Cuál jara vendo?
   Which sandbar willow do I sell?

Finally, a brief comment is in order as I close this chapter. Most of the contributors were born between 1896 and 1929, when radio programming began in this country. Many of the old-timers' parents could ill afford a radio; therefore, storytelling and riddle solving were important means of entertainment. Which of them could have dreamed that they would witness the use of television, video cameras, CD-ROMs, DVDs, and cellular telephones? The electronic gadgetry we take for granted without doubt makes the *viejitos'* childhood and adolescence seem light years away.

Answers to Riddles

JESUSITA ARAGÓN

1. *El piojo*/The louse
2. *La cebolla*/The onion
3. *La cebolla*/The onion

ELBA C. DE BACA

1. *El burro*/The donkey
2. *La lengua*/The tongue
3. *El camino*/The road
4. *El camposanto* (lit., holy saint)/The cemetery

5. *El humo*/Smoke
6. *Otro zapato*/Another shoe
7. *El hoyo*/The hole
8. *El elote*/The ear of corn
9. *Porque no se los dan*/Because they don't come free
10. *La media*/Stocking
11. *Porque la cola no puede mover al perro*/Because the tail cannot wag the dog
12. *El reloj*/The clock
13. *El huevo*/The egg
14. *Los zapatos*/Shoes
15. *Todas las que le dé la gana*/As many as it pleases
16. *Hace sombra*/It creates a shadow
17. *Estoy fumando más, pero me agrada menos*/I'm smoking more now, but enjoying it less

GUADALUPE LUJÁN

1. *La cebolla*/The onion

FILIMÓN MONTOYA

1. *La navaja*/The pocket knife

KATARINA MONTOYA

1. *La llave (por ej., la petaquilla)*/The key (e.g., to a footlocker)

ALFREDO TRUJILLO

1. *La Semana Santa*/Holy Week
2. *Un chile*/A chile
3. *Todas*/All of them

Epilogue

Hispanos—unlike the adventurers or explorers who came to New Mexico and left—stayed, but over time they have been subjected to fateful changes that are a matter of record. Col. Stephen Watts Kearny's portentous proclamation and the Treaty of Guadalupe Hidalgo are glaring examples. In the new millennium, Hispanos wage a different battle, however, right in their own backyards, right in their own kitchens.

Today they find themselves both besieged by and confronted daily with the loss of customs, traditions, and a language they have clung to for hundreds of years. Family fragmentation, alcoholism, drug addiction, poverty, AIDS, and a host of other social ills plague them as well. As a consequence, older Hispanos see their cultural patrimony fast slipping from their strong yet helpless hands in this modern age of satellite dishes, CD-ROMs, Web sites, video games, digital cameras, and DVDs. Their grandchildren and great-grandchildren, apathetic about their language and culture, can barely utter the word *tortilla*, let alone make one.

Without doubt, education is the answer to bettering one's socioeconomic lot. Many Hispanic parents, students, and even educators hold the misguided notion that in order to eradicate poverty and improve literacy, one must toss cultural heritage out the back door like dishwater. We Hispanos face the sad prospect of waking up one day in the near future divested of our cultural vestiges and unable to claim or even remember our past. And changing one's Christian name from George to Jorge, Joe to José, or Maurice to Mauricio, under the guise of cultural preservation, is nothing more than window dressing.

The elders featured in *Old Las Vegas: Hispanic Memories from the New Mexico Meadowlands,* like their contemporaries in countless small Hispanic villages in northern New Mexico, are vivid examples of a generation that unquestionably symbolizes the last remnants of centuries-old Hispanic culture and language. Their unique way of life is destined to slip into oblivion, unless we can find a way to preserve their legacy. Only that will help us put into perspective our own sense of being while humbling ourselves in the process.

Glossary

This glossary is intended to aid the Spanish speaker who is not familiar with the Spanish dialect of northern New Mexico. Many of the regional terms vary according to local pronunciation or orthography and whether a word is an archaism, such as *trujo* (*trajo*), *vide* (*vi*), or *cuasi* (*casi*), or of local invention or adoption. For example, *troca* (truck), *bos* (bus), and *pene* (penny) are Anglicisms, whereas *puelada<puela* (frying pan full of something) and *iyendo<yendo* (going) stem from the local populace. There are also countless words (e.g., *guacamole*) that have been imported from Mexico and words from the local Indian population (e.g., *chaquegüe,* mush made with blue cornmeal).

Regional Word	Standard Spanish Word	Translation
A		
a case	en casa de	at so and so's home
a case 'e	en casa de	at so and so's home
a conforme	según	according to
a'elante	adelante	ahead; in front
a más de	además de	besides
aá	allá	there; over there
abajaa	abajaba	he/she/you came down, got down
acabaan	acababan	they/you finished
acabalates	acabalaste	you had enough; you were satisfied
acabao/a	acabado/a	finished
acarriar	acarrear	to haul; to carry

acordión	acordeón	accordion
acostaa	acostaba; acostada	he/she/you went to bed; in bed
acuñaa	acuñada	wedged
a 'entro	adentro	inside
afijalo/a	fijarlo/a	to tighten it
aforraban	forraban	they lined, covered
agarraan	agarraban	they/you fought for
agarrábanos	agarrábamos	we grabbed/grasped
agarralo/a	agarrarlo/a	to grab it; to grasp it; to catch it
agarrao/a	agarrado/a	grabbed; grasped; caught
agonojando	gorgojando	infested with weevils
agüelito/a	abuelito/a	grandpa/grandma
agüelo/a	abuelo/a	grandfather/grandmother
ahi	ahí	there
ai	ahí	there
aigre	aire	air; wind
ajerraba	erraba	erred
ajuera	afuera	outdoors
alabaos	alabados	hymns of praise
alberjón	arvejón	pea
alcol	alcohol	alcohol
alderedor	alrededor	around
alegando	discutiendo	arguing
algotra	alguna otra	another; someone else
alguen	alguien	someone
almorzar	desayunar	to eat breakfast
alquerían	adquirían	they/you got, acquired
alredor	alrededor	around
amarraa	amarraba	he/she/you fastened, tied up, tied down
amarrao/a	amarrado/a	tied up
anbición	ambición	ambition
andaa	andaba	he/she/you walked, ran around
andábanos	andábamos	we walked, used to walk
antonces	entonces	then
apiao	apeado	dismounted
apiar	apear	to dismount
aprendelo/a	aprenderlo/a	to learn it
aprevinía	prevenía	he/she/you prevented, warned
aqueo/a	aquello/a	that (thing, matter)
arreglábanos	arreglábamos	we repaired
arreglao/a	arreglado/a	repaired; fixed
asentaa	asentada	settled; established
asina	así	thus; in that way
asistilas	asistirlas	to help them

atrás	detrás	behind
atrincaa	trincaba	he/she/you pressed against
automoviles	automóviles	automobiles
avisale	avisarle	to notify him/her; to inform him/her; to warn him/her
ayudale	ayudarle	to help him

B

bailaan	bailaban	they/you danced
bajao	bajado	climbed down
balanciarlo/a	balancearlo/a	to balance it
baliaron	balearon	they wounded (with a firearm)
balió	baleó	he/she/you shot (at), wounded
bañalo/a	bañarlo/a	to bathe him/her/it
barra	bar; cantina	bar
basilón	gran fiesta, baile	great party, dance
bebito/a	niño/a	child
bendicieran	bendijeran	they/you blessed
bendició	bendijo	he/she/you blessed
bestia	animal; caballo	animal; horse
bisagüelo/a	bisabuelo/a	great-grandfather/ great-grandmother
bogue	"buggy"	buggy
boguecito		small buggy
bonche	montón	mountain; bunch
bonchi	montón	mountain; bunch
borreguiaban	cuidaban borregas	they/you took care of sheep
boses	autobuses	buses
botea	botella	bottle
brel	pan	bread
bromas	pleitos	lawsuits; fights; arguments
buñelos	buñuelos	fritters; Indian fry bread
buscalo/a	buscarlo/a	to look for him/her/it
busla	burla	joke

C

cabezudo/a	testarudo/a	stubborn; pigheaded
cabresto	cabestro	rope
cachete	mejilla	cheek
cai	cae	he/she/you/it falls
caiba	caía	he/she/you/it fell, would fall
cáibanos	caíamos	we fell, would fall
caido/a	caído/a	fallen

caindo	cayendo	falling
cairían	caerían	they/you would fall
cajete	tina	tin tub; bathtub; vat
cajón	ataúd	coffin
calentalo/a	calentarlo/a	to warm him/her/it
calláranos	calláramos	(for us) to keep quiet; to shut up
calmao/a	calmado/a	calm
camalta	cama	bed
cambeo	cambio	I change, exchange
cambiao/a	cambiado/a	changed
caminale	caminarla	to walk it/her
cañaa	cañada	ravine; gully
canova	canoa	canoe
cansao/a	cansado/a	tired
cantidá	cantidad	quantity
carbulador	carburador	carburetor
carpas	tienda	tent
casao/a	casado/a	married
casorios	bodas	weddings
castigao/a	castigado/a	punished
cemiterio	cementerio	cemetery
centea	centella	lightning flash
cequia	acequia	ditch
cernícaro	cernícalo	kestrel
cerrao/a	cerrado/a	closed
chakiaa	apretón	handshake
(de manos)	(de manos)	
chamaco	muchacho	boy
chancita	buena oportunidad	chance; good opportunity
chante	casa	shanty
chanza	oportunidad	chance
chava/o	chava/o	kid; girl/boy
chequiaba	revisaba	he/she/you checked
chequiar	revisar	to check
chequié	revisé	I checked
chiflando	silbando	whistling
chifló	silbó	he/she/you whistled
chíquete	chicle	chewing gum
chivas	cabras	goats
chota	policía	police; sheriff
cirgüela	ciruela	plum
cirgüelares	ciruelares	plum tree grove
clas	clase	class
clavaa	clavaba; clavada	he/she/you nailed; nail-studded

cobija	colcha	bedspread; quilt
cobijáanos	cobijábamos	we covered ourselves (with blankets)
cobijáranos	cobijáramos	(for us) to cover ourselves (with blankets)
cociniaban	cocinaban	they/you cooked
cociniar	cocinar	to cook
colgábanos	colgábamos	we hung up
colgalo/a	colgarlo/a	to hang it up
colgao/a	colgado/a	hung up
Colorao	Colorado	Colorado
comenzaan	comenzaban	they/you began
comenzábanos	comenzábamos	we began, would begin
comenzao/a	comenzado/a	begun
comiéranos	comiéramos	(for us) to eat
comisionao/a	comisionado/a	commissioner
compraa	compraba	they/you bought, used to buy
comprábanos	comprábamos	we bought, used to buy
comprao/a	comprado/a	bought; purchased
comunidá	comunidad	community
conbinación	combinación	combination
concilario	conciliar	councilor
condao	condado	county
conforme	según	according to
conponiendo	componiendo	fixing; repairing
consiguía	conseguía	he/she/you got; obtained; achieved
contale	contarle	to tell him/her
contoy	con todo y	together with
corcovao/a	corcovado/a	hunchbacked
cortaa	cortada	cut
cortao/a	cortado/a	cut
cosechao/a	cosechado/a	harvested
costumbra	acostumbra	he/she is accustomed to
cranque	manivela	crank
creelo/a	creerlo/a	to believe it/him/her
creido	ingenuo	naïve
crencias	creencias	beliefs
creye	cree	he/she believes; you believe
creyo	creo	I believe
Crismes	Navidad	Christmas
crucifico	crucifijo	crucifix
cruzalo/a	cruzarlo/a	to cross it
cuasi	casi	almost
cuartiaron	cuartearon	they/you cracked, divided up, split
cuentar	contar	to count; to tell
cuidáanos	cuidábamos	we took care of

cuidao	cuidado	care; careful
cuilta	colcha	bedspread; quilt
cuitió	dejó; paró	he/she/you quit
curre	corre	run; scoot
curri	corre	run; scoot

D

daa	daba	he/she/you gave, would give
dale	darle	to give to him/her/you
dao	dado	given
decorao/a	decorado/a	decorated
dediao	dado al diablo	gone to hell, to pot
degollao/a	degollado/a	slaughtered
deitetivos	detectives	detectives
dejaan	dejaban	they/you allowed; left (something)
dejáanos	dejábamos	we allowed; left (something)
dejábanos	dejábamos	we allowed; left (something)
dejao	dejado	allowed; left
dél	de él	his
delicao/a	delicado/a	delicate
d'en	de en	from
dende	desde	since
deputado	diputado	deputy
derición	dirección	address
desabrochao/a	desabrochado/a	unbuttoned
desaigrar	desairar	to snub; to rebuff
desaigriar	desairar	to snub; to rebuff
d'esas	de esas	of those
desconpuesta	descompuesta	broken; busted
d'ese	de ese	of that one; from that one
desforme	deformado	deformed
desgreñao/a	desgreñado/a	disheveled
deshojalo/a	deshojarlo/a	to shuck (corn)
desmayao/a	desmayado/a	fainted
d'eso	de eso	of that; from that
desparatiar	desparpajar	to spoil; to prattle
d'este	de este	of this one; from this one
destendían	extendían	they/you spread out; stretched out
diantes	de antes	from long ago
diantre	diablo	devil
diatiro	muy travieso	very naughty, mischievous
dicía	decía	he/she/you said, used to say
dicile	decirle	to tell him/her/you

dicir	decir	to say; to tell
diécimo	décimo	tenth
dificultá	dificultad	difficulty
dijían	decían	they/you said, used to say
dijíanos	decíamos	we said, used to say
dijieran	dijeran	(for them) to say
dijieron	dijeron	they/you said
dijile	decirle	to tell him/her/you
dijir	decir	to say; to tell
dijirnos	decirnos	to tell us
dijunto	difunto	corpse; dead person
dionde	de donde	from where
diónde	de dónde	from where
direción	dirección	address; direction
diriar	desviar	to change the course of
dirisar	desviar	to change the course of
disparao/a	disparado/a	shot (a firearm)
disturbir	perturbar	to disturb
diun	de un	of a(n)
diuna	de una	of a(n)
diuna vez	enseguida	immediately; at once
doblala	doblarla	to double it; to fold it
doblao/a	doblado/a	doubled; folded
dotor	doctor; médico	doctor
duce	dulce	sweet; candy
durmía	dormía	he/she/you/it slept
durmir	dormir	to sleep

ea	ella	she
echábanos	echábamos	we put, tossed in, would toss in
echao/a	echado/a	tossed in
edá	edad	age
educao/a	educado/a	polite; well-mannered; educated
ejecutalo/a	ejecutarlo/a	to restrain him/her
eleción	elección	election
eliciones	elecciones	elections
elogía	elogio	eulogy
empacalo	empacarlo	to can it (fruit)
empacao/a	empacado/a	packed, canned
enbalsamaban	embalsamaban	they/you embalmed; would embalm
en papá	papá	Dad; Daddy; father
enboca	emboca	to push ahead

enbocaa	embocaba	pushed ahead
enbocabaan	embocaban	they/you pushed, surged
enbolaban	emborrachaban	they/you got drunk, would get drunk
enbolansa	ambulancia	ambulance
enbolao/a	borracho/a	drunk
enborrachaban	emborrachaban	they/you got drunk, would get drunk
enbrujao/a	embrujado/a	bewitched
enbustero	embustero	liar
encagao/a	encargado/a	in charge of
encerrao/a	encerrado/a	locked up; cooped up
enchira	hincha	he/she/it swells up
encontrao/a	encontrado/a	found; met
ende	desde	since
enderezalo/a	enderezarlo/a	to straighten something out; to stand something on end
enfermedá	enfermedad	illness
enojaa	enojada	mad
enpacaan	empacaban	they/you canned (fruit)
enpacaban	empacaban	they/you canned, used to can
enpacalo/a	empacarlo/a	to pack it
enpache	empacho	indigestion
enpelotaba	desnudaba	he/she/you undressed; stripped
enpeloté	desnudé	I undressed; stripped
enpelotito/a	desnudito/a	naked as a jay bird
enpeloto/a	desnudo/a	undressed
enpezaban	empezaban	they/you began
enpezamos	empezamos	we began
enpezó	empezó	he/she/you started
enpieza	empieza	he/she/it begins; you begin
enprentao	implantado	implanted
enpuesto/a	acostumbrado/a	accustomed to
enredondo	alrededor de	around
ensillao/a	ensillado/a	saddled
enterrábanos	enterrábamos	we buried, would bury
enterrao/a	enterrado/a	buried
entrao/a	atrevido/a	bold; daring; insolent
entregale	entregarle	to give (to someone)
entro	dentro	within; inside
envenenao/a	envenedado/a	poisoned; embittered
envestigan	investigan	they/you investigate
envitó	invitó	he/she/you invited
eos	ellos	they
éranos	éramos	we were, used to be
escondíos	escondidos	hidden

escupión	escorpión; alacrán	lizard; scorpion
escurana	o(b)scuridad	darkness
escureciendo	o(b)scureciendo	getting dark
escuro/a	o(b)scuro/a	dark
espelma	esperma	paraffin; wax
espinazo	espalda	back
esquina	rincón	corner; nook
estaa	estaba	he/she/it was; you were
estaan	estaban	they/you were
estáanos	estábamos	we were
estábanos	estábamos	we were
estacao/a	estacado/a	staked out
estao	estado	state; been
estilaba	destilaba	he/she/you distilled, used to distill
estiladora	destiladora	still (moonshine)
estilalo/a	destilarlo/a	to distill it
estilándolo/a	destilándolo/a	distilling it
estógamo	estómago	stomach
estrenalo/a	estrenarlo/a	to use for the first time; to premier
estrendosa	estrenua	strong; agile
estrito/a	estricto/a	strict
estuata	estatua	statue
estudiábanos	estudiábamos	we studied, would study
estudiao	estudiado	studied
estuviéranos	estuviéramos	(so that) we were
estuvites	estuviste	you were
examinalas	examinarlas	to examine them
experencia	experiencia	experience

faición	facción	facial features
fiero/a	feo/a	ugly
fierro	hierro	iron; branding iron
finao/a	finado/a	deceased
fon	diversión	fun
frega	friega	beating
fumerada	fumarada	puffs of smoke; fuss

gabacho	gavache (French)	Anglo
galopiando	galopando	galloping

ganao	ganado	cattle; livestock
ganges	pandillas; gavillas	gangs
garraron	agarraron	they/you grabbed
gaselín	gasolina	gasoline
gatiar	gatear	to crawl
golpiaban	golpeaban	they/you hit; beat up
golpiao/a	golpeado/a	beaten up
golpiar	golpear	to hit; to beat up
golpié	golpeé	I hit; I beat up
golvíanos	volvíamos	we returned, were returning
golvías	volvías	you returned, were returning
golvieron	volvieron	they/you returned
golvió	volvió	he/she/you returned
gomitándose	vomitándose	vomiting
gomitarse	vomitarse	to vomit
gómito	vómito	vomit; vomiting
grafonola	fonógrafo	phonograph
gresa	gruesa	thick
güel	bueno	well
güelo	vuelo	flight
güelta	vuelta	turn; return
güelvas	vuelvas	(until) you return
güelvo	vuelvo	I return
güen	buen	good
güeno/a	bueno/a	good
güérfanas	huérfanas	orphans
güevo	huevo	egg; testicle; ball
güey	buey	ox

H

ha	he	I have (*haber*)
ha' bido	ha habido	there has been
habelas	haberlas	to have them
habíanos	habíamos	we had
hacele	hacerle	to make him/her; to do to him/her; to force him/her
hacelo/a	hacerlo/a	to make it; to do it
hacíanos	hacíamos	we made; we did
haiga	haya	there is (*haber*)
hamos	hemos	we have (*haber*)
hanos	hemos	we have (*haber*)
hicites	hiciste	you made; did

hijadero	ahijadero	lambing season
hijao	ahijado	godchild
hijar	ahijar	to adopt (a lamb)
hinchao/a	hinchado/a	inflated; swollen
hogo	ahogo	I drown
hogó	ahogó	he/she/you drowned
honestidá	honestidad	decency; honesty

I

iba cae	iba caer	was going to fall
íbanos	íbamos	we went, used to go
imaculada	inmaculada	immaculate
imediatamente	inmediatamente	immediately
individos	individuos	people; individuals
infriadora	refrescante	cooling system
ingenio	motor	motor (car/truck)
inpuesto	acostumbrada	accustomed to
ispiando	espiando	spying
ispiar	espiar	to spy (on)
isque	dizque; se dice que	supposedly; apparently; it is said
iyendo	yendo	going

J

jala	hala	he/she pulls, tows; you pull, tow
jalaa	halaba	he/she/you pulled, towed, would tow
jalaban	halaban	they/you pulled, towed, used to tow
jalándola	halándola	pulling it, towing it
jalar	halar	to pull, tow
jale	empleo	job
jaló	haló	he/she/you pulled, towed
jalones	tirones	pulls; tugs; yanks
jallaba	hallaba	he/she/you found; discovered
jallamos	hallamos	we found; discovered
jallao	hallado	found; discovered
jallar	hallar	to find; to discover
jallaron	hallaron	they/you found; discovered
jallé	hallé	I found; discovered
jallo	hallo	I find; discover
jirbiendo	hirviendo	boiling
jirviendo	hirviendo	boiling
joso	oso	bear

jue	fue	he/she/you/it went
juera	fuera	outside; out; away
juéranos	fuéramos	(so that) we went
jueron	fueron	they/you went
juerte	fuerte	strong
juerza	fuerza	strength; force; power
jugáanos	jugábamos	we played, used to play
jugábanos	jugábamos	we played, used to play
jui	fui	I went
juíanos	huíamos	we fled; escaped, would escape
juimos	fuimos	we went
juir	huir	to flee; to escape
juntaan	juntaban	they/you united; assembled; would get together; socialized
jurao	jurado	jury; sworn
juventú	juventud	youth
juyendo	huyendo	fleeing; escaping
juyó	huyó	he/she/you fled

L

l'acha	el hacha	hatchet; ax
l'acordión	el acordeón	accordion
l'agua	el agua	water
'l agüelo	el abuelo	grandfather
'l aire	el aire	air; wind
'l alfabeto	el alfabeto	alphabet
'l anillo	el anillo	ring
'l asilo	el asilo	asylum
l'azúcar	el azúcar	sugar
l'edá	la edad	age
l'escuela	la escuela	school
'l escusao	el escusado	outhouse
'l espinazo	el espinazo	backbone; spine
'l esposo	el esposo	husband
l'estiladora	la destiladora	the still (moonshine)
'l estógamo	el estómago	the stomach
l'estuata	la estatua	the statue
l'etrecidá	la electricidad	electricity
l'hecho	lo hecho	what is done
l'hizo	lo hizo	he/she/you did it
l'iban	lo iban	they/you were going
l'iglesia	la iglesia	the church

l'iscuela	la escuela	the school
l'istoria	la historia	the story
l'ochó	lo echó	he/she/you threw
'l ojo	el ojo	the eye
ladiaba	ladeaba	he/she/you tilted
ladiara	ladeara	(for you) to tilt
ladié	ladeé	I tilted
lao	lado	side
lastimalo/a	lastimarlo/a	to injure him/her; to offend him/her
lavaderos	lavadores	washboards
lazalo/a	lazarlo/a	to rope it; to lasso it
lego	luego	then; afterwards; later (on)
leperaa	trucos; engaños	tricks
levantaa	levantaba	he/she/you raised; got up
levantáanos	levantábamos	we raised; got up
leyer	leer	to read
ligaa	ligada	bound; tied
ligao/a	ligado/a	bound; tied
llegaa	llegaba	he/she/you arrived, would arrive
llegáanos	llegábamos	we arrived, would arrive
llegábanos	llegábamos	we arrived, would arrive
llegao	llegado	arrived
llenaa	llenaba	he/she/you filled
llenala	llenarla	to fill it
llevaa	llevaba	he/she/you carried; took away; wore; led
lleváanos	llevábamos	we carried; took away; wore; led
lloraa	lloraba	he/she/you cried, would cry
logo	luego	then; afterwards; later (on)
lonche	almuerzo	lunch
lonchera	cubo para comida	lunch pail
loo	luego	then; afterwards; later (on)
lotro/a	el (la) otro/a	the other one

m'hija/o	mi hija/o	my (dear) daughter/son
macánico	mecánico	mechanic
maiz	maíz	corn
malcriao	malcriado	brat; ill-mannered
mamao/a	mamado/a	nursed; fed
mamases	mamás; madres	mothers
mandaan	mandaban	they/you sent; ordered, used to order
manejaan	manejaban	they/you drove; handled, would handle; managed

manijaba	manejaba	he/she/you managed, used to manage
manijar	manejar	to drive; to handle; to manage
matala	matarla	to kill it/her
matao	matado	dead; killed
medecina	medicina	medicine
medianito	chiquito	small; tiny
medianochi	medianoche	midnight
meecina	medicina	medicine
mentao	mentado	well-known
mérica	médica; curandera	folk healer
mesmo	mismo	same
mestro/a	maestro/a	teacher
metíanos	metíamos	we used to hide
m'hijo	mi hijo	my son
mintir	mentir	to lie
mitá	mitad	half
mixtiaron	mezclaron	they/you mixed
mojao/a	mojado/a	wet
monquiando	traveseando	being naughty, mischievous
monquiar	travesear	to be naughty, mischievous
montaja	montaje	assembly; montage
moo	modo	manner; way
moralidá	moralidad	morality; moral values
moretiada	moretón	black and blue bruise
muchichito/a	muchachito/a	little boy/girl
muchito/a	muchachito/a	little boy/girl
mudaan	mudaban	they/you moved, used to move
muncho/a	mucho/a	a lot
mure	muy	very
murían	morían	they/you died, would die
murir	morir	to die
murirte	morirte	to die
murre	muy	very
muvimiento	movimiento	movement

naa	nada	nothing
naar	nadar	to swim
nadien	nadie	no one
naguas	enaguas	skirts
naide	nadie	no one
naiden	nadie	no one
nalgaa	nalgada	spanking

Navidá	Navidad	Christmas
necesidá	necesidad	necessity
necidá	necesidad	necessity
nesitaa	necesitaba	he/she/you needed
nicle	cinco centavos	nickel
nito	niñito	my good (dear) boy
nitriato	nitrato	nitrate
niun	ni un	not even one
niuno/a	ni uno/a	not even one
nochi	noche	night
Nochibuena	Nochebuena	Christmas Eve
nodriza	enfermera	nurse
nojao	enojado	mad, angry
nojar	enojar	to get mad, angry
nójase	enójase	he/she/you got mad, angry
nojó	enojó	he/she/you got mad, angry
nojotros/as	nosotros/as	we; us
nomás	sólo; solamente	only
noo	nuevo	new
nuevecientos	novecientos	nine hundred

ofecina	oficina	office
ójali	ojalá	one hopes; hopefully
olvidates	olvidaste	you forgot
onde	donde	where
ónde	dónde	where
ondequiera	dondequiera	wherever
oportunidá	oportunidad	chance; opportunity
ora	ahora	now
orita	ahorita	right now
oyindo	oyendo	hearing; listening to

pa	para	for
paá	para allá	over there
pacá	para acá	over here
pa cas' 'e	para casa de	headed for (mother's) house
pader	pared	wall
pahi	para ahí	there

pal	para el	for the
pallá	para allá	over there
pa' (no) listarse	para alistarse	to get ready, dressed
pantión	panteón	family plot; cemetery; mausoleum
papalote	molino	windmill
papases	papás; padres	fathers
paquel	para aquel	for that one
par	para	for
parao/a	parado/a	stopped; standing up
pariaditos	paraditos	standing stiff, straight up
parriba	para arriba	up there
partila	partirla	to chop it; to smash it; to break it
pasáamos	pasábamos	we spent, passed
pasáanos	pasábamos	we spent, passed
pasao/a	pasado/a	past
pasiaban	paseaban	they/you strolled, visited
pasiador	vagabundo	vagrant; bum
pasiándose	paseándose	visiting
pasiar	pasear	to take a walk; to visit
pasteo	pasto	pasture
pataas	patadas	kicks; stamps of the foot
pa trae	para traer	to bring; to cause
patrás	para atrás	to the back
pegales	pegarles	to hit them; to kick them
pelao/a	pelado/a	bald
peliaba	peleaba	he/she/you fought, would fight
peliamos	peleamos	we fight/fought
peliando	peleando	fighting
peliaron	pelearon	they/you fought
pelié	peleé	I fought
pene	centavo	penny
penitensaria	penitenciaría	penitentiary
pensaan	pensaban	they/you thought
perdelo/a	perderlo/a	to lose him/her/it
persinalo/a	persignarlo/a	to bless him/her
persínelos	persígnelos	bless them
pesao/a	pesado/a	heavy; boring; difficult
pidir	pedir	to ask for
pinabete	pinoabeto	pine tree
pior	peor	worse
pisotiaran	pisotearon	they/you trampled; disregarded

planiaron	planearaon	they/you planned
platicale	platicarle	to tell him/her
plebe	muchachos	boys
podelo/a	poderlo/a	to be able to
podío	podido	able to
poemos	podemos	we are able to
pograma	programa	program
poído	podido	able to
polecía	policía	police
ponelo/a	ponerlo/a	to wear it; to place it
polvaerones	polvaredas	clouds of dust
poníanos	poníamos	we put on, would put on
porecito/a	pobrecito/a	poor thing
portunidades	oportunidades	opportunities
pos	pues	well
preguntates	preguntaste	you asked
prencipio	principio	beginning
prendelo/a	comenzarlo/a	to start (the car)
prendío	prendido	turned on; lighted; started (the car)
probe	pobre	poor
prusición	procesión	procession
pu' si	pues si	well, then
puea	pueda	can; is able
puee	puede	he/she/you can
pueo	puedo	I can
pus	pues	well

quebrale	quebrarle	to break
quebrao/a	quebrado/a	broken
quedaa	quedaba	he/she/you remained
quedáranos	quedáramos	we would stay
quemao/a	quemado/a	burned
qu'era	que era	that was
queríanos	queríamos	we wanted
que'sa	que esa	that that
quisque	dizque; se dice que	supposedly; apparently; it is said
quitábanos	quitábamos	we took off, would take off
quiteles	quitarles	to skin (a hide)
quitao/a	quitado/a	removed

R

rasguñao	rasguñado	scratched
reborujito	burujo; reburujito	brawl
recibites	recibiste	you received
regalao/a	regalado/a	given; rewarded
regüelto/a	revuelto/a	choppy; rough; untidy
reguroso	riguroso	strict
reló	reloj	wristwatch; clock
requiaso	golpe	blow
resequedá	sequedad	dryness
Resureción	Resurección	Resurrection
retirao/a	retirado/a	remote; secluded
rezale	rezarle	to pray to
rifaa	rifaba	raffled off; drew lots for
rií	reí	I laughed
rir	reír	to laugh
roando	rodando	rolling
robaan	robaban	they/you stole; robbed
rofe	áspero, duro	rough; uncouth; unrefined
rula	regla	ruler

S

sabíanos	sabíamos	we used to know
sacáanos	sacábamos	we removed, would remove
sacábanos	sacábamos	we removed, would remove
sacao	sacado	removed
salites	saliste	you left
salivia	saliva	saliva
sanaa	sanaba	he/she/you got well; cured (someone)
sartificao/a	certificado/a	certificate
sei	sí	yes
semos	somos	we are
sentábanos	sentábamos	we sat down, would sit down
sentao/a	sentado/a	seated
sepoltura	sepultura	grave; tomb
setiar	poner	to set; to put; to place
sherifas	policía	sheriff
shipiaban	mandaban	shipped
shotas	policía	police
siguí	seguí	I followed
siguía	seguía	he/she/you followed

siguimos	seguimos	we followed
siguir	seguir	to follow
sinke	lavabo	sink
siñor	señor	sir; gentleman
sintemos	sentimos	we felt
sirvir	servir	to serve
soldao/a	soldado/a	soldier
sonaan	sonaban	they/you sounded; rang; beat up
sopone	suponer	to suppose; to assume; to imply; to suggest
soponía	suponía	he/she/you supposed; assumed; implied; suggested
subile	subirle	to rise (temperature)
subío	subido	climbed
suriguanga	friega	beating

T

'tonces	entonces	then
'toy	estoy	I am
'tras	atrás	here; over here
taa	todavía	yet; still
táanos	estábamos	we were
tamién	también	also
tapao/a	tapado/a	covered
tapolio	lona	tarpaulin
taramote	terremoto	earthquake
tare	tan	so; so very
tavía	todavía	yet; still
telefón	teléfono	telephone
teníanos	teníamos	we had
testiábamos	probábamos	we tested
testiador	probador	tester
tirale	tirarle	to throw to him/her
tirao/a	tirado/a	thrown/unkempt
toavía	todavía	yet; still
tocaa	tocaba	he/she/you played (an instrument)
tomaan	tomaban	they/you drank
tomao	tomado; borracho	drunk
too/a	todo/a	all
trabajaa	trabajaba	he/she/you worked
trabajáanos	trabajábamos	we worked, used to work
trabajábanos	trabajábamos	we worked, used to work
trae	esfuerzo	try

tragaa	tragaba	he/she/you swallowed, would swallow
trai	trae	he/she brings/you bring
traiba	traía	he/she/you brought
tráibanos	traíamos	we brought, would bring
traila	traerla	to bring it
trampao	trampado	packed (dirt)
trancaban	atrancaban	they/you blocked
tranpaba	trampeaba	he/she/you rode the rails
tranpar	trampear	to ride the rails
tras	detrás	behind
trataa	trataba	he/she/you tried
tresquilando	trasquilando	shearing
tripa	manguera	hose
troca	camión	truck
tronpean	trompean	they/you collide
truenando	tronando	thundering
trujiera	trajera	(for you) to bring
trujimos	trajimos	we brought
trujo	trajo	he/she/you brought
tualla	toalla	towel
turra	zurra	flogging, whipping
'tuvo	estuvo	he/she was; you were

U

un' hacha	una hacha	an axe
un' herida	una herida	a wound
usaa	usaba	he/she/you used
usté	usted	you
ustees	ustedes	all of you

V

vagamundiar	vagamundear	to lead a vagrant's life
vanidá	vanidad	vanity
vaquetazo	vaqueta	razor strop
varejonazo	azote con una vara	blows with a stick
velo/a	verlo/a	to see him/her
venao	venado	deer
vendío	vendido	sold
veníanos	veníamos	we came, were coming
verdá	verdad	truth; true
vestíos	vestidos	suits; dresses

vía	veía	he/she/you saw, would see
vide	vi	I saw
vido	vio	he/she/you saw
vinemos	venimos	we come
vinía	venía	he/she/you came, would come
viníanos	veníamos	we came, would come
vinir	venir	to come
vistío/a	vestido/a	dressed; suit
vivemos	vivimos	we live, lived
vivíanos	vivíamos	we used to live
volaan	volaban	they/you flew
voltiaba	volteaba	he/she/you turned back, turned a corner
voltialo/a	voltearlo/a	to turn it over, upside down
voltiaos	volteados	turned over
voltiar	voltear	to turn over, upside down
voltiaron	voltearon	they/you turned over
votáanos	votábamos	we voted, used to vote

Z

| zoquete | barro; lodo | mud |
| zumbío | zumbido | roar; humming |

Interviewees

Interview Data

The information provided here is to help orient the reader regarding each informant's life experiences; it is not meant to serve as a comprehensive summary of the interview.

Jesusita Aragón

Born March 26, 1908, Las Vegas, New Mexico. Interviewed April 11, 1994, in Las Vegas, for one hour. Sheepherder as a young girl. Nationally known midwife. Delivered first baby at age thirteen. Midwife for over eighty years; has delivered several thousand babies. Shared various facets of folklore (e.g., folk sayings).

Andrés Archuleta

Born February 4, 1905, in Trujillo, New Mexico. Interviewed April 22, 1994, in Las Vegas, for one hour and fifteen minutes. Principal features of interview: ranch life, religion, education, witchcraft, politics, philosophical outlook on life's travails.

Severa Archuleta

Born November 26, 1910, in Trementina, New Mexico. Interviewed in Las Vegas, April 22, 1994, for approximately thirty-five minutes. Principal features of interview: household chores, religious activities (including baptisms and weddings), education.

Elba C. de Baca

Born September 14, 1918, in Las Vegas, New Mexico. Interviewed November 21, 1998, in Las Vegas, for one hour and twenty minutes. Well-known folklorist. Principal features of interview: popular holidays, religious customs and traditions.

Filiberto Esquibel

Born August 7, 1928, in Cañada del Medio, New Mexico. Interviewed April 18, 1994, in Las Vegas, for an hour and a half. Well-known musician, but spoke on a variety of topics: music, education, politics, traditions, folklore, cultural values.

Carmelita Gómez

Born May 12, 1909, in Aguilar, New Mexico. Interviewed May 2, 1994, in Las Vegas, for thirty-five minutes. Principal features of interview: anecdotes and family stories.

Reynaldo Gonzales

Born April 13, 1914, in Los Juertes, New Mexico. Interviewed May 23, 1994, in Las Vegas, for approximately one hour. Principal features of interview: ranch and farm life, moonshine, witchcraft stories, personal pranks, and corrupt politicians in Las Vegas.

Fred W. Korte

Born November 7, 1915, in Buena Vista, New Mexico. Provided a typed list of folk sayings in Spanish on December 4, 2000. Plays accordion and composes songs. Knowledgeable about folklore.

Guadalupe Luján

Born December 11, 1910, in Las Vegas. Interviewed May 4, 1994, in Las Vegas, for one hour and twenty minutes. Active in local politics since 1930s; as small boy saw Theodore Roosevelt in nearby Montezuma. Principal features of interview: corruption and voter fraud, "Wild West" killings, and other stories.

Arsenio Montoya, Sr.

Born June 18, 1918, in Piedra Lumbre, New Mexico. Interviewed January 26, 1994, in Las Vegas, for an hour and a half. Principal features of interview: cowboy life, family traditions, education, politics, WPA, bootlegging in Las Vegas. In the 1930s sang in Las Vegas with Lydia Mendoza, famous singer in Texas and throughout the Southwest.

Cesaria Montoya

Born February 5, 1929, in San Pablo, New Mexico. Interviewed April 4, 1994, in Las Vegas, for an hour a half. Principal features of interview: holidays, games, dances, religious customs, politics, schooling, witchcraft and superstition, humorous stories.

Filimón Montoya

Born June 30, 1915, in Cañón de Fernández (Taos County). Interviewed May 23, 1994, in Las Vegas, for one hour and twenty minutes. Came to Las Vegas in the 1950s. Principal features of interview: father shearing sheep for a living, respect (or lack of it) among elders and youth, traditional holidays, religious customs, politics, games, the supernatural, humor.

José Nataleo Montoya

Born July 3, 1929, in San Pablo, New Mexico. Interviewed on May 23, 1994, in Las Vegas, for one and a half hours. Father a sheepherder. Principal features of interview: ranch life, fiestas, religious ceremonies, politics, education, witchcraft and ghosts.

Katarina Montoya

Born February 10, 1919, in El Ojo, New Mexico. Interviewed on May 23, 1994, in Las Vegas, for about forty-five minutes. Principal features of interview: Christmas, politics (she comes from a political family), education, family customs, and folklore.

Isabel Romero

Born November 5, 1896, in Sabinoso, New Mexico. Interviewed April 8, 1994, in Las Vegas, for one hour and fifteen minutes. Cowboy (on Bell Ranch), sheepherder, goatherd. Grandfather was a buffalo hunter on Llano Estacado. Principal features of interview: ghosts and other supernatural phenomena.

Alfredo Trujillo

Born May 27, 1911, in Terromote, New Mexico. Interviewed February 26, 1999, in Las Vegas, for an hour and a half. Moved to Las Vegas in the 1940s. Self-taught musician; plays guitar and sings. Dislikes politics. Knows old Spanish dances and a variety of folklore, ghost stories.

María Trujillo

Born October 1, 1911, in Levi, New Mexico. Interviewed January 27, 1999, in Las Vegas, for twenty minutes. Principal features of interview: folk sayings and educating her children.

Alfredo Ulibarrí

Born February 14, 1923, in Las Vegas. Interviewed April 11, 1994, in Las Vegas, for fifty minutes. Principal features of interview: family traditions, education, politics, superstitions, and ghostly apparitions.

Teresina Ulibarrí

Born in La Lagunita, New Mexico, on August 14, 1926. Interviewed on April 13, 1994, in Las Vegas, for approximately one hour. Farm girl. Principal features of interview: foods eaten during Lent, dances and fistfights at political functions, children's games, witchcraft.

Cruzita Vigil

Born in Corazón, New Mexico, on August 24, 1901. Interviewed January 28, 1994, in Las Vegas, for two hours. Principal features of interview: family traditions, religious and popular holidays, folk healing, the evil eye, and superstitions.

Suggested Reading

Arellano, Anselmo F., and Julián Josué Vigil. *Las Vegas Grandes on the Galli-nas: 1835–1985*. Las Vegas, NM: Editorial Teleraña, 1985.

Bryan, Howard. *Wildest of the Wild West*. Santa Fe, NM: Clear Light Publish-ers, 1988.

Buss, Fran Leeper. *La Partera: Story of a Midwife*. Ann Arbor: University of Michigan Press, 1980.

C. de Baca, Carlos. *Vicente Silva: The Terror of Las Vegas*. Truchas, NM: Tate Gallery Publication, 1968.

C. de Baca, Elba. *Customs and Traditions*. Booklets I, II & III. Las Vegas, NM: Self-published, n.d.

Gottschalk, M. C. *Pioneer Merchants of the Las Vegas Plaza*. Las Vegas, NM: Self-published, 2000.

Nahm, Milton C. *Las Vegas and Uncle Joe: The New Mexico I Remember*. Nor-man: University of Oklahoma Press, 1964.

Otero, Miguel Antonio. *My Life on the Frontier: 1864–1882*. Albuquerque: University of New Mexico Press, 1987.

Perrigo, Lynn. *Gateway to Glorieta: A History of Las Vegas, New Mexico*. Boul-der, CO: Pruett Publishing, 1982.

Robe, Stanley L., ed. *Hispanic Folktales from New Mexico: Narratives from the R. D. Jameson Collection*. Berkeley & Los Angeles: University of California Press, 1977.

———, ed. *Hispanic Legends from New Mexico: Narratives from the R. D. Jame-son Collection*. Berkeley & Los Angeles: University of California Press, 1980.

Steele, Thomas J., S. J., and Rowena A. Rivera. *Penitente Self-Government: Brotherhoods and Councils, 1797–1947*. Santa Fe: Ancient City Press, 1985.

Tobias, Henry J. *A History of the Jews in New Mexico*. Albuquerque: University of New Mexico Press, 1992.

Index

chiquiao(s), 16–17, 61–62. *See also* special dance
chiropractor or bonesetter, 112. *See also* sobador/a
Christmas Eve, 193
Christmas, 94, 99,192–93, 196
Christmastime, 99
Christopher Columbus, 112
ciboleros, 31. *See also* buffalo hunters
Cobos, Rubén, 242
Cofradía de Nuestro Señor Jesucristo, 195
cofradías, 177. *See also* confraternities
confraternities, 117. *See also* cofradías
corridas del gallo, 15, 58. *See also* rooster pull/race
country remedies, 113. *See also* remedios del llano
coyote, 165–66
Crismes, 93, 98 190–91
culebra mamona, 162. *See also* milk snake
curandera(s), 112–13, 115–16, 158. *See also* folk healer
curanderismo, 112. *See also* folk healing

Delgado, Lorenzo, 215–16, 231–32, 234–35, 237
devil, 143, 166, 173–74
Día de Resurecíon, 188
Día de San Agustín, 56
Día de San Juan, 73
Día de San Lorenzo, 58
Día de Santa Ana (Santana), 73
Día de Santiago, 58, 73
diezmos y primicias, 176. *See also* tithes
dispensa, 113, 159. *See also* pantry
dichos, 240–242, 258
dolor de cintura, 115. *See also* lower-back pain
Domingo de Ramos, 188, 207
Domingo de Resurecíon, 189
don, 115. *See also* gift of God
Don Quixote, 241

Doren, Tom, 233, 236
Durán, Polonio, 221, 223

Earp, Wyatt, 8
Easter, 189–90
el agüelo, 140, 191, 193
el coco, 139–40, 149. *See also* bogeyman
el diablo, 142, 166, 173
el diantre, 142
el mal ojo, 114, 128, 129, 131–34, 140.
El Tiempo Santo, 187
embrujados/enyerbados, 115. *See also* bewitched
embrujo, 140. *See also* bewitchment
empacho(e), 114, 135. *See also* indigestion
enchanted places, 140. *See also* lugares encantados
Encinias, Luis, 217, 219, 234, 236
entierros, 140. *See also* buried treasures
escribano, 77. *See also* scribe
Escuela de la Imaculada Concepción, 83, 110
Escuela de Nuestra Señora de los Dolores, 83
espíritu malo, 167. *See also* evil spirits
Esquibel, Filiberto, 73, 102, 114, 134, 143, 212, 225, 242, 247
evil spirit(s), 142, 167

fallen fontanel, 114. *See also* caída de la mollera
Fidel Hotel, 236
Fielding, Romaine, 9
floor manager, 16, 62, 65. *See also* bastonero
Flynn, Jim, 9
folk healer(s), 112,159. *See also* curandera(s)
folk healing witches, 152
folk healing, 112. *See also* curanderismo
folk sayings, 240–242, 255

malevolent witches, 152. *See also* malhechores
malhechores, 150. *See also* malevolent
witches
Manuel Durán, 5
manzanilla, 113, 119. *See also*
chamomile tea
marbles, 15. *See also* bolitas
Marcha de los Novios, 179
María Santísima, 98, 207. *See also*
Blessed Virgin Mary
Martínez, Félix, 76
mayordomos, 56, 176, 185
Meadow Home, 221, 223
médica/o, 112–13, 115,126
medicine cabinet, 113. *See also* alu-
cena
Midnight Mass, 177. *See also* Misa del
Gallo
midwife, 112, 119–20, 123, 127, 159.
See also partera
Mieder, Wolfgang, 242
Miércoles de Ceniza, 188
Miguel Archuleta, 5
milk snake, 162. *See also* culebra
mamona
mint tea, 113. *See also* yerba buena
Misa del Gallo, 177, 192, 194. *See also*
Midnight Mass
Mix, Tom, 9
Montoya, Arsenio, Sr., 16, 38, 58, 78,
177–78, 197
Montoya, Cesaria, 16, 21, 60, 97, 114,
132, 154, 212–13, 256
Montoya, Filimón, 26, 106, 159, 178,
184, 188, 206, 212, 229, 265, 267
Montoya, José Nataleo, 44, 64, 71,
131, 162, 217, 252
Montoya, Katarina, 88, 93, 114, 128,
252, 260, 265, 267
moonshine, 61–62, 67–68, 70–72. *See
also* mula
Mora County, 211
morada, 177, 186, 189–90

Mount Calvary, 190
mula, 61, 66–69, 71. *See also* moonshine

NAFTA (North American Free Trade
Agreement), 4
National Guard, 236–37
Nativity, 192–93
Navidá, 190–91, 195
New Mexico Highlands University, 10
Newlyweds' March, 182
Nochibuena, 191
Normal University, 83–84. *See also*
New Mexico Highlands University
North and South Public Schools,
83–84
North Public School, 84
novena, 197–98
Nuestra Señora de Guadalupe, 207
Nuestra Señora de los Dolores, 5, 207
Nuestra Señora del Rosario, 199

Old Town and New Town, 6
Old Town Historic District, 11
Old Town, 85. *See also* Plaza Vieja
oremos, 191, 193
oshá, 113
Our Lady of Guadalupe, 208
Our Lady of Sorrows of the Large
Meadows, 5
Our Lady of Sorrows School, 84
Our Lady of Sorrows, 208
Our Lady of the Rosary, 201
owl(s), 162, 168. *See also* lechuza or
tecolote

paisanos, 41–42. *See also* roadrunners
Palm Sunday, 189, 208
pantry, 160. *See also* dispensa
partera, 112–13, 116, 123, 158. *See also*
midwife
Penitent Brothers, 176
Penitents, 177, 186, 231–32
plains, 14. *See also* llano

Trujillo, María, 253

Ulibarrí, Alfredo, 28, 94, 170, 178,
187, 199, 212, 215
Ulibarrí, Teresina, 52, 172, 255, 259
un pie torcido, 115. *See also* sprained
ankle

Vásquez de Coronado, Francisco, 2, 3
velorios, 177, 195–96. *See also* religious
wakes
Viernes Santo, 189
Vigil, Cruzita, 36, 126, 130, 135, 173,
209
Vigil, Donaciano, 76
Virgen de Guadalupe, 13
Virgil, 193
visiones, 140. *See also* hallucinations

Wagon Mound, 38–39
War of Valverde, 47
Wells, H. G., 3
West and East Las Vegas, 6, 12
white ghost, 142, 169–72. *See also*
bulto blanco
William Becknell, 4
Wilson, Woodrow, 233, 236
witch(es), 150, 152, 160–61, 168, 174
witchcraft, 159
WPA (Works Progress Administration),
233

yerba buena, 113. *See also* mint tea
Young Democrats, 236